The New World of Philosophy

To Bracha

and the land she helped to build

THE *New World of Philosophy*

ABRAHAM KAPLAN

VINTAGE BOOKS

A DIVISION OF RANDOM HOUSE

New York

VINTAGE BOOKS
are published by ALFRED A. KNOPF, INC.
and RANDOM HOUSE, INC.

Thanks are due for permission to quote material from the publications of the following:

Harcourt, Brace & World, Inc., *Collected Poems 1909–1935* by T. S. Eliot, Copyright, 1936, by Harcourt, Brace & World, Inc.; *Poems 1923–1954* by E. E. Cummings, Copyright, 1923, 1951, by E. E. Cummings.

Holt, Rinehart and Winston, Inc., *Complete Poems by A. E. Housman*, Copyright 1940, © 1959, by Holt, Rinehart and Winston, Inc. Quotation on p. 314.

"Freud and Modern Philosophy" originally appeared in the volume *Freud and the 20th Century*, edited by Benjamin Nelson. It is reprinted here by permission of the publisher, Meridian Books, The World Publishing Company. Copyright © 1957, by The World Publishing Company.

MANUFACTURED IN THE UNITED STATES OF AMERICA

PREFACE

THESE LECTURES ON CONTEMPORARY WORLD PHILOSOPHIES were delivered at U.C.L.A. in the fall of 1959 and the spring of 1960 under the auspices of the Extension Division of the University of California. I want particularly to thank Mr. Leonard Friedman and Miss Lois Smith of the Liberal Arts Program for their conception and arrangement of this lecture series. The chapter "Freud and Modern Philosophy" is based on the Freud Centenary Lecture delivered in 1956 before the Society of Psychoanalytic Medicine of Southern California; it originally appeared in the volume *Freud and the 20th Century,* edited by Benjamin Nelson, and published by Meridian Books, Inc., and is reprinted here, with some revisions, by their permission.

The Asian philosophies I was enabled to examine at first hand on a grant from the Rockefeller Foundation, and the manuscript was prepared in the leisure provided by the Center for Advanced Study in the Behavioral Sciences; to both these institutions I wish to express my profound thanks. I am grateful also for the editorial help given me by my friends Jason Epstein and Nathan Glazer of Random House.

Most of all I want to thank the audience who listened to these lectures, with more patience than I deserved, I am afraid, and sometimes with more understanding than I dared confront.

STANFORD, CALIFORNIA NOVEMBER, 1960

CONTENTS

Introduction

AMONG MEN who say one thing and do another, professors of philosophy must rank almost as high, proportionately, as candidates for public office. If a philosopher writes a treatise on modesty, he will not neglect to sign his name to it (an observation for which credit must be duly given to Epictetus, if I remember rightly). He may declare himself a solipsist, and appeal to all his readers to agree with him; proclaim that time is unreal, and point out that he arrived at this truth only after many years of reflection; or present a closely reasoned argument to urge that the good life is one of unthinking spontaneity. The philosophy that a man professes, in short, is often quite other than the one he lives by; and in our time, professional philosophy is in danger of becoming more and more only something professed.

I once knew a great philosopher of science who adhered to an uncompromising probabilism: nothing can be known with absolute certainty. One of his critics held, on the contrary, that some things are sure. Science rests on certain presuppositions which are literally beyond question, and so must be accepted as being indubitably true. Yet the probabilist was as convinced of the soundness of his view as the most zealous dogmatist would be; and the critic put forward his position with doubts and hesitations. If the style is the man, the living philosophy is expressed, not in what is said, but in the manner of its saying.

The difference between professed and living philosophy is not a matter of insincerity, a tactic to win assent. I do not mean to imply a failing in contemporary philosophers, but rather in much contemporary philosophy. As happens recurrently in art, religion, and elsewhere, philosophy has become so institutionalized as to serve the profession, but not those whom the profession was supposed to serve. A philosophy which speaks, even indirectly, only to philosophers is no philosophy at all; and I think the same is true if it speaks only to scientists, or only to jurists, or priests, or any other special class. For the business of philosophy, as I see it, always was—and remains—to articulate the principles by which a man can live: not just as a scientist, citizen, religionist, or whatever, but as the whole man that he is. To describe a man's philosophy is to say how he orients himself to the world of his experience, what meanings he finds in events, what values he aspires to, what standards guide his choices in all he does.

Now there always is some orientation or other; there are always at work certain patterns of meaning, preferred values, operative standards. Every man has a philosophy, in short; and if it is not provided—formulated, criticized, improved—by those identified as philosophers in the prevailing division of labor, others will inevitably perform that function. At various periods of history various groups have performed it—priests, poets, scientists, statesmen, and occasionally even professors of philosophy. In our time, journalists, psychiatrists, literary critics, and nuclear physicists seem to be carrying the burden. I do not say that academic philosophers are so ripe in wisdom as to presume to tell others how to live—such a presumption is itself enough to show that a man is a fool. Yet sometimes modesty only masks irresponsibility, and the man who seems anxious not to presume may only be lacking in courage. Those who are professionally occupied with philosophy must at least make the claim that they are no worse fitted, by endowment and training, to perform the philosophical function than are those for whom it is an avocation, and who are in fact performing it. But the word "philosophy" means the love of wisdom; and the love of wisdom, I suppose, is like any other sort of love—the professionals are the ones who know least about it.

Yet professionalism in itself is not to be condemned; at worst, in a society as complex as ours, it is a necessary evil. I am only pointing out that this profession, like any other, stands in need of justification. Now let me say at once that, as far as I am concerned, the satisfaction of intellectual curiosity is justification enough for any pursuit. Aristotle opens his *Metaphysics* with the observation that "All men by nature desire to know"; they were the opening words, too, of the first lecture in philosophy I ever heard, and seemed to me then quite enough reason for changing my course of studies. If knowledge is all, however, science provides sufficient scope for the most insatiable curiosity; and it is just this sort of curiosity, detached from any concern for immediate applications, that is responsible for most of the great scientific advances. Still, from a purely intellectual standpoint, I find chess also fascinating and unfathomable. The fact is that many philosophers today pursue their subject as though it were a game, and though I think chess is a better one, I am certainly in no position to condemn them for playing theirs.

But the point is that there is something else to be done. In the arts and sciences, in law, medicine, politics or religion, questions continually arise which, because they are so speculative, so broad in scope, or so inextricably involved with values, are habitually dismissed as being too philosophical in character to be considered there. I have no quarrel with those who hold that such questions belong in philosophy; but what is to be done if philosophers also refuse to consider them? I am saying only that the division of labor in society must not be allowed to go so far as to leave no place at all for those great questions which cannot be divided, and for which every man presupposes some answer or other in going about his business or just in living his life. That those of us who have some professional responsibility for dealing with such questions can do no better with them than anyone else is a sorry enough confession to make, though I think that honesty demands no less. But I do not know why philosophy should keep the name if it abdicates the responsibility.

Some decades ago the great social scientist Max Weber wrote a famous essay on politics as a calling. I wish some sociologist would write an essay today on philosophy as a calling, and on the social or psychological forces which transform a vocation into merely an occupation. I am afraid that nowadays, in the English-speaking world at any rate, we would have to say that anyone for whom philosophy may be a calling would be well advised to stay away from schools of philosophy. Such advice is no different, after all, from what we might give to a young man who aspires to write poetry or to emancipate his people. These things are not academic pursuits; and I say, in the case of philosophy at least, so much the worse for the academy.

In the lectures that follow, I am interested in philosophy, not just as an academic subject matter, but as the impulse and expression of a people's culture. I have included, therefore, several movements of thought which do not belong to philosophy in the narrowest sense but rather to science, religion, or politics, on the ground that these movements seem to me to bear significantly on the orientations, meanings, values and standards by which some men choose to live. I begin with a distinctively American philosophy, pragmatism, then Anglo-American analytic philosophy, European existentialism and psychoanalysis, then behind the Iron Curtain to communism. Continuing eastward, I discuss Indian philosophy, Buddhism, Chinese philosophy, and Japanese Zen, which, I suppose, brings us back to the United States by way of the West Coast.

As a survey of philosophies in the world today, this suffers from a number of conspicuous omissions. I have said nothing about such philosophers as Bergson, Santayana, Whitehead, and Croce, for they have had few followers, even within the academy. The Judaeo-Christian outlook I judged to be too familiar, and at the same time too heterogeneous, to lend itself to this survey. The most serious omission is Islamic thought, of enormous importance in a vast region stretching from Morocco to Indonesia; I can only plead ignorance and the political exigencies which made it impossible for me to acquaint myself with this movement of thought at first hand.

In these lectures I have tried to convey a sense of the commonality of human problems. I do not mean to say that the world's philosophies today are at bottom all the same; on the contrary. They could not serve as philosophies to live by if they did not embody within themselves the distinctive traits which differentiate one culture from another. I meant, rather, that sense of kinship expressed by the Roman poet who wrote, "Being human, nothing human is foreign to me." For though the fantastic developments in communication and transportation, and the demands of politics and economics, have given us all a world-wide perspective, our thought remains, for many of us, shamefully parochial. "East" and "West" are still thought of by many as defining distinct mentalities, whether they are interpreted as referring to the two sides of the Iron Curtain or of the International Date Line. And on a smaller scale, Anglo-American philosophy on the one hand, and continental European philosophy on the other, are almost wholly indifferent to one another. The world of art has for some time been quite genuinely world-wide in the scope of its awareness and appreciation; this is only just beginning to be true in the world of ideas.

A number of themes can be identified as recurring elements in the various world philosophies. I am not talking about anything so abstruse as a supposedly perennial and universal philosophy, but about something much simpler, and I think more useful: a few guides to the understanding of what most of these philosophies are getting at. The similarities that we find here are in the pattern of what has been called "family resemblance": what makes the members of a family look alike is not that there are some traits which appear in all of them, but rather that each member resembles some of the others in one trait or another, and that none of them looks wholly different from the rest. In my eyes, the world philosophies show a family resemblance; and how could it be otherwise in the family of man?

In this spirit, I would mention first a theme of *rationality,* broadly enough conceived to include various kinds of emphases on intellect and understanding. The world is viewed as some sort of systematic unity—causal or historical, constituting a purely natural order or perhaps a moral order as well, but in any case making sense in its togetherness. Existentialism's category of "the absurd," and Zen's receptivity to nonsense puts them somewhat apart in this respect. But for the most part, the philosophies at work in the world today view human life against a background of something intelligible to the human mind, and so regard knowledge as being of prime importance. It may be knowledge of nature, as in pragmatism and analytic philosophy; or knowledge of society, as is especially characteristic of communism and Confucian thought; or knowledge of the self, which is so central in psychoanalysis, Indian philosophy, and elsewhere. At any rate, philosophy is usually thought of as a rational enterprise; it need not surprise us that philosophy thinks highly of the uses of reason.

There is a second theme of *activism:* understanding is not sufficient unto itself but serves as a guide to action. The business of philosophy is neither the construction nor contemplation of a world picture; knowledge does not provide us with a picture at all, but with a map by which to find our way. Only analytic philosophy at one extreme and Taoism at the other are content with scientific understanding or mystic contemplation; for the rest, that there is something to be done is central to the philosophy. Pragmatism and communism explicitly make action the primary context of all meaning and value. Existentialism and psychoanalysis are concerned with putting the individual effectively into that context, the one in its emphasis on involvement or commitment, and the other in its emphasis on the externalization of conflict, and of the impulses of love and hate. In Asian thought, action is fundamental as the performance of duty—the Indian *karma-yoga*—or as the locus of self-discipline, so central in Buddhism and especially Zen. And when action is viewed in relation to its rational base, education comes to the focus of attention, as it has in pragmatist and Confucian thought, or in communist indoctrination.

A third theme is *humanism,* the centrality of man in the philosophy itself, if not in the world philosophized about. The continuity of man and nature is widely recognized—in the West, as a mark of post-Darwinian thought, and in the East, as part of an outlook in which the familiar dualisms of man and nature, mind and the world, subject and object, never have taken hold. In many of the philosophies, a theory of human nature, of the mind and self, is either the starting point or the culmination of the whole movement of thought: this is especially true, I think, of pragmatism, existentialism, psychoanalysis, and Buddhism. For the communist and Confucian, it is a theory of man in society that serves in this way. A number of the philosophies are further distinguished by the place which they provide for man's emotional nature, the workings of the mind at the lower psychic levels. This is exemplified by the close connection of existentialism with literature, by the bearing of psychoanalysis on the understanding of art, and of Taoism and Zen on its creation.

Finally, I would mention as a family trait of world philosophies today a preoccupation with *values,* especially moral and spiritual values. In several of the Western philosophies, most notably the analytic school, the concern is with the basis on which values can be grounded. Asian thought, by and large, takes this basis for granted, or refers it back to some conception of human nature; in either case, values are viewed as being no more problematic than facts. In almost all the philosophies, the specific content of the realm of value is left open; and by some of them the life of man is viewed as nothing other than the filling in of this content—existentialism, psychoanalysis, and pragmatism, I think, all take this view. The one specific value on which the various movements of thought converge is freedom, but variously interpreted in psychological, social, moral, or spiritual terms. The last is by and large taken in a naturalistic sense, without dependence on a God or a realm of being transcending the world of human experience. I am struck by the observation that most of the philosophies proceed from a profound sense of the disvalue in life, rather than from the awe and wonder in which Aristotle saw the birth of philosophy. A certain joyousness may be found in Taoism and Zen, but for the other philosophies the life of man, as it is, leaves much to be desired. All of them are in striking agreement that the accumulation of possessions and the perfection of the machine are very far from fulfilling our highest human aspirations.

No doubt other strands of thought can be identified as running through several of these philosophies. But for us the difficulty is not in finding similarities but in doing justice to differences. It is relativism and subjectivism that remain the bugbears of our thinking. We say that every man is entitled to his opinion; but how can we acknowledge that title without conceding that our own opinion is no better than any other? Or putting it the other way around, how can we act with vigor and confidence in our own perspectives and yet recognize the possibility, and even the reasonableness, of other points of view? We are caught, most of us, in the dilemma of absolutism or subjectivism. On the one hand, there are the "God's truth" philosophies, for which all others are heresies and the work of the devil; I have known men espousing even such a sweetly reasonable view as that of analytic philosophy who nevertheless act as though they alone were in possession of God's truth. If only there were not conflicting claims to truth, or if, indeed, God Himself, in unmistakable accents, proclaimed which was His truth! But on the other hand, the subjectivist, for whom you pays your money and takes your choice, makes whatever is chosen worthless, save as an expression of a momentary whim or fancy.

I do not think we escape the dilemma with an eclecticism which pretends to be better than all by making a concoction of the best from each. In my judgment, it is often the worst that is chosen, or at any rate it loses its worth when we set out to make a hash of it. It seems to me that the rich diversity of the world's cultures is rapidly giving way to an empty sameness, in the pursuit of what I have elsewhere described as a realm of value rich and creamy with homogenized goodness. We are cultivating a cultural uniformity amidst unyielding political differences; the hope of the world, as I see it, lies in exactly the reverse: a political unity within which cultural and individual differences can flourish. I do not look forward to a state of society in which all men espouse one world philosophy, but rather to a state in which each man espouses his own philosophy, but one in which he can live at peace with all the world.

For philosophy, as I see it, has in a certain respect more kinship with art than with science. We do not expect every culture, much less every individual, to create and appreciate one and the same style of art, while we do expect them ultimately to arrive at and accept the same scientific truths. And a living philosophy is even more like the creation of art than like its appreciation: when it comes to philosophy, there are no spectators, only participants. The pictures that we paint of ourselves and the world, the ideas with which we furnish our minds—these are as intimately our own as anything could be. An acquaintance with the work of others serves us best when we make it a guide and stimulus to the release of our own creativity.

What is new in this new world of philosophy is not something in the ideas themselves. The distinctively Asian schools date from antiquity, and the main lines of the Western schools can also be traced back as far as our historical scholarship will carry us. What I think of as new is the possibility of reabsorbing the past into a living present, and more especially, of doing so in a perspective which, for the first time in human history, can be genuinely world-wide in scope.

The association of philosophy with age is, I believe, a mistake; fullness of years may bring wisdom, but the love of wisdom is more passionate in the young. It is they in whom the sense of wonder is most intense, whose horizons spread widest, whose determination to make something of themselves and this great world is most unflinching. Politics in our time has made of the "brave new world" a name of bitterness and fear. As we grow in our understanding of other people and other ways, and thereby of ourselves, I do not know what better task our philosophies can set themselves than to restore the youthful hope in this brave new world, that has such people in it.

LECTURE ONE

Pragmatism

There is something peculiarly appropriate about the use of closed-circuit television for a lecture on pragmatism. It is *not,* I must say at once, that pragmatism is a philosophy which promises fast, fast, fast relief; nor that it is so distinctively the philosophy of American business (as Europeans have so often charged) as to be itself only an egghead commercial. Pragmatism does address itself to the problems of everyday life in this messy world, and it is indeed an intellectualized expression of the American genius for solving problems. But the appropriateness that I have in mind refers to something different. It is that the complexities of cameras, lights, and wiring, with all the constraints they impose in an academic setting, confront us with the recurrent question—Who is to be master, man or the machine? Now pragmatism is distinguished, I think, from all other philosophies in making this question central, in tackling it with all the seriousness it deserves as basic to the modern predicament. Whether it be the hydrogen bomb, the so-called cybernetic revolution, or just the workings of the social mechanism in general—there is no doubt that the problems of life in the mid-twentieth century turn on our capacity to master the instruments we have devised for the conduct of life. Pragmatism may best be characterized as the attempt to assess the significance for human values of technology in the broadest sense.

The word "pragmatism" comes from a root which means an act, deed, or affair. This derivation goes far to express the spirit of the pragmatic movement. Just as Socrates brought philosophy down from the clouds into the market place, pragmatism brought it back from the academy into the laboratory and factory, studio, workshop, and home. For some centuries, the practitioners of philosophy in the Western world have been not philosophers but professors. And correspondingly, the philosophical issues with which they have been occupied have had the character of academic questions—that is, questions whose answers were not expected to have any practical consequences. In the nineteenth century the prevailing philosophy was an idealist metaphysics transcending the actualities of human experience. In the twentieth it became an abstract mathematical logic, equally removed from the problems of men. The pragmatic reconstruction in philosophy, as John Dewey has termed it, is by no means a replacement of "theoretical" by "practical" considerations: on the contrary, a cardinal tenet of pragmatism is the repudiation of this antithesis. No one is more insistent than the pragmatist on the practical import of sound theorizing. His reconstruction of philosophy aims at putting soundness into philosophical theory, not at taking the theory out of philosophy. And that means giving philosophy significance in terms of human action in general, rather than in terms of only the acts characteristic of academicians whose specialty happens to be "philosophy."

It has set about doing this by viewing philosophy always in the perspective of the whole cultural context in which it serves *as* philosophy. Pragmatism, that is to say, insists on regarding philosophy primarily as a human endeavor—serving human purposes in various ways and more or less effectively, subject to the same limitations as every other human endeavor, and sharing also in the unlimited reach of the human spirit. Philosophy may be the most academic of disciplines, but the academy is, after all, a part of society. What could be more academic than Einstein's theory of relativity? But what formula has had more explosive impact on society than "$E = mc^2$"? If "academic" means remote, speculative, and really of no importance, it is because thought has become sterile or because society has emasculated the thinker. There are men who, confronted with an oppressive problem, find refuge in the counsel, "O well, let's be philosophical—let's just not think about it!" If philosophy has come to this, it is a reflection, not on the uses of reason, but on the irrationalities of our use of it.

The nineteenth century was more alive to the power of ideas; and the impact on the twentieth century of the ideas of Karl Marx has brought us to a belated awareness that a philosophy may be of more than academic interest. Such awareness is itself of philosophic significance. The philosophic enterprise is directed toward giving clarity and coherence to the fundamental presuppositions of culture, the ideas and principles that underly the science, art, religion, politics, and morality of a particular society. The task of philosophy is both analytic and synoptic—laying out the parts of our basic ideas and reassembling them into a working whole.

But philosophy does something more: it has also a creative task. For philosophy does not merely follow a track parallel to the course of social movements, reflecting them but at some remove, in a symbolic dimension remote from reality. It is a part of the process of social change. Unless, indeed, the philosophy is a merely academic speculation, it is an instrument for such change, formulating new values and providing a conceptual framework by which they can be grasped and realized. This is the creative, or one might even say, the prophetic role of the philosopher in society. His task does not end with the explanation and justification of things as they are, though many philosophers have, to be sure, contented themselves with being little more than apologists for the old order. In this changing world, the business of philosophy is, in Dewey's phrasing, to mediate between the stubborn past and the insistent future. If philosophy today is to have any significance outside the academy—as the great philosophies always *have* had for their cultures—it must provide us with some scheme of ideas by which we can make clear and coherent both the claims on us of established institutions and practices, and the promise for us of a freer, fuller life held out by the new ways of the emerging future.

Pragmatism, therefore, approaches philosophy as it approaches all ideas—and indeed, all human endeavors—by asking, not "What does it mean?" but rather "What is it supposed to *do?*" For its meaning lies in its purpose, or rather, in the way in which it works to fulfill its purpose. For the pragmatist, philosophy must be understood functionally, as an ideational structure and process serving social ends, playing a significant part in the continuing effort of every culture to make the most of human life, as that culture conceives it.

If we now ask, "What *is* the task for twentieth-century philosophy in the Western world?" the answer that pragmatism gives is direct and to the point. In its simplest and most fundamental terms, it is to assimilate the impact of science on human affairs. The business of philosophy today is to provide a system of ideas that will make an integrated whole of our beliefs about the nature of the world and the values which we seek in the world in fulfillment of our human nature. There is no doubt that far and away the most significant development in Western culture in the past three or four centuries has been the rise of modern science and the transformation of civilization by the technology based on that science. But in the course of this transformation, a radical bifurcation has grown up between man and nature, value and fact, which confronts us with the dilemma of either turning our backs on science or else resigning ourselves to living in a world without human meaning or purpose. Pragmatism conceives the task of philosophy for modern man to be nothing other than finding a way out of this dilemma.

The history of modern philosophy is, for pragmatism, a history of successive attempts to cope with this problem, and the elaborate constructions of epistemologists and metaphysicians are to be understood in terms of their bearing on this fundamental cultural crisis. On one side we have science and technology, on the other side, religion, morals, politics, and art. The tradition of realism and empiricism—from John Locke and David Hume to Bertrand Russell—has turned largely in the direction of science, and has provided for human values no more solid a foundation than a subjective emotional involvement. The idealist tradition—represented most influentially by Hegel and the conventional religionists—may do justice to human aspiration but cannot give any intelligible account of science and scientific method consistent with its own presuppositions. Other philosophies—like those of Descartes, Immanuel Kant, and contemporary neo-orthodoxy—try to resolve the dilemma simply by accepting it, thinking to settle the conflict between science and religion, between rational good sense and emotional sensibility, by assigning to each its own domain within which its sovereignty is to be undisputed.

Pragmatism cannot rest content with either of the one-sided philosophies, which simply ignore the problem, nor yet with any dualistic philosophy, which mistakes a formulation of the problem for its solution. As against the scientific philosophies of our time, the pragmatist is determined to restore man to the position of centrality which is rightfully his—not because the world is mindful of man, but because it is the human mind with which we inescapably look out on our world. As against the several idealisms, the pragmatist insists on the realities of conditions and consequences, causes and effects, in which ideals must be grounded if they are to have any impact on human life. And as against the philosophies which compartmentalize experience, the pragmatist argues that man cannot live divided against himself, affirming in the name of religion or morality what he must deny in the name of science. By circumscribing for each its own sphere of influence, we do not forestall conflict but only mark out the battle lines.

Pragmatism is thus both a humanistic and a scientific philosophy, and that it is both in an integrated rather than a dualistic sense is perhaps its most distinguishing characteristic. Most philosophers,

Williams James once observed, are either tough-minded or tender-hearted. The pragmatist is tough-minded in his determination to live in the world as it is, rather than in the fantasy worlds of the metaphysicians and theologians. Since it is science which provides us with the best warranted knowledge of the world as it is (and in the broadest sense of science, the *only* knowledge), his philosophy must be firmly grounded in science. Not, to be sure, in the content of science, which changes from day to day as our knowledge grows, but in the *method* of science: controlling the abstract intelligence by its application to the concrete facts of observation and experience. And being human, for us it is the facts of human life that are most important. Most scientific philosophies derive from the natural sciences, and especially from physics and mathematics; for pragmatism, it is biology, psychology, and the social sciences that have been most influential; indeed, James and Dewey themselves made important contributions to psychology, and George Herbert Mead (perhaps the last of the great pragmatists) is as well known to sociologists as to philosophers.

But the pragmatist is tender-hearted, too, at least in the sense that he is unwavering in the conviction—or the faith, if you will—that human values and purposes are a part of nature, natural events like any other, matters of fact for which any scientific account of the world must provide a place. It is striking that all the philosophies that have any considerable influence in the world today agree in giving primacy to the human significance of the world process. In this respect, pragmatism can take its place alongside existentialism, communism, and the various religious philosophies. It differs from these, not in assigning only a minor role to man and his works (as the scientific philosophies are charged with doing by many of their critics), but in the scientific basis that it puts forward as the ground of its perspectives. The religionist relies on theology; the communist —for all his talk of "scientific" rather than "utopian" socialism—replaces social science by ideology; and the existentialist substitutes literature and its metaphysics for a scientific psychology. Modern man is caught up in a cultural dualism which threatens to split his personality as it has already fragmented his institutions. The pragmatist, attacking this dualism, is in the position of fighting a war on two fronts: more scientific than one side, more human than the other, he finds himself repudiated by both. But fortunately for him, both by temperament and by philosophic conviction he thrives on conflict.

But even more important to the pragmatist than the resolution of this conflict is the way we go about resolving it. Contrary to the popular reading of the word "pragmatic," his emphasis is not on results but on method. In his analysis, science turns out to be essentially a method of inquiry, democracy a method of arriving at public policy, morality a method of integrating impulse wth intelligence, and even art and religion he conceives as methods of organizing and realizing potentialities of human value. If pragmatism is concerned always with bearings on action, it approaches action in terms, not of what we do, but of how we do it. The pragmatic philosophy itself it characterizes by its *way* of philosophizing, not by a distinctive body of philosophic doctrine: William James' first book on pragmatism bore the subtitle "A New Name For Some Old Ways of Thinking."

Old or new, the pragmatic way of thinking means, first, to put every problem into its concrete behavioral and social setting, to analyze every idea as an abstraction from some context of action. Accordingly, this is sometimes called the principle of *contextualism.* Every experience occurs in what Dewey calls a biological and cultural matrix, and the conceptions that grow out of and are tested by experience are inevitably conditioned by that matrix. We have already seen how the pragmatist approaches philosophy in general as a human enterprise carried on in specific social situations; and he approaches particular philosophic problems in the same way. Contextualism implies that both the data and solution of these problems are *relative*—relative, that is, not to the mere think-so of the philosopher, but to the factors at work in the context in which the problem arises and is to be solved. And it implies also that data and solutions are ultimately *concrete,* rooted in the particular existents that make up the context, not in the abstract generalities of a fictitious world of ideas. Contextualism means that no problem can be solved once for all, for the simple reason that we can confront a problem only in the situation in which we happen to find ourselves; in other situations, the problems that we will face will also be quite other. There are no ultimates, no absolutes, because there is no ultimate and absolute context—or if there is, it is the habitat of God alone. For man, "sufficient unto the day is the evil thereof"; the pragmatist adds only, "and the good thereof as well."

The pragmatic method is secondly a *genetic* method. The pragmatist asks always, How did it get this way? What was its origin, its purpose, its function? How did the context in which it arose shape the character it now presents to us? It is noteworthy that of the four most influential thinkers of the past hundred years—Darwin, Marx, Freud, and Einstein—three of them explicitly applied the genetic method to their subject matters, and the fourth applied it to the basic concepts of his subject, if not to the subject itself. The historical, evolutionary, functional approach has been invaluable in the human sciences. But throughout most of its history, philosophy has been influenced rather by mathematics and the natural sciences, and so has occupied itself with the quest for fixed relations among timeless essences. Pragmatism takes time seriously.

In the third place, the pragmatic method looks for continuities and gradations rather than separateness and sharp differences. Wherever the pragmatist encounters polarities—and his way is beset by them: mind and body, reason and emotion, the individual and society, man and nature—he sets himself the task of overcoming them by reconstituting them as aspects of a seamless whole. Dichotomies imposed on the facts are to be recognized as the impositions that they are, the results of transposing distinctions in our ideas into differences in things. The integrated personality and coherent culture for which the pragmatist strives he puts forward as an ideal rooted in the wholeness of the world of actuality. What God has put together man has torn asunder: this is the original sin of traditional philosophy. It demands, not the merely ritualistic expiation of a monistic metaphysics, but a thoroughgoing reconstruction of our ways of living in God's world.

But both the guilt and its atonement are viewed by pragmatism in a wholly naturalistic perspective. The pragmatic method repudiates the appeal to any transcendent beings or processes. We must make sense of experience only in terms of what experience itself discloses. To explain anything in this world by referring to a world "above," "beyond," or "beneath" is to make a metaphysics out of a metaphor. Of course there is a difference between what merely appears to be such and such, and what really is such and such; but there is no such thing as "Appearance" and "Reality." The world really *is* what experience shows it to be. When we say that something is only apparent, we are contrasting it, not with what transcends experience, but with what would be disclosed in other experiences. Transcendent metaphysics converts a functional and contextual difference to a substantive and absolute distinction. Talk about what lies outside *any* experience remains just talk: its truth cannot possibly make any difference—that is, truistically, any difference that anyone could possibly experience.

In its naturalism the pragmatic method thus repudiates what Herbert Feigl has called the "seductive fallacy," the fallacy of invoking a mysterious something more. For the naturalist there are no mysteries. There are many things which we do not know, many which we will probably never know; but there is nothing in principle unknowable, nothing which cannot be made intelligible and be intelligently dealt with in terms of human experience. The stock metaphor of a vast and measureless ocean of ignorance on which human knowledge precariously borders embodies a truth of enduring relevance. The naturalist yields to no one in the humility, the sense of awe and wonder, evoked by that limitless horizon. But what lies at his feet is wondrous in just the same way. The gods that rule the sea have dominion over the land as well. It is one world after all.

Thus pragmatic naturalism also repudiates the reductive fallacy, the fallacy of "nothing but." Experience must be accepted on its own terms. If it is futile to try to understand man by assigning him a transcendent soul, it is equally pointless to deny his distinctive humanity by pretending that he is "only" a complex physical and biological system. Neither view is true to experience: the one because it is not the whole truth, and the other because it is not nothing but the truth. The pragmatic method is an attempt to provide a rational basis in experience for our beliefs about both facts and values, or rather, to provide beliefs which can be given such a basis. Experience must come first, or our thinking is nothing but projection and rationalization: imposing on the world the content of our own prejudices, then justifying the prejudices by pretending to find them built into the nature of the world as it is.

With this sketch of the pragmatist conception of the aims and methods of philosophy, we can proceed to more substantive matters.

The primary question which pragmatism raises, in common with so much of contemporary philosophy, is the question of meaning. Under what conditions does a statement *have* meaning, and *what* meaning attaches to it in the light of these conditions? The whole pragmatic movement begins with a consideration of these questions, in a paper published in *Popular Science Monthly* in 1878 by Charles Saunders Peirce, a man who is coming to be regarded more and more as the greatest American philosopher, perhaps one of the greatest of the modern world. His essay was called "How to Make Ideas Clear," and it is in this essay on semantics that the defining principles of pragmatism were first explicitly set forth.

Peirce's criterion of meaningfulness and of the proper way to analyze meanings has come to be known as the *pragmatic maxim.* It has been given many formulations, first by Peirce, then by James, and in our own time by Dewey, Mead, C. I. Lewis, and other philosophers. What these formulations amount to is this: In order to understand what is meant by any proposition, we must ask ourselves, "Suppose this proposition were true; what conceivable bearing might it have on the conduct of our lives?" When we have fully answered this question, we have said all there is to say about the meaning of the proposition. And if we are unable to specify any respect in which its truth or falsehood could conceivably have any bearing on our lives, then we are also unable to specify any meaning whatsoever for that proposition. William James, with his characteristic flair, puts it more simply: "A difference that makes no difference *is* no difference." It is only a matter of words. This is essentially the content also of the so-called "verifiability theory of meaning" of the logical positivists, that meaning lies in the mode of verification, and a proposition which is in principle unverifiable has no meaning at all. And it is much the same as the viewpoint of "operationalism," which identifies the meaning of a scientific concept with the operations by which we determine whether or not the concept applies to a particular case.

Pragmatism arrives at this position, not on the basis of an abstract logical analysis, but as a result of that focus on concreteness which is the heart of the pragmatic method. Meanings occur always in a human context, which is to say, a context of action: words mean only because people mean something by them. Language is an abstraction from concrete acts of speech, and such acts have their origin in the desire to achieve some human end. Meaning, in short, must be analyzed by reference to its genesis in a context of purposive behavior. Meanings are a part of the natural world, continuous with all the sorts of events that make up experience. There is no separate realm of meaning, peopled by ghostly essences or forms utterly different in their makeup from the things and processes of concrete experience. Because semantic verbs are transitive, we suppose that there must be entities peculiarly suited to serve as their objects, thereby mistaking an all-too-human grammar for the creative Word of God Himself. When a man "means something," what is happening is a process like "catching a cold" or "taking a walk." The cold is not a mysterious entity that exists apart from the act of catching it, just as the walk a man takes is constituted by his act of taking it. Meanings come to be when human beings perform certain actions. They do not constitute another world, but provide another dimension, an additional degree of freedom, to the one world which is the locus of purposive behavior.

When a man asserts a proposition, he is expressing a belief; and every belief is a rule for action. When I say, "This desk is made of wood," my meaning is to be understood as follows: If you want something that will float on water, you can make it of this stuff; if you want to warm yourself, you can set fire to it and it will burn; if you need material that can be sawed and hammered, you can use this; and so on. In other words, a meaning is to be analyzed as an indefinite set of propositions, hypothetical in form, with the antecedent of each hypothetical stating a human purpose, interest, value, or goal, and the consequent of the hypothetical indicating the outcome of appropriate action. This is what James called the "cash value" of the idea—its import for the fulfillment of purpose. When Alice, floating down the rabbit hole, decided it didn't matter whether she said that cats eat bats or bats eat cats, because she couldn't tell which was true anyhow, she was being a pragmatist.

Traditionally, meanings were thought of as creations of the human mind, or at any rate, as eternal essences or forms capable of being grasped by the mind because they are rational or intellectual in their own nature. This procedure, the pragmatist argues, is trying to explain what we do not understand on the basis of what we do not know. In these terms, the "mind" is a mysterious faculty invoked for the express purpose of having commerce with equally mysterious "meanings." The pragmatic method requires that we go the other way around. We must begin with what we know and experience, the actions of human beings engaged in purposive behavior in concrete settings. Out of such behavior meanings emerge as rules or habits of action, brought into play by concrete objects which, because of their function in behavior, can be identified as symbols. And the "mind" is nothing other than the use of symbols. Undeniably, many details and even larger features of this process are obscure; but at least, we know how to make them less so, by adding to our knowledge of human behavior. The mind, as a metaphysical substance, must remain forever impenetrable. We are tempted to think of it as a substance because the word "mind" is a substantive.

The situation would be much more clearly conveyed if the word were a verb, or better yet, an adverb. To say something about the mind is to talk about certain ways we have of doing things, not about a secret agent who does them for us.

Pragmatism thus rests on a behavioral psychology; over half a century ago it argued that "consciousness" is expendable. The position was *not* that what a man strives for would be best attained if only he could stop intellectualizing and act instead on the basis of natural impulse—very much the contrary! What was repudiated was "consciousness" as an explanatory category, not as an instrument of successful action. The pragmatist rejects mentalism in psychology and metaphysics, but if anything he is even more hostile to any kind of anti-intellectualism. He has no use for the notion of an abstract intellect, but every use in the world for an intellect conceived as manifested in intelligent behavior.

This kind of behavioral psychology is not to be confused with the behaviorism that made such a stir a few decades ago. For that was a reductive, a "nothing but," psychology. It made the cardinal error of identifying mental processes with their physical, organic manifestations—as though playing chess can be described as nothing but changing the positions of little bits of wood: to the chess-player, "wood-pushing" means precisely thoughtless, unintelligent play. What the behaviorist did not realize is that meaning, and therefore mind, is a social phenomenon: it is something that happens in the interaction among organisms and not within any one of them. A gesture (including, in particular, a spoken word, which is, as it were, a vocal gesture) becomes a symbol only when the person making it is able to respond to it from the standpoint of other people. We are using symbols only when in ourselves we play the role of other people, only when what we say and do means to us what it would mean to anyone else who speaks our language. Mind, as George Herbert Mead put it, is the capacity to make gestures and respond to them from the standpoint of "the generalized other." We become selves only through this basic identification with others. An infant isolated from other human beings, if he lived, would no more have a mind or self than he would have a language—not even the Hebrew with which the Creator endowed Adam.

Behaviorism also blundered in concentrating on subcutaneous responses, as though mental processes go on only inside the skin. The pragmatist urges that we do our thinking, not only with the brain, but also with the liver and stomach and kidneys and everything else that makes up a whole organism. But even more important in his conception, we think with paper and pencil, and pieces of chalk, with pliers and microscopes and cyclotrons—in short, with whatever instruments we use in any kind of problem-solving activity. Mind is an abstraction derived from the concreta of intelligent behavior. It is purposive and social through and through. It is capable of grasping meanings because meanings are themselves abstractions from the very same contexts of interpersonal purposive behavior that gives man a mind.

From this analysis of mind and meaning it is only a short step to the pragmatist theory of truth. The truth of an idea lies in the fulfillment of purpose which the idea makes possible. In James' not always happy phrasing, the truth is what works, what is expedient in our thinking. The attribute of truth accrues to an idea when we put the idea to work. It becomes true as we use it, for its truth is nothing other than its usefulness.

Now it is easy to misunderstand this doctrine, and Europeans especially have widely misunderstood it. Obviously, a scoundrel's purpose may be better fulfilled by falsehood than by truth, a lie may work some of the time, a deception may prove expedient, and even self-deception has its uses. But all this is entirely beside the point, for it places the idea only in a personal and limited context, which is just what the pragmatist wants to get away from. No proposition becomes true only because it pleases us to believe it, or to have others believe it, any more than something we eat becomes nourishing merely because we enjoy its taste or because gourmets commend it. Whether or not an idea is useful is not a matter of subjective feeling, nor even of an objectively warranted judgment based on only a single context of application. What counts is whether it works in the long run, and really works out—that is, achieves the ends to which it serves as a means, regardless of the recognition withheld or bestowed on its achievement. James once characterized as "an impudent slander" the charge that pragmatists claim that an idea is true if it makes us happy to think so. Whether the charge is malicious I cannot say; but it seems to me beyond question that it *is* a misrepresentation.

The pragmatist theory of truth amounts, I think, to this: that candidates for truth are fundamentally not descriptions but predictions, and what they predict is the outcome of possible action. Empiricism is essentially retrospective in its outlook: the credentials which it demands of an idea before admitting it to the realm of truth are those which certify its origins. Unless a proposition derives either from sensation or else from reflection on the relations of ideas among themselves, Hume insisted, it must be committed to the flames as sophistry and illusion. But pragmatism, in spite of its reliance on the genetic method, turns here, not to the origins of the idea, but to its destination. What counts is not its antecedents, but what we can do with the idea, what we can made of it, what it promises for the enrichment of our lives. For knowledge is not merely a record of the past—not even the kind of knowledge we call "history." It is a reconstruction of the present directed toward fulfillments in the emerging future.

To be sure, we must not confuse our knowledge of the truth with what it is we know. And does not truth itself consist simply in correspondence with the facts, whether the facts—including the fact of correspondence—are known or not? Aristotle with characteristic directness defined truth as saying of that which is *that* it is, and of that which is not, that it is not. This is perfectly straightforward and unobjectionable. But the pragmatic theory of truth is not an alternative to this so-called correspondence theory; it is an attempt, rather, to explain what the correspondence consists in. Pragmatism conceives of a true proposition as being rather like a "correspondent" in a divorce case. The truth of the proposition is a matter of its interactions with things, its involvement in affairs; it does not consist in some mysterious abstract resemblance to facts.

Strictly speaking, of course, it is we who are involved, not propositions. The proposition serves in our transactions, and its truth is the measure of its service. A true proposition corresponds to the facts in the sense that it leads us to the facts, guides us in our dealings with them, brings our efforts to their consummation. In the pragmatist conception, truth belongs to propositions, we might say, in the colloquial sense: to assert a proposition is to make a proposal or invitation to some reality. The proposition is true when the offer is accepted, and has a happy outcome.

At bottom, what is at issue is the conception, not of truth, but of knowledge. Knowledge is *of* the truth, and truth has significance for us, obviously, only as and when it is known. How philosophers conceive of truth, therefore, is largely determined by their conception of knowledge, not the other way around. For all we know of truth is only what belongs, tautologically, to the object of knowledge. And what the pragmatist is repudiating is the notion that in knowing we are no more than spectators of the passing show. The classical realist theory of knowledge yields only what I have ventured to call a "keyhole epistemology," as though we pry out Nature's secrets without ever intruding on her privacy. This ideal of so-called objectivity does not make a virtue out of a necessity, but a necessity out of a secret vice. It projects onto inquiry, both in science and in everyday life, the frame of mind of the merely academic in the worst sense of that word. Setting aside the pretensions of philosophy, every actual case of knowing is one in which we are involved with what we know. We must do something with the object of knowledge for it to *become* known: manipulate it, take it apart, experiment on it. Even just looking, if it is to yield cognitions, is not a matter of pure passivity. For scientific observation, surely, is not "just looking," or at any rate, it is not *just* looking: we throw light on the object, or pass x-rays through it, or bounce radar off of it. We know only as the outcome of our doings. The old saw that seeing is believing does not characterize the scientific mentality but its opposite. The task of inquiry is largely one of discovering what it is that needs to be done so that we *can* believe what we see.

Indeed, the knower is involved with the known even in the fuller sense of emotional involvement. The passion for truth is, after all, a passion, and however detached a scientist may be, he can scarcely deny an interest in his subject matter, often even a consuming interest. A consideration of the part played by judgments of value in inquiries into matters of fact must be postponed. But we must see to it that our theory of knowledge provides for such a part. Like other involvements, that of the scientist carries with it certain responsibilities. To embark on the cognitive enterprise is to enter into a commitment—a commitment to truth. The pragmatist conception of knowledge would be wholly untenable if it evaded that commitment. How to discharge the commitment to truth is the next question, therefore, that pragmatism faces. The answer to the question constitutes pragmatist logic.

The logic of pragmatism is usually identified as "instrumentalism." This is a very appropriate label, because the keynote of the pragmatist logic is the treatment of ideas as being essentially instruments for the solution of problems. As I have already pointed out, for the pragmatist, thought of any kind is an activity of problem-solving. Aristotle conceived of God as continuously engaged in nothing but thinking. The pragmatist god, if there were one, could never think at all: he would have nothing to think about—not even, as Aristotle claimed, thought itself. God has nothing to think about because He already has all the answers; all His interests are completely satisfied, all His purposes are already fulfilled. He has only to say, "Let there be!" and there is, and He can see that it is good. But for man, as T. S. Eliot has it:

> Between the conception
> And the creation
> Between the emotion
> And the response
> Falls the Shadow

In this chasm that separates the wish from its fulfillment thought finds its locus.

Now, thought will not serve as an instrument for problem-solving unless it is a real problem that we are thinking about. The problem is real when it is rooted in the situation in which we find ourselves as defined by the purposes which we have brought into it. The problem is unreal, artificial, misconceived when it is generated by conditions localizable only in the subjectivity of the thinker. A man shut in a room may suffer the agonies of Edmund Dantes even though the door is not locked; but his predicament is not genuine. For him, the question of how to emancipate himself may appear to be profoundly philosophical, but it has a simple and down-to-earth answer: open the door and walk out. His despair is that of the man who complains bitterly that he has nothing to eat but food. Such agonizing may generate metaphysics, but it has abandoned logic.

This is not to say, however, that the only real problems are practical ones, in a sense in which these are contrasted with problems of theory. A theoretical difficulty may be perfectly genuine—when it arises in a context of theorizing and can be given a solid ground in that context. However universal the natural law to which the scientist aspires, he himself is in a particular situation; though he is concerned with an abstract generality, his concern itself is quite concrete and particular. It is this concrete particularity that makes his problems genuine, for it is this that thwarts his purposes and invites thought about how to fulfill them or redirect them in the light of the real conditions that set his problem.

Now, whenever we face a problem, there is always something about our situation that is not problematic. Every problem presents itself to us as a difficulty projected against a background of what G. H. Mead called "the world that is there." Not everything can be problematic all at once. You cannot meaningfully formulate a problem without specifying data for the problem, and these data are not themselves problematic—or at any rate, they are not problematic in that context. Modern philosophy is still often victimized by the influence of Descartes, who supposed that the only safe proceeding for a philosopher is to begin from scratch, to assume that he knows nothing, and then to admit one at a time only those ideas which satisfy the most critical scrutiny. This Descartes called methodological scepticism; it has had many followers and not only among sophomores. But from the standpoint of pragmatic logic, such wholesale scepticism is nonsense. In philosophy, Charles Peirce pointed out, as anywhere else, there is only one place to begin, and that is where you are. To a request for directions on how to reach Killarney Castle even a Dublin policeman wouldn't answer, "Sure, and I just wouldn't start from here!"

No human being already capable of thought ever *is* at scratch. Not even a philosopher can start to think in total, utter ignorance, however tempting that description may be as applied to some of our philosophical opponents. We begin always with *some* knowledge about *some* features of reality. Classical epistemology set itself the problem of justifying the movement in thought from the self to the world, the problem of proving, that is to say, that there is such a thing as an external world, that the whole of experience is not merely a shadow play of my own dreams and fancies. Such a problem may be appropriate for a Society of Solipsists, each convinced, of course, that he is the founder and sole member of the organization; for the rest of us, it is the problem itself that is a play of shadows. Our thought does not begin with the self, and problematically move out to the world. We are in the world to begin with, and thought is directed to the question how we can move from one part of it to another. Thought concerns itself with moving from some particular context in which a problem presents itself to the other contexts continuously emerging in the endless flow of experience.

The answer to this question, in its most general terms, constitutes nothing other than logic. Logic is simply the most general formulation of the procedures of successful inquiry, or problem-solving. Some decades ago a famous textbook of elementary logic was published called *An Introduction to Logic and Scientific Method*. John Dewey's criticism of this book was focused on one word, and that a word in the title, the word "and." For this word implied that logic and scientific method were two separate things. But logic is nothing else than a statement of the methods to be pursued in order to arrive at warranted beliefs. The system of such beliefs is what we call science; what we call logic *is* just the method of science. Logicians sometimes talk as though their relation to scientists is that of the baseball commissioner, or at least an umpire, to the players: laying down the rules and judging whether they have been obeyed, with the power to thumb anyone out of the game for being "illogical." It is true, of course, that logic formulates norms of inquiry, and rules of proof if not of discovery. But for the pragmatist the authority of these norms derives from the cumulated experience of the scientific enterprise itself. It is not grounded in the metaphysical constitution written by God for the order of nature: when a man thinks logically it is not that he is expressing "Thy will be done," but rather that he is bending every effort of an all-too human intelligence to achieve a fully human end.

Thus logic, like the rest of philosophy, is basically something that men do, and occurs always in a concrete bio-social context. Logic is not more absolute and unchanging than anything else in human affairs. Pragmatism agrees that logic is concerned not with how men *do* think but with how they *ought* to think. But it insists that the force of logical norms derives from their grounding in what as a matter of fact happens when we think in one way or another. For several centuries philosophers have been anxious to avoid what they call "psychologism"—that is, confusing questions of logic with matters of psychology. For the pragmatist, logic is either inseparable from psychology or else it has nothing to do with thinking: thought, after all, is inescapably a psychological process. The point really to be made is that the psychology in question must not be mentalistic or subjectivist. If it is behavioral and objective—if, in other words, it occupies itself with what experience reveals to be the relations between the human being and his environment—then it is indispensable to the logician. For the logician aims at nothing other than a specification of those general ways of acting on the environment that actualize man's capacity to solve his problems.

To be sure, many factors of interest to the psychologist have no particular logical significance. They are highly personalized, or peculiar to some special feature of just that problematic situation. But that men are generally given to wishful thinking and rationalization, that emotional excitement interferes with accurate perception, or that mental "sets" thwart the creativity of the free imagination—these are surely matters of logical as well as psychological interest. And what has just been said about psychology applies also to the other human sciences. Pragmatism unequivocally repudiates the communist notion of "class science": though different classes have different beliefs, the class consciousness of the believer is irrelevant to the truth of the belief itself. Yet the class structure of society may very well have a logical bearing. The culture of the European Renaissance gave birth to modern science while those of ancient Greece, India, and China did not; and one of the reasons generally pointed to is that in the ancient cultures it was beneath the dignity of the speculative thinker to soil his hands with the experimental manipulation of his materials. If true, this is surely of importance not only to the sociologist or historian, but also to anyone who hopes to appreciate what is involved in scientific method.

The pragmatist logic, in short, is concrete and substantive, rather than formal and abstract. Yet it must be said, in all fairness, that the astonishing growth of logic in the last century or so has been largely a matter of its purely formal development. But from the pragmatist point of view, formal logic is, in effect, a branch of mathematics. Apart from its intrinsic interest and beauty, its value as an explication of the norms of thinking or problem-solving is limited to the methods of mathematics itself, and the most developed parts of the exact sciences. Formal logic can provide an elegant reconstruction of knowledge already acquired, but throws little light on the procedures actually followed to acquire it. It is not that the pragmatist is seeking a logic of discovery rather than a logic of proof, but rather that he refuses to identify the formalist reconstruction of scientific method with the procedures of discovery and of proof that the scientist actually employs. The use of mathematics in science is, after all, a *use,* and cannot be understood in abstraction from the human purposes which make it useful. If the pragmatist logic has not fully availed itself of the subtleties and ingenuities of the formalist achievement, neither has the formalist fully appreciated the role of personality and culture in determining the patterns of thought which, in specific situations, further man's search for truth.

It is truth that is the goal of logical thinking and not the merely formal consistency of a self-contained system. For man is not self-contained, and it is just this fact that makes thinking necessary. The requirement of consistency amounts to the injunction, "First to thine own self be true." But beyond the self lies God's world to which thought reaches out. And it is how the world responds to our advances which determines whether there is any truth in us. In the scientific enterprise man is not engaged in reconstructing the blueprint of the work of Creation but in laying out his own work which lies before him. The value of a scientific discovery lies in the further discoveries which it enables us to make, just as falsehood drives us further and further into our own fantasy world. As the Talmud has it, the reward of a good deed is the opportunity to perform another, and the punishment of sin, the necessity to sin once more. We cannot judge the truth of a proposition by its accord with an idea in the mind of God but only by its usefulness in promoting other ideas by which we can get on in God's world.

And this is to say that truth is after all an ideal, not a specific objective attained time after time. It is the receding horizon rather than the mileposts on the road of inquiry. But the road is an endless one, and truth acquires human significance only if it is conceived in terms of progress along the road rather than as housed in a destination never to be reached. The measure of the solution to a scientific problem is not in the questions answered but in the new questions raised, not in how much ground we have traversed but in how much now lies open to us. Peirce's maxim "Do not block the road of inquiry" is thus the basic tenet of the pragmatist logic. New questions always arise: no thought and no action solves any problem once for all. If it is true that thinking is impelled by the need to resolve a difficulty in which we find ourselves, it is truistic that human life —and the life of the mind as much as any other—is nothing but one damned thing after another: man is born to trouble, as the sparks fly upward. As no solution is final, no thought can be said to have finally reached its goal. The outcome of the pragmatist logic is that nothing is certain, and certainly not the "truths of science." In a world of chance we must take our chances, and do the best we can.

Pragmatism, then, conceives logic as the most general formulation of the effective ways of solving problems, and conceives science and technology as the use of these ways in thought and action. It is on the basis of these conceptions that it approaches its fundamental task of integrating fact and value: science and technology on one side, and morality, religion, art and politics on the other. The pragmatist theory of value is central to the philosophy and stems directly from its logic.

In the pragmatist analysis, what we call "facts" all involve an element of value. For purposes are embedded in all our meanings, and every purpose determines a value. Discourse, even the most theoretical and abstract, is a segment of purposive behavior; to empty it of any reference, however indirect, to human value is to rob it of all human significance. What we call a fact is, tautologically, what we have *taken* to be factual. In so conceptualizing it, we have entered into a transaction with things: it is only in the context of such transactions that things acquire significance for us. They are marked out in our thought as the things that they are because it suits us to do so, because we find it useful, satisfactory. To be sure, our thinking so does not make it so; but this implies only that judgments of value are as fallible as any other (if there are any other!). It is only because the values implicated in discrimination of facts are ordinarily not problematic in the context of the discrimination that we tend to overlook their essential role. We contrast facts with values, not because they are different modes of being or the referents of different modes of signification, but simply because so often when we are specifying the facts we can take for granted the values implicated in the specification.

Correspondingly, values are themselves facts, patterns and events as natural as any other. And when science is conceived in terms of its distinctive method rather than its content in a specific cultural situation (usually the content of about a half-century ago!), it becomes clear that science is as applicable—at least, in principle—to the realm of value as to the more restricted domain so often assigned to it. The proper contrast is not between fact and value, but between old values and new, shared values and those in conflict, unreflective values and those that we have thought through—most fundamentally, between values which we uncritically project onto facts, and those which intelligent reflection on the materials of experience discloses in the facts themselves.

It is in the same perspective that the pragmatist views the conventional opposition between reason and emotion, knowledge and feeling. The philosophic task is not to mediate between them, but to make clear that the opposition itself is ill-conceived. Emotions are not, except in pathological cases, encapsulated from the world; on the contrary, they spring from and are directed toward features of the environment. They are grounded in happenings in the world and not merely in our own subjectivity—this is their genesis—and they hold out prospects for certain other happenings in the world and not merely in our own subjectivity—and this is their function. And the determination of what is going on in the world, and how it may be expected to affect our own purposes—just this is the work of reason. From the genetic and functional point of view, therefore, the proper contrast again is not between reason and emotion, but between rational emotions and irrational ones; not between knowledge and feeling, but between feelings grounded in what we know about ourselves and our situation, and those which are the product of ignorance, error, confusion, or caprice. The radical dualism which besets our culture is the institutionalization of a faulty philosophy. When we try to defend values by declaring them out of bounds to inquirers into fact, we succeed only in dehumanizing science and technology and in deranging politics, religion, morality, and art.

For the pragmatist, judgments of value fall within the domain of science in the sense of being subject to critical appraisal on the basis of intelligent reflection on facts. What a value judgment judges is that a certain act or situation will have certain consequences of experienced satisfaction or frustration. It declares that something will or will not serve as a means for the attainment of a desired end. And it does something more: it considers conditions as well as consequences. It judges not only the appropriateness of some means to a pre-assigned end but also the appropriateness of the end to the available means. Means and end reciprocally determine one another: we choose the road on the basis of our destination, but also pick the destination on the basis of the condition of the roads. "When I'm not with the girl I love, I love the girl I'm with" may, after all, express a healthy pragmatism. To acknowledge the centrality of conditions and consequences in the pursuit of value is only to express the determination to make the best of the world as it is, and as it can be made to be; anything else is a futile and dangerous romanticism.

Clearly these relations between means and ends are all matters of fact, to be validated by inquiry of just the sort that is needed to establish any other point of knowledge. Now it is universally acknowledged that whether a certain means will lead to a given end is a factual question. But how am I to know which end to take as "given"? It appears that the pragmatist tells me only to regard this end as in turn a means to other ends, and those as means to still others; but how shall I choose ultimate goals and values? The pragmatist presents us with what Philip Blair Rice has aptly called "the mountain-range effect": we climb one ridge only to find another lying before us, and so endlessly, without ever finally crossing the mountains. And this, indeed, is just the point that the pragmatist urges: there *is* no crossing over. All values lie in what he calls the "means-end continuum." All values are instrumentalities—every good is good for something. The only thing of which it could be strictly true that it is good in and of itself would be one that existed in and of itself—depending on no conditions and producing no consequences. With Spinoza we could call it God, but *sub specie temporalis* it is nothing at all. Of course the distinction between inherent and instrumental value is genuine and important: "How goodly are thy tents, O Jacob!" is the voice of a prophet and not of a tax assessor. But this distinction, like all others, the pragmatist insists on treating as contextual and functional, not as absolute and substantive. Values are inherent when we view the continuum retrospectively: they are the ends to which other means have brought us, performance of past promise, consummation of all our efforts to date. And the very same values are instrumental when viewed prospectively, foreshadowing the good that is yet to come. The words of a prophet, however divinely inspired, must await their fulfillment.

The issue, in short, is whether there are any final ends, ultimate and absolute. Pragmatism flatly says no. Its critics concede at once that the injunctions of technology take the form of hypothetical imperatives: "If you want *x*, do *y!* But moral injunctions, they insist, have the form of categorical imperatives: "Thou shalt!" and "Thou shalt not!" with no ifs, ands, or buts. It is this that pragmatism categorically denies. For values cannot realistically be conceived in isolation. They are not only conditioned by circumstances, but also by the indefinite multiplicity of other values with which they are implicated in the real world. To insist that something is a value "no matter what" is to repudiate either the world of causal connection or everything else in the realm of value. The proper analysis of what is called a "categorical imperative" is "*Since* you want *x,* do *y!*" It is not that there are no qualifications, but that the qualifications are not brought into question. They are not problematic in the context of *that* valuation, but that is very different from saying that there is nothing there that ever *could* be problematic. In every valuation, as a matter of principle *all* our values are at stake, just as every scientific experiment tests, not merely the hypothesis in question, but the whole body of scientific knowledge that bears on the design and interpretation of the experiment. Pragmatism is not reducing morality to technology but unfolding the moral commitments in technology itself.

We have values, and we judge of values. Of course, having them is not an intellectual or cognitive process; but judging them is. We prize many things, but to certify them as values we must also appraise them. The rational man is one who values only what evaluation reveals to be worthy of it. A value judgment is not a mere expression of the fact that we then and there find something to be satisfying, but a hypothesis that it will prove to be satisfactory; not merely that we are interested in it, but that indeed it is to our interest. These are commonplaces of our analyses of lesser values; the irony is that when we aspire to the greater good, we seem impelled to take leave of our good sense.

It follows from this position that values are inescapably relative. For a hypothesis about values, as about anything else, depends on the facts, and facts are always specific to the particular occasion. The relativism of the pragmatic position is an immediate consequence of its contextualism. The moment we are prepared to deal with particular cases we must acknowledge that circumstances alter cases. Of course, one man's meat is another man's poison; but why should we feel it necessary to prescribe the same diet for all men? The sameness lies only in the laws of biochemistry, and it is precisely these that demand our accommodation to individual differences. Pragmatism thus leads to an awareness of the richness and complexity of the moral life, and of every value domain. The world of value is a pluralistic one: "In my Father's house are many mansions." Where values differ it is not necessarily the case that one is genuine and the other spurious, one right and one wrong, one superior and the other inferior: they may just be different. We need not accept other people only because, after all, they are just like us; they may be quite unlike us and still have claim to our acceptance. Community does not entail conformity to a single inflexible standard; on the contrary, the sense of community is deepened by the acknowledgment and acceptance of the right to differ.

What is fundamental is that this relativism is not a matter of subjectivity: pragmatism espouses an *objective relativism.* Values are relative to the persons and circumstances to which the valuation refers. But once this reference is specified, it is no longer a matter of anyone's think-so as to whether what is taken to be good *is* indeed good. This is not relative to the judger, but only to those whose good is being judged. And here we can expect as much agreement as our knowledge of the facts and our capacity to understand them allows. What is needed is continuing inquiry, continuing application of intelligence to the experience of what is never more than a provisional good.

It is this provisional character of the good in the pragmatist philosophy that underlies, I believe, much of the hostility to it, especially from the side of the religious philosophies. For pragmatic humanism, after all, does not put man at the center of the moral universe. It is true that human needs are a necessary condition of value, but they are not in themselves a sufficient condition. It is the objective world —the laws of Nature, and, if you will, of Nature's God—which is ultimately decisive. But the religionist wants to be certain of what the decision is, and it is this certainty that pragmatism fails to provide. For in assimilating value judgments to scientific hypotheses, the pragmatist perforce subjects them to the same fallibilistic logic. The resolution of a moral issue confronts us with new moral dilemmas, just as the successful scientific theory generates new problems. The formation of habit from impulse, and of character from habit, and the guidance of this process by deliberate choice—intelligent or otherwise, as we ourselves make it—goes on as long as life itself. It is said that when Dewey was asked, "What do you do when you are tired of climbing mountains only to find, when you have crossed them, still another range before you?" he replied simply, "When you are tired of climbing, you die."

Its theory of value is applied by pragmatism characteristically to social and political questions. Indeed, in the English-speaking world, it is virtually the only contemporary philosophy with a clear-cut bearing on that vastly important segment of human life today which is defined by the political. Even more distinctive is the fact that the pragmatist approaches such questions on the same basis as his philosophy of science and theory of value. Most contemporary philosophies are restricted in their outlook, and correspondingly restrictive in their influence, focusing almost exclusively on science (like the logical positivists), or on morality (like existentialism), on religion (like Zen), or on politics (like dialectical materialism). Pragmatism is philosophy in the grand style at least in the respect that its social philosophy is all of a piece with its logic, ethics, and metaphysics.

And this social philosophy can most simply be described as providing meaning to the old-fashioned and much abused term *liberalism*. It is, first of all, a philosophy of social protest. A pragmatist is always dissatisfied, always striving for betterment. His very logic demands it of him, for, on his theory, to be conscious of a situation is to be aware of what is problematic in it, and complacency implies thoughtlessness. At the turn of the century William James found it necessary to insist over and over again that the fight against evil is a real fight. Nowadays there are few philosophies that touch on social questions at all which keep up the pretense that all is for the best in this best of all possible worlds. Yet there is still a strong residual idealism, especially in the religious philosophies, committed to the view that in the end virtue must triumph and the right prevail. For pragmatism, the philosophic task is not to concoct a proof that the nature of man and the universe guarantees that human values are secure, but rather to provide ideational instruments by which through human effort in this precarious world they can be made more secure. James, I think, would have enjoyed the current definition of an optimist as a man who believes that this is the best of all possible worlds, and of a pessimist as one who's afraid that the optimist is right. His own position he described as "meliorism": the question is not whether it's best or worst, but how to go about making it better.

Pragmatism is thus, in the second place, open to new possibilities, new social forms and patterns. James unceasingly attacked the frozen, block universe of nineteenth-century mechanistic materialism. In the present century, the notion that the future is closed finds expression in various historicist philosophies, which argue that the social process is inexorably moving toward a predetermined end—world communism, the welfare state, or whatever. Inexorability in any form is uncongenial to the pragmatic temper. Liberalism repudiates all pre-assigned patterns, whether the assignment is made by the past, as in conservative philosophies, or by a fixed future, as in "progressive" ones. It regards social forms as continuing hypotheses as to the realization of social values, subject to continuing criticism and reformulation by the free intellect.

Pragmatism is therefore in the third place receptive to social planning, for it is committed to a policy of taking thought about our problems, rather than relying on the pre-established harmony of the classical economics to solve them for us. Coöperative effort for the attainment of common ends may have as important a place in the social process as competition, and public enterprise may be as important as private. But this is not to say that pragmatism is a "philosophy of the Left": pragmatism repudiates the image of social philosophies as falling on a single dimension from left to right. For while it is predisposed toward a socialized economy, it insists on an uncompromising individualism in the political structure. Economic security must be sought within a framework of political freedom—civil rights and civil liberties are primary values for liberalism. Thus contemporary pragmatists like Sidney Hook have been intransigent critics of the communist regimes. For whatever humane ends are pursued are inexorably shaped by the inhuman means employed for their attainment. Under these conditions, a free and secure social order becomes a mere utopia, not a working ideal guiding decisions actually taken. The final outcome is a destruction of the very values alleged to be pursued. It is this tragic paradox which Dewey formulated by pointing out that the best is the worst enemy of the better.

Finally, pragmatic liberalism is committed to democracy, not as a specific set of social policies, but as a method of arriving at policy. And in a word, the method is the application of intelligence to social problems. A faith in democracy, as the pragmatist conceives it, is a faith, first, in the capacity of human nature to determine what—in the long run and in the widest set of contexts—will be experienced by man as good; and a faith, second, in the capacity of human intelligence to discover the actions by which, in the world as it is, this good can best be achieved. Now both the experience of value and the use of intelligence are localized only in individuals; both the ends and the means of social action can be defined only by reference to individuals. The pragmatist therefore insists that it is the individual which is the focal point of social reconstruction—not the class or state, the race or nation, or an abstract "humanity."

It is in this perspective that education comes to play such an important part in the pragmatic philosophy—more important, perhaps, than in any other Western philosophy since Aristotle. Understandably, Dewey has had an immeasurable influence on educational practice in the United States and elsewhere, though it must be said that much of what is called "progressive education"—especially by its critics—has nothing to do with Dewey.

The outcome of the pragmatist social philosophy, then, is to assign to each individual the ultimate responsibility for active participation in the process of dealing with social problems. Democracy, Dewey once said in a memorable phrase, must be achieved anew by each generation. It does not consist in a political mechanism which can be inherited, but in habits of thought and action which each man must acquire for himself. Pragmatism, I think, would enthusiastically endorse a maxim to be found in the *Ethics of the Fathers:* "The work is not yours to finish, but neither are you free to pass it by."

And now a few concluding remarks, directed especially to certain widespread misconceptions of pragmatism. I know of no better way to get at these than to say a few words about the pragmatist philosophy of art. I think it very revealing that according to Dewey the best way to judge a philosophy is to look at its esthetics. The reason is that it is in art that we find the *summum bonum:* art is most distinctively the domain of inherent value. It is satisfying in immediate experience, and satisfactory in subsequent critical judgment. A philosophy that has no room in it for art cannot really provide room for anything else—art is the last for which the first was made. Properly conceived, technology, politics, and morals (as C. W. Morris has pointed out) are handmaidens of art, aiming at the extension of esthetic quality throughout experience, and in the experience of all men. Pragmatism thus insists on the continuity of art with life; Dewey is nowhere more eloquent, I think, than when he elaborates the charge that in our culture art has become "the beauty-parlor of civilization."

I call attention to the great importance that pragmatism attaches to art as the locus of inherent value because pragmatism is so often misunderstood as acknowledging only instrumental value, measuring everything only by the standards of efficiency and success. Over and over Europeans have characterized pragmatism as in this sense "the philosophy of the American businessman." Dewey once replied to Bertrand Russell's making this criticism with the defense that it would be as fair to account for Cartesian dualism by the Gallic propensity for keeping a mistress as well as a wife; to which Russell is said to have rejoined, "Precisely!" The fact is that what the ideals of efficiency and success leave out is just what pragmatism itself insists upon as being most fundamental. From its point of view, it is as much a blunder to appraise means without regard to the inherent value of the ends to which they lead as to appraise ends without regard to the instrumental value of the available means. Efficiency and success, as these are usually understood, subjectively isolate values which objectively are only fragments of a complex value system. The question, "For what shall it profit a man, if he shall gain the whole world, and lose his own soul?" is thoroughly pragmatic. Living the good life, as pragmatism conceives it, depends on the fullest possible realization of *all* the values which as a matter of fact are implicated in the contexts of all our actions; and what these are is determined by what *we* are, by what we bring into each situation, as well as by what the world demands of us in that situation. The amateur pilot who radios "I'm lost, but I'm making good time" may be efficient, but he's no pragmatist. To identify pragmatism with the ideals of efficiency and success is as much a vulgarization as to identify psychoanalysis with uninhibited sexuality and aggression.

In short, the aim of life as the pragmatist sees it is, in Dewey's words, to make the stability of meaning prevail over the instability of events. It is to give to experience that quality of significance which emerges, as in the creation of a work of art, only when through our own efforts we have so transformed recalcitrant materials as to given them a human meaning and value. But this transformation is never complete, and what it yields is at best significant only for us whose efforts have brought it about. It remains for others to take up the unfinished work, and do with it what *their* purposes demand, in their life situation. In a sense, pragmatism cannot offer itself as a "philosophy of life." For this suggests that the philosophy is finished, and what remains is only to apply it in action. It suggests that the philosophic enterprise as a whole is essentially complete, offering to each man an array of world views by which he can live. But the pragmatist position is that the question of the meaning of life does not yet have an answer, and cannot have one as long as life goes on. It must be answered by each of us, not in terms of meanings already provided, but only in terms of the meanings, which, with the deepest sensibilities and fullest exercise of intelligence, we ourselves can provide. In a world so undeniably unstable as this one, a world in which meanings are so hard to come by at all—to say nothing of being made stable—in such a world it may well be that the pragmatic temper of mind holds out as much hope as a rational man can realistically entertain.

QUESTIONS

How much of an influence has pragmatism had outside the United States in recent years?

IN THE FIRST DECADE or two of the present century, pragmatism had a considerable impact in various parts of the world, particularly in China. More recently, however, its influence in Asia, South America, and elsewhere is negligible as compared with that of the so-called analytic movement in Western philosophy. But this is true only if we are speaking of what the influenced thinkers themselves identify as stemming from pragmatism. Early in the history of the pragmatic movement James forecast its future by describing the three stages through which every new theory passes: its critics first condemn it as absurd, then dismiss it as trivial and obvious, and finally claim it as their own discovery. This process can be traced especially clearly, I believe, in contemporary British linguistic philosophy. Over a period of twenty years or so this philosophy has gradually come round to the realization that language is, after all, an instrument, that meanings involve purposes, and that the proper analysis of any discourse demands appreciation of the full particularity of the contexts of its use. Pragmatists have been doing philosophy in this perspective for almost a century, only to have the British denounce them for confusing logic with psychology and sociology. I have had occasion elsewhere to counter the witticism of a great contemporary English philosopher in one of his early books that "all good fallacies go to America when they die, where they are resuscitated as discoveries of the local professors" with the rejoinder that recent years make it plain that thereafter they return to England, where they enjoy a second childhood.

Is there any relation between pragmatism and the communist conception of ideas as weapons in the class struggle?

THERE ARE indeed certain points of resemblance here, which Sidney Hook especially has explored. "Philosophers hitherto have tried to understand the world; the point, however, is to change it"—this is a Marxist thesis which, properly construed, might very well have been enunciated by a pragmatist. In both conceptions, knowledge is an instrument of active intervention in affairs, not a purely passive mirroring of a world to be taken as given. In both, science is viewed, not as the product of disembodied intellect, but as the outcome of the activity of real human beings, acting in concrete social situations. In both, therefore, the social matrix of inquiry is important, not merely as directing attention to one set of problems rather than another, but also, and more fundamentally, as providing the materials—both conceptual and physical—with which the problems are formulated and solved.

But there is a world of difference between them nevertheless. What the communist does not realize is that, while ideas are relative to the social context, it is still an *objective* relativism which is involved. Philosophical and scientific theories may serve as ideologies, but even that service is subject to objective appraisal in terms of the real needs to be met in the situation in which they are promulgated, and the real constraints which the situation imposes. The communist has no place for objectivity because it is he who defines his own reality, by what he calls "class consciousness," and he cannot therefore aspire to anything more than a "class truth." Ultimately, such a so-called truth rests only on the dogmas of a political orthodoxy: "revisionism" is a cardinal sin whose wages literally is death, and not, as in pragmatism, the very purpose of continued inquiry. Nothing could be less in keeping with the pragmatic temper than the closed mind and closed system of communist thought. And nothing, finally, could be less pragmatic than the apotheosis of action which makes up the core of the communist faith. For pragmatism, meanings are related to action only because the purpose of action, at bottom, is to institute meanings. We do not think merely in order to do, but to see to it that all our doings shape a world worth thinking about.

What part can pragmatism play in uniting people behind shared values?

I THINK that a pragmatist would first point out that there may be more danger in an artificial and spurious unity than in genuine and open differences. Unity, agreement, shared values have come to be something of a fetish in the world today. We are constantly assuring one another that in the last analysis we are all aiming at the same thing, and differ "only" in the means for attaining it. What we fail to recognize is that the solution to any problem does not and can not wait upon the last analysis but must meet the constraints of the situation as given. The means chosen become ends in that act of choice. Bombs exploded in a "preventive" war are just as destructive as in an "aggressive" one; a dictatorship ruling in the name of the proletariat is just as repressive as the tyranny of a ruling class. Abstracting ultimate ends from proximate means on behalf of unity generates an easy and dangerous optimism. Both White and Black are aiming at checkmate; but behind this purely verbal unity is the crucial difference that White wants the black king checkmated and Black the white one. The pragmatic approach to social problems requires that we do as much justice to differences of interest as we are usually prepared to do to shared interests.

Having said this, I must now acknowledge that the pragmatist nevertheless puts his emphasis on the shared interests, for though it is differences that constitute the data of our problems—and this is why they must not be overlooked—it is agreements that point to possibilities of solution. What is always shared is the world we all live in: nature and the laws of nature, together with the particular matters of fact governed by those laws. Whatever our purposes, we must all of us continuously redefine them in terms of causal conditions and consequences that transcend any particular set of purposes, however extensive. No matter how great the differences in our private worlds, sooner or later we must all come to terms with the one world in which we all live. And this is what we share: air that can be breathed without glowing in the dark, food for ever-growing populations, and that something more than bread alone by which the human spirit everywhere is nourished. There are many common roots of human endeavor; the concrete question is always whether we can reach down far enough to resolve the conflicts of divergent purposes.

What pragmatism insists upon is that we not deceive ourselves, either with a too optimistic conception of how much agreement there is, or too pessimistic a conception of how irreconcilable the disagreement is. No disagreements among human beings are absolutely irreconcilable, for we share a common humanity; and equally, no agreements are entire, for we are distinct individuals occupying different contexts, viewing the world in different perspectives, and so pursuing different values. Pragmatism has no prescription for world unity, and would not prescribe it if it could. It insists only that we face our problems realistically, and cope with them intelligently. And this requires doing justice to both components—values shared and not shared—of every conflict situation.

Doesn't the pragmatist's relativism make of values a purely personal matter?

Of course there is a sense in which values are personal, more intimately bound up with the personality, indeed, than anything else which makes it individual. What I am is defined not by what I have but by what I seek: the aspiration is the man. But this is to say that values are personal only in the sense that it is they that make the person, not the other way round. Values are not personal if this implies that they are purely private, or the product of mere whim or caprice.

First of all, as I have already indicated, the relativism in question is an objective one. Whether the shoe fits depends on who wears it, of course; but that fact didn't do Cinderella's sisters a bit of good—on the contrary, it is that fact which found them out. And what is to the present point is that objectivity is a matter of inter-subjectivity: the basic test for the objective is, "Do you see what I see?" To be sure, it is only the subjectivity of the qualified observer that counts, and only observations made under appropriate conditions. The business of the logic of inquiry is just to formulate these qualifications and conditions. Values that have been sustained by inquiry, that is, objectively *e*valuated, are as public as any other matters of fact.

In the second place, the person is already social in its own nature.

There is no basic antithesis between the individual and society: individuality has a social content and is expressed through social forms. A person's values make up a more or less loosely integrated value system, and this system largely derives from the ambient culture. G. H. Mead sometimes distinguished between what he called the "I" and the "me" as the aspect of personality which acts or which is acted on by social norms. Values are in part the spontaneous creation of the freely acting individual, but only in part. They are also the embodiment—or introjection, as the psychoanalyst would say—of the standards of the various persons and groups with which the individual identifies himself. And it is only through such identifications that he becomes a person who can have any values at all.

Finally, pragmatism emphasizes the social nature of values because in its analysis values, if they are not just words, must be grounded in the concreta of action. And action is social through and through, in its conditions as much as in its consequences. The pragmatist ethics is one of the few which take seriously Aristotle's dictum that man is a social animal. For it, the term "social ethics" is a redundancy: like Adam himself, Robinson Crusoe becomes a moral agent only on a Friday. Not just moral values, but values in general, of whatever species, have their locus in the ways of man to his fellows. In short, values are impersonal in their validation, personal in substance, and social in significance. They are personal in the pejorative sense—private and subjective—only in just those respects in which there is nothing of good in them. The only truly private place is Hell.

Does pragmatism make any provision for religion?

Much depends on what we conceive to be essential to religion. There is a sense of "religion" in which pragmatism not only assigns it a role, but as important a role as the most ardent of religionists would insist on. It is not, however, a sense which the ardent religionist is likely to admit as at all a proper one. Specifically, pragmatism can interpret religious ideas, like any others, only in terms of what lies within experience. It therefore has no place for the conception of a deity who sets the ball rolling and stands off to see whether or how soon it will crash at the bottom of the hill; no place for a deity who promulgates a moral law and sits in judgment on his subjects; no place, surely, for a deity who suspends any laws for his favorites, or intervenes between an act and its consequence; no place for an immortal soul which suffers or enjoys forever the destiny it has chosen or been ordained; no place for a providence that moves all things to a predestined good. In short, pragmatism cannot countenance any religion inextricably involved with a transcendent theology and metaphysics.

But when these are set aside, it cannot lightly be assumed that nothing recognizably religious is left. In fact, in some of the world's great religions none of these things plays any significant part; and I believe the same is true of the core of mysticism in all religion. What remains is an abiding sense of the meaning and value that is possible in life, and an acceptance of the responsibility so to live as to make the most of the possibility. Pragmatism might speak of such possibilities as God in the making; in a more old-fashioned religious idiom we can call it the worship of the God who is not yet.

In this conception, faith is not the evidence of things unseen, but it *is* the substance of things hoped for. Such a hope serves as a unifying principle providing drive and direction to all of life's efforts. In this way, pragmatism makes room for religion, as I believe every mature philosophy must; only, it must be a correspondingly mature religion.

Yet I think it may not be unfair to say that pragmatism is weakest just where it comes closest to these fundamental questions. I believe that religion transcends the pursuit of the good, and sees beyond the tragedy of the inevitable failure of the pursuit. Pragmatism, I am afraid, cannot account for the moral hero—the martyr who dies, not that a greater cause may triumph, but because his life has a meaning neither enhanced by triumph nor degraded by defeat. The pragmatic ethic may lead when all is said and done to no greater virtue than prudence. But there is a kind of divine madness well known to the fool of God; and it may be, in the end, that to court such foolishness is after all the highest wisdom.

How can pragmatism justify its emphasis on intelligent conduct in view of the enormous role of irrationality in human life?

I THINK it is this question that puts its finger on the most serious difficulty that confronts the pragmatist. For pragmatism is perhaps the most thoroughgoing attempt to build a conception of what man is, what he can hope for, and what he ought to do, on the basis of his being capable of intelligent behavior. To be sure, pragmatism recognizes very well that rationality is a precarious and limited acquisition of the human animal. But its sense of these dangers and limitations is, I am afraid, rather superficial. It acknowledges such biological constraints as the urgency of impulse and the rigidity of habit, and such sociological ones as the vested interests that put obstacles in the path of free inquiry. But the course of civilization has confronted us with the deep-seated irrationalities of the psychiatric clinic brought into positions of power and prestige. The challenge to the future of civilization carries with it as a minor corollary a challenge to the philosophies which still conceive of man as a rational animal. Whether the challenge can be met is as uncertain in the one case as in the other.

But the pragmatist may have a last word in self-defense. Philosophers have their commitments too, and perhaps the most basic is the commitment to rationality. The philosophic enterprise, it might be urged, is unthinkable without—what else but the power of thought? To raise a philosophical question is to assume that we have sense enough to know the answer if we should find it, or at least to understand it if it is put before us. Perhaps it would be more realistic to recognize that man's irrationality will either prevent us from finding the answers, or else prevent us from recognizing them as answers, or at any rate prevent us from understanding them. But if we are to be *that* realistic, we would have to give up being philosophers to start with. And even that would be a pragmatic solution after all!

LECTURE TWO

Analytic Philosophy

THERE IS NO DOUBT that the broad philosophical movement which I am loosely designating as "analytic philosophy" is far and away the most influential one in the English-speaking world. In almost every American university, certainly in the British ones, philosophy has virtually come to mean just this kind of enterprise. For the younger generation of students of philosophy, at any rate, the ideas of this movement are thought to be by far the most exciting and promising. To an increasing extent, this is coming to be true also in other parts of the world, especially in India—which, of course, is still very much subject to British influence, intellectually, at least—and in Japan, where, since the Occupation, American ideas have been steadily replacing German and French influence. The analytic movement has also had some impact in South America, and now at last is even not altogether without honor in its own countries of the European continent.

It is particularly appropriate that we should be discussing analytic philosophy here at U.C.L.A., because this university has had the privilege of numbering on its faculty some of the founders and world leaders of the movement. Analytic philosophy can probably best be traced to the inestimably important work carried on by Bertrand Russell at Cambridge in the first decades of this century; and Russell, as some of you may remember, taught here at U.C.L.A. in the late 'thirties. From Cambridge, the new ideas moved across Europe to Vienna, where a group of philosophers formed the so-called Vienna Circle to explore and develop these ideas; one of the founders of this Circle was Rudolf Carnap, who is now a member of our department, and is generally recognized as the most influential philosopher in the United States today. At about the same time, or a little later, a group was also formed in Berlin, headed by the distinguished Hans Reichenbach, who joined the University in the mid-'thirties and taught here until his death a few years ago. Having been myself a student of all three of these men, and bearing in mind the Talmudic precept that a man's teacher is as a father to him, I take particular pleasure in expressing my filial gratitude by putting their ideas before you. But need I caution you that the sins of the children are not to be visited on their parents? I alone am responsible for whatever misrepresentations of their work this brief survey may contain.

So then, in talking about analytic philosophy I am not speaking of something exotic, a system of thought belonging either to a totally foreign culture or to a special sub-culture of our own. It is a point of view quite widespread in American intellectual life, and has been taking root here for at least a generation.

I am grouping together under the label "analytic philosophy" a number of somewhat diverse standpoints for which several designations have been current. Probably the most familiar, though now rather out of date, is "logical positivism"; others have been "logical empiricism," "scientific empiricism," and just "scientific philosophy." The British developments have been known as "logical atomism," "Cambridge analysis," "Oxford analysis," and sometimes simply "language philosophy." What I am calling "analytic philosophy" applies to the loose grouping of whatever schools and individual standpoints these various labels stand for, together with certain aspects of pragmatism and operationism. I choose this designation because it is suggestive of the conception of the aims and methods of philosophy that is characteristic of the movement as a whole. And that is that philosophy is essentially a kind of logico-linguistic analysis, not a set of super-scientific truths about man and nature, nor a sustained exhortation to live one's life in a particular way.

One of the most outstanding figures in this movement is a man whose name is not widely known to the general public, but who would probably be recognized by the profession as among the three or four most important philosophers of the present century—Ludwig Wittgenstein, who also died a few years ago. He was at one time a pupil and later a colleague of Russell's at Cambridge, and early in the 'twenties published a remarkable little book called *Tractatus Logico-Philosophicus.* With a Latin title, the book was written in German, and printed with the English translation on facing pages; the text runs to not more than about ninety pages, but in the last half-century no single work on philosophy has been more influential in the English-speaking world. The conception of philosophy manifested in this book, and made explicit elsewhere in Wittgenstein's teaching, is that the business of philosophy is "not a body of propositions, but to make propositions clear." And one of the early members of the Vienna Circle was fond of saying that he looked forward to the time when there would be no books written on philosophy, but all books would be philosophically written.

Now this turn in the history of ideas was a very attractive one in the intellectual atmosphere then current. For the philosopher was now apparently abandoning his pretension to the grasp of an ultimate reality formulated in the world-systems of the traditional metaphysics, especially in the nineteenth-century idealisms. No longer is there such a thing as philosophical truth accessible only to those who have mastered some arcane dialectic or transcendental logic. If philosophy is still the love of wisdom, it is not the vain pursuit of a remote goddess, but the very earthy enterprise of achieving intimacy with the body of knowledge made available in the sciences. The material of philosophy is neither the world as given nor as transformed in the perspectives of art and religion, politics, and morality. The material of philosophy is science, and its business is to analyze the methods, terms, and laws of science so as to make clear their logical structure and empirical content.

The men who entered upon this activity of philosophical analysis had marked scientific interests; many of them, indeed, had been trained in one or another of the sciences, especially physics and mathematics. Now philosophy of science, in one form or another, is as old as philosophy itself, at least in the Western world—the pre-Socratics, with whom our histories of philosophy conventionally begin, were largely occupied with cosmological speculations. Indeed, it is scarcely a hundred years since the sciences themselves were explicitly differentiated as such, and the label "natural philosophy" replaced by "physics," "chemistry," and the rest. What was new—though nothing in the history of ideas is without precedent, as scholars never tire of documenting—or, the important difference from the scientific interests of an Aristotle or Kant was that now we were to have, not just a philosophy of science, but a thoroughgoing scientific philosophy. Kant, indeed, had explicitly raised the question how it was that science had achieved so much and philosophy so little, and explored the possibility of applying the method of science to philosophical problems. In this respect, as in a number of others, he is the most important precursor of the modern movement (though the influence of Hume was perhaps more direct). At any rate, philosophy itself was now to become a science, and thereby regain the respectability which the intellectual community had for some time denied it.

This means, first of all, that clarity becomes an important ideal of philosophy. What appears as profundity in the traditional thinkers is often no more than obscurity; as Nietzsche had already said of some of them, they muddy the water that it may appear deep. Metaphor and the other resources of rhetoric have no part in scientific discourse, and therefore have no place in philosophy either; Plato's dialogues may be literary masterpieces, but they cannot serve as a model for the philosopher. Russell once urged that the educator would be well advised to put less emphasis on Plato, and more on the things that Plato himself thought important, like mathematics. It is not that Plato's philosophy is false or mistaken, but that we cannot hope to settle the questions that he raises, or even appraise his answers to them, unless we can formulate them as clearly as the scientist does his own problems.

Nor is there anything about the philosophical subject-matter which makes such formulation impossible. There are no limits to the application of the scientific method, no boundaries to the domain of clear thought, clearly expressed. It was Wittgenstein who formulated the principle which has remained a slogan for the movement: "Whatever can be said at all can be said clearly." Wittgenstein had in his own temperament a certain mystic streak which—unfortunately, to my mind—was not taken up by his followers. He therefore also held that there were indeed some things which could not be said at all; accordingly, the last sentence of his *Tractatus* reads, "Whereof one cannot speak, thereof one must be silent." If the philosopher is not silent (and even mystics have been known to write books), he must say whatever he has to say as clearly and as carefully as the scientist. This is the first principle of analytic philosophy, and perhaps contains in itself all the rest. But for *this* to be made clear, the notion of clarity itself desperately needs clarification.

The British wing of the analytic movement sought clarity largely through the use of what they called "ordinary English"—the language spoken, as was once said, by dentists and nursemaids. (In many ways the British school differs markedly from the one I shall chiefly deal with.) But the most dramatic developments of analytic philosophy came about through the application to philosophy of artificial language systems—not of the type of Esperanto, but like the calculi of mathematics. On the Continent, and subsequently in America, most analytic philosophers held that only in such artificial languages could philosophical issues be posed with the clarity and precision necessary to their resolution. Just as the advance of science depends on the development of appropriate symbolisms and new branches of mathematics, so also philosophy, if it is not to remain a matter of futile and endless dispute, must develop its own notations and logical systems.

In this respect, the analytic movement has brought to fruition a long tradition in the history of ideas—that manipulation of the appropriate symbols can reveal the structure, if not of things themselves, at least of our ideas of things. This tradition goes back, perhaps, to the ancient Pythagoreans, runs through the medieval cabbalists, and is already quite explicit in the early Renaissance. By the seventeenth century it is given a modern cast in the ideas of the great German philosopher Leibniz, who, at the same time as Newton, created the branch of mathematics we usually call just "the" calculus. Leibniz formulated the ideal of a universal symbolism—a symbolic logic, we would say today—in which all philosophical questions could be formulated and then more or less mechanically resolved, just as the scientist proceeds by putting his ideas in mathematical terms and then carrying out suitable mathematical transformations. Let us hope, Leibniz said, that the time will come when two rival metaphysicians, meeting one another, will no longer engage in bitter and endless controversy but, putting their arms about one another in friendliest fashion, will say instead, "Come, let us calculate!"

As we shall see, this ideal of a universal symbolism has been very nearly realized in the contemporary movement, with the development of symbolic logic, and most recently in the form of what mathematicians know as set theory. For certain of the analytic philosophers the metamorphosis of philosophical speculation into mathematical calculation has become virtually complete. But if I correctly sense the trend, a reaction has set in, and more and more philosophers are asking whether clarity and precision are enough and, even more, whether the gain in philosophic knowledge compensates for the loss in philosophic wisdom. For the new symbolic systems in which philosophy is now formulated are "languages" only in a very special sense; the analytic philosopher, confronted with the basic problems of modern society, has put himself in the awkward position of the college draftee whose sergeant asks him to "talk algebra." It is already almost forty years since Wittgenstein warned (in the preface to his *Tractatus*) that the problems which can be definitively solved with the new techniques amount to very little. Philosophy in the old style may not have gotten very far, but its human content and cultural relevance seem unassailable; analytic philosophy must be credited with dramatic achievements, but just what significance attaches to them remains open to question. I believe this is the central issue in the assessment of the whole movement, and it must be kept in mind throughout what follows.

The new philosophy, then, is scientific in its ideals of clarity and precision. But even more, it aspires to scientific status in allowing for progress, for cumulation of results. Traditionally, philosophy presented the appearance of a number of world views, each essentially complete in itself, and impossible to assess in terms of some other philosophy without begging the fundamental questions. One is either a Platonist or Aristotelian, Spinozist or Thomist, Cartesian or Kantian, and so for the rest. And the choice between the great systems seemed to be a matter of taste or temperament; no wonder the controversies were endless. Edward FitzGerald was writing as a European and not as a Persian when he rendered Omar with:

> Myself when young did eagerly frequent
> Doctor and Saint, and heard great argument
>   About it and about: but evermore
> Came out by the same door wherein I went.

Now, says the analytic philosopher, the time has come to put an end to such pointless disputation. When a philosophic thesis is formulated in sufficiently exact language, there is no longer room for debate—the thing can be settled one way or the other, and once for all. Philosophy could make progress if only the philosopher would rather be definitely wrong than vaguely right.

To this end, the philosopher must also resign himself to dealing with lesser questions than the nature of man and the universe as a whole. We must take up philosophical problems piecemeal, and though they may appear trivial considered singly, in the aggregate they will amount to more than the sweeping generalizations about which philosophers have never been able to agree. It is in just this way that science at last entered on the road of progress. Galileo did not speculate about the structure of the cosmos and the laws of being *qua* being, after the manner of his scholastic predecessors; he contented himself with determining how fast a ball rolls down an inclined plane. His contemporary, Descartes, in the *Discourse on Method,* formulated a principle as important for philosophy as for science: problems must be broken down into their simplest parts, and only then can we hope to make progress.

Of course, there are those who insist (and I among them) that the business of philosophy is to pull things together, to make a coherent whole out of the congeries of ideas and perspectives to be found in the various domains of culture, and relating to all the various aspects of experience. But such a synthesis, the analytic philosopher would rejoin, can be made only after analysis has provided it with reliable materials. In principle, of course, he is quite right, but in practice it seems that the materials are never sufficient, or never sufficiently reliable. I have had occasion elsewhere to criticize what I call the "ordinal fallacy"—first this, then that; first I will achieve power, then use it for the public good; first I will acquire adequate knowledge, then embark on moral action; first I will master my medium, then I will find something to say in it. I cannot be persuaded that a strategy will succeed in philosophy that fails daily in politics, art, and morals.

There is, however, one undeniable advantage to this policy of piecemeal philosophizing, clearly demonstrated in the history of science. That is that it allows for contributions to be made by men of only moderate ability. For the advance of science—make no mistake about it!—depends, not just on the occasional genius, but on the steady day-by-day contributions from the mediocre. From the outside, it is inevitable that we identify science with the work of the few scientists who have achieved fame, but it is in the very nature of fame that it be limited to a few. The corpus of science, since the seventeenth century, at any rate, is to be found, not in the rare prize-winning publication, but in the continuing output of the scientific journals. In modern society the division of labor and its technological organization has become as important in the sphere of ideas as in other types of production. From the broadest historical point of view, I believe that contemporary philosophy can best be characterized by the simple fact that today there are journals of philosophy, just as there are journals of chemistry or botany—some dozens published in English alone. Whether this in itself is a sufficient condition for philosophical progress I have grave doubts; but there can be no doubt that it is a necessary condition—this much must be conceded to the analytic philosophers. The next step—one which has already been taken hesitantly here and there—is to organize philosophical "projects," with teams expertly disposing of foundation and government subsidies. Such collective farms are a far cry from the garden of Epicurus, but they unquestionably produce a higher yield per acre. I am fearful of voicing my misgivings, lest I brand myself a reactionary. But, but, but . . .

It is surely plain by now that the analytic philosopher focuses largely, and perhaps exclusively, on the phenomenon of language. Language is not merely the instrument for philosophizing, as it is for all thinking; it is also the raw material and in a way the end product of philosophizing. For Wittgenstein, philosophical problems as such arise only when "our language has gone on vacation." When it is no longer subject to the discipline of ordinary life, language breaks out of its restraints and leads us into awkward and puzzling idioms which we mistake for metaphysical difficulties. From this standpoint, the enterprise of philosophy is, again in his terms, "nothing other than a battle against the bewitchment of our intelligence by language." We find ourselves in perplexity because, without realizing it, we have been misled into interpreting extraordinary locutions as though they were the straightforward constructions to which we have become accustomed in extra-philosophical contexts.

As I have said, it is particularly in Britain, and more especially in the Oxford school, that this conception of the nature, aim, and method of doing philosophy has been developed. I have forgotten what wit it was who explained this development with the observation that by the mid-twentieth century the British Empire had nothing left to defend but the English language. Be that as it may, the prevailing British conception is that when a man is occupied with a philosophical problem he is suffering, as it were, from a certain kind of illness, a disease of language; and the symptoms of this illness consist in the fact that he uses words in a very strange way without a clear sense of this strangeness. He says odd things (the word "odd" is a very popular one in this connection, closely followed by "queer"), things that no man in his right linguistic senses would ordinarily be tempted to say—like "Time is unreal" or "The Absolute slumbers in eternal repose" or "The Nothing nothings" (a basic tenet of the existentialist Heidegger). Such pronouncements have, to be sure, an air of profundity, but they are no more than profound nonsense, due to misusing words or grammar, unconsciously distorting them while consciously insisting on applying the ordinary rules for their interpretation.

In this perspective, the activity of the philosopher is a work of linguistic therapy, directed toward restoring the patient to a condition of semantic well-being. In fact, the British school has sometimes been given a label derived from this conception, and referred to as "therapeutic positivism." It is not that philosophy is to replace psychotherapy in the strict sense, but only that it has the same aim with respect to its problems that the psychotherapist has with respect to the problems that his patients bring to him. In both cases, the situation is that the problems presented are not solved, the questions are not answered; rather, the patient is brought to a realization of the pathological conditions which motivated the questions and produced the spurious sense of something problematic. When words are restored to their ordinary uses philosophical problems simply disappear, just as neurotic conflicts vanish when their unconscious dynamics are laid bare. In Britain the task of the analytic philosopher is essentially to overcome the functional disorders of language induced by the distortions of usage characteristic of traditional philosophic reflection.

In America, analytic philosophy by and large has little sympathy with ordinary language. On the contrary, the growth of science has always necessitated departures from the ordinary meanings of words, and for some purposes even the construction of whole new notational systems (like zoological nomenclature or chemical symbols), to say nothing of the language of mathematics. Accordingly, the philosopher must construct certain quite extraordinary languages, designed precisely to protect us from the snares and pitfalls which beset our paths in the ordinary ways of words. Thus Carnap and others work characteristically by first setting up some artificial language, specifying with great exactitude and explicitness first the vocabulary of this language, then the "formation rules" according to which terms can be combined into sentences, and finally the "transformation rules" by which one sentence (or a set of them) can be transformed into others, which are then said to follow from the first. Philosophical issues are translated into technical questions concerning the properties, both internal and in application, of the language so constructed.

From this point of view, what usually happens when philosophers engage in dispute is that one of them operates with a language of one sort and the other with a language of quite a different structure, but neither of them with a clear idea of what their languages are. Consequently, they not only cannot come to agreement, but at bottom cannot even understand one another—and worst of all, they remain unaware of what is responsible for their misunderstanding. In place of the conflicting schools and positions of traditional philosophy, Carnap propounds a so-called principle of tolerance: not that all philosophical views are equally acceptable, but that a man is entitled to use whatever language he wishes, provided only he makes quite clear what the rules of his language are. You claim that if something is necessary, this is itself necessary and not merely contingent; another philosopher disagrees with you. I say, formulate for me the rules of your language, and I shall see whether or not in that language what you claim is correct. Until the language is specified, the argument is pointless; and if you specify a language which settles the issue in one way, we can also, if we choose, construct another language with different rules so as to yield the other outcome. Questions of fact depend only on fact, and on language merely in the trivial sense that the words single out the fact which is in question. But such questions are the exclusive province of science; philosophical questions are *essentially* linguistic questions, and so cannot be dealt with except by relating them to some language or other of specified structure.

But all languages must satisfy certain conditions in order to be usable as languages at all. In a word—though it is a confusing one—they must be capable of transmitting *meanings*. For analytic philosophy sense and nonsense are the basic categories of philosophical analysis. It might be supposed that all philosophical questions could be put as follows: Given such and such a set of propositions, which of them are we to classify as true and which as false? But from the point of view of analytic philosophy this way of putting the matter is grossly improper. Indeed, philosophy has no place at all in this formulation, because it is the business of science, and science alone, to decide what is true and what is false. The work of philosophy is a prior one, and the above formulation simply takes it for granted that the work has already been done. For in addition to the true statements and the false ones there is a third class—the meaningless statements, without content and so neither true nor false. It is the business of philosophy to settle which statements are meaningless and which have meaning. Once this question has been settled, science can take over and decide with respect to meaningful statements which are true and which false. Philosophy is not the queen of the sciences, yielding a supra-scientific truth; it is their handmaiden, serving humbly and faithfully the enterprise of scientific knowledge, the only kind of knowledge worthy of the name.

Now, how shall we determine whether a statement is meaningful?

In a variety of formulations, essentially the same principle has been proposed, one usually called in the literature "the verifiability theory of meaning." In fact, of course, it is not a theory at all, but a rule proposed for the construction of languages. The rule amounts to something like this: admit as meaningful only those statements with regard to which there is some possibility, at least in principle, of some bit of evidence tending either to verify or else to falsify the statement in question. The possibility may be a bare logical possibility, not necessarily a physical possibility, to say nothing of actual feasibility. The evidence must consist ultimately in something that is directly experienced, and such that we can discriminate, at least under ideal conditions, whether we have experienced it or not. And it is only some degree or other of verification or falsification that is called for, not establishing or refuting it beyond any question. But if no experience that any human being could ever possibly have would add or detract anything whatsoever from the verification of a statement, then the rule denies any meaning to the statement and excludes it from the language. Certain qualifications must be introduced to accommodate the statements of logic and pure mathematics, but these need not concern us here.

From this standpoint, analytic philosophy is a type of empiricism, and is often called "scientific empiricism" to distinguish it from the older varieties. All empiricisms agree that knowledge must be based on experience. What is distinctive of the position we are now considering is that it relates to experience not only truth but also meaning. We might call the former "epistemic empiricism" and the latter "semantic empiricism." Obviously every semantic empiricist is also an epistemic one, but the converse is not true. Kant, for instance, insisted that we can know only what is based on experience, but he considered statements about God or the soul, for example, as perfectly meaningful even though they are beyond experiential verification. It is on this basis that he was able, as he said, to limit reason in order to make room for faith. In this sense the analytic philosopher is not lacking in faith; it is rather that there is nothing for him to have faith in—the statements which he is asked to accept on faith he neither accepts nor rejects, because on his principles they are without content altogether.

This is the situation, he claims, with regard to all the statements characteristic of traditional metaphysics. The distinctive pronouncements of idealists and materialists, rationalists and realists, and all the other "ists" in the history of philosophy, simply fail to make any discrimination, however indirect, among our experiences. Whether objects are ideas in the mind of God, products of the creative "I," or material substances with their qualities, is all one so far as our experiences are concerned. However vigorously a man proclaims that life is but a dream, he must still distinguish in exactly the same way as everyone else does between what he calls a dream chair that he can dream he sits on, and a mere dream of a dream that unpredictably dissolves into his dream of Aunt Mary. Nothing that anyone can possibly experience could tend in the least to substantiate his claim, because of course to speak of "waking up" is to beg the question, since what *we* understand by "waking up" is for him only a dream of waking. It is not that his claim is a mistaken one; in the strict sense, he is making no claim at all—or at most, only proposing that we change the usage of words like "dreaming" and "waking."

In short, for analytic philosophy the questions raised in traditional metaphysics are unanswerable because they are not genuine questions. Philosophical arguments have been interminable because in principle there is no way to establish that one side is right and the other wrong. It is like playing a game without ever having decided what the object of the game is, and so of course no one can ever say "There! I've won!"—or at least, he can never convince the other players. Even the race in *Through the Looking-Glass* had some point to it—games don't *have* to be competitive; but traditional metaphysics seemed to serve no purpose except to provide an occupation for other metaphysicians. The situation is well summed up in the undergraduate definition of philosophy as a game whose object is to formulate its own rules. What is crucial, from the standpoint of analytic philosophy, is that metaphysical questions are unanswerable because of defects in their formulation, and not because of any alleged limitations of the human mind. For we are speaking of what is verifiable in principle and not in fact; and if there are principled limitations on human knowledge, precisely corresponding limitations operate on meaningful discourse. What we cannot possibly know we cannot even say that we cannot know. To understand a statement is to know what the world would be like if it were true, and some possible experience could then disclose whether or not the world *is* like that—for of course, what we mean by "the world" is just that which discloses itself, however partially, in experience.

In my opinion what the analytic philosopher is getting at here is quite right, in the main, as a criterion of meaningfulness; but I cannot agree that its application condemns most traditional philosophy to the domain of nonsense. For verification even of a scientific hypothesis is more complex and indirect than I think most analytic philosophers allow for; and the hypotheses, if I may call them such, that make up the substance of the various philosophies are still more subtle in their bearings on experience. Of course, if the truth of a philosophy would make no difference there is no sense in bothering with it at all. But it is coming to be more widely recognized that how a philosophical conviction makes a difference still stands in need of considerable analysis. The positivism of a few decades ago was sweepingly and even militantly anti-metaphysical, but this attitude has gradually yielded to the realization that a philosophy may have a good deal to do with experience even if we cannot trace out with any exactitude what its connections are with what we see and touch. A man or a culture may find it easy to live with a certain philosophy or awkward, according to the growth of his knowledge or, as we say, the fruits of his experience. This, in my opinion, is a verification of sorts, and quite enough to give his philosophy meaning. But how to specify *what* meaning it has and how to change its meaning so as to make it more livable—these are plainly quite different and much more difficult matters.

At any rate, analytic philosophy directs attention to the undeniably real danger of occupying ourselves with questions that are unanswerable not because they are profound but because they are lacking in meaning altogether. If we do not seriously consider questions like "How high is up?" it is not because we do not know enough yet about the frontiers of space but because we already know too well the rules of grammar which such questions violate—it simply makes no sense to ask for the magnitude of a direction rather than a distance.

Now the questions posed by philosophers do not violate grammar in this simple sense. They violate what we might call a logical grammar, of which ordinary grammar is occasionally a distorted reflection, but which cannot at all be identified with the rules of ordinary languages. That half a loaf is better than nothing, and nothing is better than wisdom, does not justify the suggested conclusion; it is not the grammar of the word "nothing" which is at fault here, but its logical syntax. Grammatically, "nothing" is as proper a subject for a proposition as any other common noun; but logically, it must obey quite different rules.

This difference between logical and grammatical form was made strikingly apparent to the philosophical community early in this century by Bertrand Russell, with a justly celebrated analysis of one of the shortest and most important words in the English language, the word *the,* especially in the construction called the definite description—that is, phrases of the form "the such and such." I use Russell's original illustration. Sir Walter Scott was the author of the Waverley novels, so the expression "the author of Waverley" describes a particular individual, just the one who is named by "Sir Walter Scott." Now suppose someone were to ask, "Is Sir Walter Scott the author of Waverley?" This is a perfectly sensible question, yet to a philosopher it is a very puzzling one. The puzzle has nothing to do with ignorance of literary history—let us stipulate that as a matter of fact Scott *did* write Waverley. The puzzle is that both parts of the question name the same person, so it is as though we were asking "Is Sir Walter Scott Sir Walter Scott?" And this is no longer a sensible question. Apparently the definite description is like a name in some ways but not in others, and ordinary grammar does not help much to make the distinction. The confusion is also apparent in the anecdote which Russell tells about a man who was once invited by a friend to visit him on his yacht, and who, after looking about him with disappointment, said, "I thought your yacht was bigger than it is." To which the reply was, "How *could* it be?"

The difficulty becomes more serious in the case of descriptions which do not apply to existing individuals, or, as we are tempted to say, which describe nonexistent things. To pursue Russell's classic illustration, consider the proposition, "The present king of France is bald." Let us agree that, however unstable French politics is, right now there is in fact no king of France. Then the puzzle is, whom are we talking about when we assert that the present king of France is bald? If we say simply that we are talking about no one, the same would have to be said with regard to, say, "The present Czar of Russia is bald." Yet there is surely some sense in which these two propositions are about different people. But since neither of the people in question exists, we are tempted to assume some kind of shadowy unreal existence, just to provide us with two different people for the two propositions to be about. Something of this kind was the solution arrived at by Plato: propositions are about Ideas—not ideas in the usual sense, because, of course, in talking about the present king of France I am not saying anything about the contents of my own mind, or anyone else's, but about a person who happens not to exist. Platonic Ideas have their own reality, independent of anyone's think-so, yet quite distinct from ordinary existence in space and time. It is easy to see that such a theory raises many difficulties, and it is these that Russell proposed to dispose of by laying bare the logical grammar of the word "the." The illustrations may be trivial, but the principles involved are of enormous importance.

Russell's solution is to point out that although the phrase "the such and such" is the grammatical subject of the sentence in which it occurs, it is not the logical subject of the proposition conveyed by the sentence. Indeed, we are misled by the grammatical form of the sentence to suppose that it is only a single simple subject-predicate proposition which is being asserted, but in fact the logical structure is much more complex. From a logical point of view, the statement "The present king of France is bald" must be understood as the joint assertion of the following three propositions: (1) There is an x such that x is now a king of France; (2) for all y, if y is now a king of France, y is identical with x; (3) x is bald. Our original statement is not deprived of meaning because there is no present king of France, nor do we need a shadowy king to serve as subject of any proposition here asserted. Such a mysterious entity was needed only so long as we confused logical and grammatical subjects. The definite description does not name an entity which the proposition is about; it only plays a part according to the rules of English grammar. What we must do is to learn not to be misled by the grammar of our language, but to speak a logical language and not merely a grammatical one.

Quite often our philosophical problems result from a failure to realize when we are concerned with some feature of language and when we are concerned with some feature of the world as it is, independently of the rules of the particular language we are using to refer to the world. For we not only speak *with* language, but also sometimes speak *about* language, and often the same words serve both purposes. Children are often amused by this duplicity of language—"smiles" is the longest word there is, because there is a mile between the first and last letter. But for grown-ups to be taken in by this duplicity is far from amusing. Philosophers, in particular, have sometimes supposed themselves to be dealing with some special realm of being when in fact they were unknowingly just talking about words. Analytic philosophy has been especially insistent on keeping this distinction clear.

Accordingly, Carnap and others call the language that we talk about the *object language* (in the sense of the object of inquiry, not in the sense that it talks about things); but when we speak about the object language, what we are using is called the *metalanguage*. In the metalanguage we only mention the words of the object language, we do not use them. The statement, "'Smiles' is the longest word there is" is in the metalanguage; it says nothing about smiles but talks only about the *word* "smiles." (Of course, the preceding statement is in the meta-metalanguage.) The philosopher must always be clear as to whether his statements are metalingual, and so only about language, or whether they are in the object language, and so about matters of fact in the (non-linguistic) world. When he is perfectly explicit in this respect, he is said to be using the *formal mode* of discourse, and when object and metalanguage are not discriminated, the *material mode*. Philosophical perplexities arise in the material mode, and vanish when we transform them into the formal mode.

Thus philosophers have said that the world consists of substances with their attributes, and evolved elaborate metaphysics to explain the distinction and connection between these two. But in the formal mode we may say simply: The world can be described in a language whose sentences consists of subjects and predicates. Instead of saying that a rose is a thing and its redness a property, and that things cannot exist without properties nor properties without things, we can say: The word "rose" is of one kind, the word "red" of another, and no sentence can consist of words of only one sort. Or we may feel that things somehow have an independent existence, while properties are dependent on things, which might be rendered in the formal mode by pointing out that, in our language, in places where a word like "rose" appears we may also, according to the rules, use a proper name, but not in places where a word like "red" appears. I will not pretend that these formulations in the formal mode are wholly adequate, but they may serve here, I hope, for purposes of illustration.

A more interesting application of this line of analysis is provided by the concept of existence, to which philosophers have devoted so much attention. Some centuries ago Kant already made clear that existence is not an attribute of things, like their size or color, even though grammar allows us to speak of existing things in the same constructions in which we speak of large ones or colored ones. We know nothing whatsoever about something if we are told only that it exists, and we cannot know about anything that it does not exist (for in that case, of course, there *is* nothing of which we know this).

Existence is a concept that can be applied only in connection with attributes, or, what comes to very much the same, classes of things. To say, for instance, that lions exist or that there are lions is to say that the formula "*x* is a lion" does not always yield a false proposition when we successively replace the variable "*x*" by all the proper names that can, by the rules of the language, serve as values of the variable.

But the case of lions, we may feel, is a simple one, because they are after all real things; what about entities like numbers, or properties of things, like colors? Do these exist? Suppose there were no red things whatsoever in the world; would there still be such a thing as redness? Would the color red still exist? These are typical questions of the material mode, to be resolved by reformulations which make explicit reference to language. In the famous formula of the brilliant logician Willard van Quine, "To be is to be the value of a variable." Whenever we use the concept of existence we do so in connection with reference to *something* of a kind, and this is conveyed by a variable. The details of this analysis need not concern us here—I may say that even among the analytic philosophers there is by no means complete agreement on the many issues that arise. What is important is the characteristic way in which formulas like Bishop Berkeley's "To be is to be perceived" are replaced by statements about languages and their structure.

The role that analytic philosophy assigns to logical syntax and semantics must not be confused, let me warn you, with the claims of what has widely come to be known as "semantics," or, more distinctively, "General Semantics." The so-called General Semantics is, at its best, an application of some of the simple results of the logical analysis of language to concrete problems of communication, of the kind that are dealt with by teachers of journalism, public speaking, and the like. I do not mean to be in the least disparaging about such concerns—they are of enormous practical importance. Unfortunately, many of the devotees of what they call "semantics" seem to have made of it a kind of magic helper for every problem facing either the individual or society, from psychoneurosis to the cold war. To be sure, language is a factor of every problem for which what somebody thinks is a datum. But it is only one factor; and very often, whatever disorders of language may be involved are as much effects as causes of the underlying difficulty. Let me admit that a paranoid would be cured if he no longer treated his own name and Napoleon's as synonyms, and that there would be no fixation if "mother" as the patient uses it today were recognized to have a different referent from what it had when he used it in childhood. But I cannot see that semantic naïveté or sophistication has much to do with either the etiology or the cure of these conditions.

To return, then, to the philosophical considerations. I have said so far that the analytic philosopher associates philosophical perplexities with misleading or obscure constructions and idioms in our language, and proposes to resolve them by laying bare the logical structure either of the natural language being used or of the artificial one created for just this purpose. The question then arises, What are we to understand by the logical structure as distinct from the grammatical one? What is this logic to which there is such frequent reference? To answer this question in full is virtually to give a history of the analytic movement. For this movement grew out of a series of quite remarkable developments in logic which extend back not much beyond the middle of the nineteenth century and which reached a climax in the early decades of the twentieth. This new logic, as it came to be known (though by now it is already the "classic" form), was incomparably richer, more powerful, and at the same time more exact and rigorous than the discipline which had remained largely unchanged for some two thousand years. As Russell remarked—with the authority of one of the most important contributors to the development—while the old logic put thought in fetters, the new logic gave it wings.

It did so by enormously broadening the kinds of inferences with which logic can deal—the traditional syllogism is a very special and rather uninteresting case, usually dealt with in only a lecture or two in modern introductions to the subject. And it also brought logic into intimate connection with mathematical thinking, which, since medieval times, has had incomparably more to do with scientific inference than did the patterns codified in the traditional logic. In the last several decades, the new logic has advanced with giant strides, so that more progress has been made in the discipline during Russell's lifetime, say, than in the millenia which separate him from Aristotle. In recent years it has also turned out that this logic has a number of exciting applications, not only to certain mathematical and physical theories, but even to the technology of computing machines, which are constructed on principles exactly and elegantly formulable in terms of the new logic. Whether or not the rational animal is stuck with Aristotle, the thinking machine has a more up-to-date brain.

Now I can best convey to you some idea of the content of this new logic by considering its bearing on the conception with which it is associated of the aims and methods of philosophy. Very early in the development of the logic, analytic philosophy formulated the goal of constructing an ideal language for philosophical purposes, a language whose grammar would coincide with the requirements of logic itself. English, for instance, has built into it such illogicalities as gender, which often has nothing to do with the sex of the referent, and which in any case is, in general, irrelevant to the logical content being conveyed. Its syntax often involves transformations of words —in connection with case, tense, number, and the like—which can be understood historically, perhaps, or on the basis of the psychophysiology of speech, but which again have nothing to do in general with *what* is being said. The philosopher, in short, aimed at a language which would be perfect from a logical point of view, one which would manifest in the notation itself only that structure which must be taken into account in understanding what is being said and in drawing valid inferences from it.

Naturally, it was recognized that such an ideal is, from the nature of the case, impossible of attainment. But the point was to try to describe what such a language would have to be like. And, of course, it must be a language sufficiently rich for the purposes of science. So that, instead of asking, "What are the fundamental principles of reality?" or, "What conditions must be satisfied by any being for it to be?" analytic philosophy asks, "What would a language have to be like for us to be able to say in this language all that there is to be said?" Now there are some difficulties here that I believe a focus on language tends to blur, for "what there is to be said" cannot in turn be decided only by reference to an ideal language without going in a circle. The question whether a particular language is an adequate one depends, of course, on the purposes for which it is to be used. The preoccupation with science characteristic of analytic philosophy, and especially with physical science, is responsible, in my opinion, for serious shortcomings in its treatment of language, which in turn reinforces certain misconceptions in its perspectives on other aspects of culture than science. But I must return to this point later.

Now whatever the structure of an ideal language, it is built around a core of logical necessity; the paradigm of any logical inference is, "Since such-and-such, therefore necessarily so-and-so." But if we recognize such necessity, are we not after all admitting the existence of certain fundamental principles of reality, the discovery of which is nothing other than the objective of traditional metaphysics? Are not the laws of logic universal and necessary only because they are the laws of being as such? Or, if we interpret them as laws of thought, must we not subject our thinking to these laws only because otherwise thought would be incapable of grasping reality? To such questions the analytic philosopher replies flatly in the negative. Logical necessity derives entirely from the rules of the language whose logic is in question; we need not appeal to anything outside language in order to account for its force. The analysis proceeds as follows.

All the statements which can be made in any language fall into two fundamentally different categories. One, called "synthetic" statements, consists of those which cannot be established or refuted without some reference, however indirect, to the facts of experience. The other kind are called "analytic," and their truth can be certified merely by consulting the rules of the language in which they are formulated. Suppose I report the discovery that no pauper has a bank account, or that all brothers are males, or that quadrupeds have four legs. Plainly, none of these discoveries registers anything other than an awareness of the rules governing the use of these words in the English language. If a man had a bank account it would be a misuse of language to call him a pauper, just as it would be a misuse of language to refer to a woman as being anyone's brother, or to call an organism with only two legs a quadruped. To be sure, the bank account may be empty, "brother" may have a moral rather than biological sense, and a dog may lose two of his legs without ceasing to be a quadruped. But these apparent exceptions only point to the vagueness and ambiguity of ordinary language. In a sufficiently precise locution, such questions would not arise. (It must be pointed out, however, that many philosophers, even within the movement, have recently expressed grave doubt whether the concept of "analytic" can be given a precise definition.)

At any rate, the classical position in the movement has been that the truths of logic owe their necessity and universality to the fact that they are analytic statements in the sense roughly specified above. It is a matter of logic and not of meteorology that tomorrow it will either rain in Los Angeles or else it will not. (A heavy dew does not affect the logical necessity here, but only makes it harder for us to decide whether or not we should say that it is raining, and whichever decision we make verifies the "prediction.") The reason why this *must* be true is not to be formulated by the claim that it is impossible for a thing both to be and not to be in the same respect at the same time. This is in the material mode, and conveys the misleading impression that the reason lies in the nature of things such as rain, whereas in fact it lies in the rules of the English language governing the usage of such words as "or" and "not."

Specifically, the word "not" is used in English in such a way that, if a given sentence is true, the new sentence produced by adding the word "not" (or some synonym) in the appropriate place is false; and if the given one is false, the new one is true. And from a logical point of view, this is the whole meaning of the word "not"; any other connotation it may have has nothing to do with what is being said by the statements in which it occurs, but affects only personal feelings or associations. The rule for the word "or" is that, when it stands between two full clauses—and there are rules for transforming other occurrences into this type—then if either clause taken singly is true, the whole statement is true. (In some uses, the so-called "exclusive 'or,'" the whole statement is true only if no more than one of the two clauses is true.) Now let us suppose that as a matter of fact it does rain tomorrow in Los Angeles. Then the first clause of my "prediction" is true, and so, by the rule for "or," the "prediction" itself is true. Suppose in fact it does not rain. Then the first clause is false; but by the rule for "not" that makes the second clause true, and so again the "prediction" is true. The truth of the statement can thus be established by reference just to the rules of language; no meteorological data whatever are needed. And it is this fact which is responsible for its necessity.

Statement which in this way are true no matter what is the case are called "tautologies," and correspondingly, those which are necessarily false are "contradictions." Synthetic statements are those which would be true if one thing were the case and false if another were the case; they can be established only by experience, because only experience can reveal what *is* the case. The new logic developed elegant techniques by which it can be determined even in a routine way whether a given statement is a tautology, synthetic, or contradictory (there are, indeed, machines capable of performing this task of logic). Logical necessity, in short, takes this form. If q is true whenever p is, and p is as a matter of fact true, then q must be true—and this "must" only reflects the fact that the whole statement is a tautology.

In this way, as Ernest Nagel has spelled out, logic is freed from ontology. Its truths do not depend on the nature of the world, but only on the conventions we ourselves have adopted to govern our ways of speaking about the world. Yet it is important to keep in mind that, though it is for us to decide which conventions to adopt, once we have made our decision we are no longer free. Each decision carries with it certain others, what Reichenbach called "entailed decisions," to which our original commitment binds us. If I have decided to spend five dollars, I have willy-nilly decided to spend at least four; that is already an inescapable consequence of my first decision. I am not free to make my choice at every point, and logic itself will tell me where my hands are tied by choices that I have already made. But they are tied only in this hypothetical sense, that *if* I choose *A,* then I commit myself to *B.* On the principle of tolerance I can, if I choose, use a quite different language, governed by different rules; but then I must abide by the consequences.

The new logic is thus a paradoxical affirmation of both freedom and necessity. It is in this respect most fundamentally, I think, that it reflects the spirit of mathematics. For it is essentially a mathematical logic. It is often called "symbolic logic," but this is not a distinctive designation, for the traditional logic also used symbols. It is mathematical in that it proceeds by laying down postulates concerning its fundamental terms, and other terms introduced by explicit definition, specifying rules for operating on these postulates, then deducing the consequences of the postulates determined by these rules. This is the heart of the mathematical method, as we know it since Euclid, and as refined and made rigorous in the work of the great twentieth-century mathematician David Hilbert. It is free in its choice of postulates, and subject to necessity in the consequences which follow from the postulates chosen.

But the new logic is mathematical in substance as well as in procedure. Indeed, the greatest triumph of the analytic philosophy came about through the application of its logic to certain fundamental questions concerning the nature of mathematics. The postulational method made clear that the truths of mathematics were hypothetical: *if* the postulates are true, then the theorems are also true, for they follow by logical necessity from the postulates. But *are* the postulates of mathematics true? Can we show them to be tautologies in themselves? So long as we conceive of mathematics as dealing with unspecified entities—*x*'s and *y*'s—with regard to which we say only that if certain postulates about them are accepted, then certain theorems will also apply, then Russell's characterization of mathematics is unexceptionable: it is the discipline whose practitioners don't know what they are talking about nor whether what they say is true. But mathematics seems to be about numbers and other such entities; can these be given a logical analysis?

The answer—technical complications aside—is a resounding "Yes!" By the end of the nineteenth century mathematicians had succeeded in reducing their entire subject-matter to the arithmetic of the natural numbers. Everything in mathematics could be rigorously derived from that fundamental part of the subject which talked only about addition and multiplication and so on of the familiar whole numbers. This achievement was summarized in the memorable declaration by one of the great mathematicians of the period: "The natural numbers were created by God, all the rest is the work of man." Then a number of investigators—most notably Gottlieb Frege, and shortly after the turn of the century Bertrand Russell and Alfred North Whitehead—showed that this most fundamental part of mathematics is in turn derivable from logic itself. This remarkable thesis was developed in the monumental three-volume *Principia Mathematica* which Russell and Whitehead published between 1903 and 1914, and which played almost as important a part for the formal sciences in our time as Newton's *Principia* had for the physical sciences some scant three centuries earlier.

The key to their reduction of mathematics to logic lies in the explicit definition they introduce for the concept of number itself, and for the particular numbers. I content myself with giving you their definition of the number 2. The number 2 is a class whose members are themselves classes, and in particular all those classes, say *alpha,* which satisfy the following condition: that there exists an x and there exists a y such that x is a member of *alpha* and y is a member of *alpha* and x is not identical with y, and further such that, for all z, if z is a member of *alpha,* then either z is identical with x or else z is identical with y. Moreover, when I say that there exists an x which is a member of *alpha,* I am not invoking any mysterious concept of existence, for this is only another way of saying that it is not the case that, for all x, x is not a member of *alpha.* What is important is that in this way the number 2 is reduced to such logical elements as classes, class membership, "or," "not," and so on. Russell and Whitehead then proceeded to show that the familiar truths of arithmetic are only extensions—logical consequences—of the tautologies relating these logical elements. Henceforward it becomes impossible to say where logic leaves off and mathematics begins.

Now this was an extraordinarily exciting and influential development. In the following decades, logic has developed as virtually a branch of mathematics, and correspondingly, many lines of mathematical inquiry have been opened up as in effect branches of logic. In particular, the application to mathematics of the logical analysis of language systems of which I spoke earlier generated a rich and powerful discipline known as meta-mathematics, cultivated by such men as Alfred Tarski and Alonzo Church, and leading to the establishment not merely of particular theorems, but even of whole classes of theorems all at once. Probably the most significant outcome of that development was the work of Kurt Gödel, who demonstrated that no mathematical system can possibly be sufficiently resourceful to permit us to prove all the true propositions which can be formulated in the system. Every formalism is inevitably incomplete, and the ideal of a universally comprehensive mathematics must be abandoned. But by now it must be clear that we have moved very far indeed from the problems of philosophy as these have been conceived not only in the past, but by most people today.

To return once more, then, to the philosophical considerations—and it is a mark both of the vigor and the failing of this movement that it keeps straining away from philosophy! The formulation of a logic cannot be the whole work, after all, even of a scientific philosophy. For even the most advanced sciences cannot consist of pure mathematics alone, but must contain synthetic propositions. For only these convey information about the world, and do more than express the conventions we have adopted to govern our ways of speaking about the world. The part played by mathematics in science is essentially this, that it allows us to transform given propositions into others that necessarily follow. It does not enlarge our knowledge save in a psychological sense. If we know that something is a sphere then, from a logical point of view, we already know that its volume is $4/3\pi$ times the cube of its radius. Of course, without mathematics we would not realize that we already know this; but the whole content of what we know derives just from the knowledge that the object in question is a sphere, and *that* mathematics cannot tell us, but only observation and measurement can. To be sure, we might *deduce* that it must be a sphere from other scientific laws, like the operation of surface tension on a raindrop. But then these other propositions, in turn, cannot be purely mathematical in character. In short, mathematics helps us derive scientific conclusions, but does not provide the premises from which the derivations proceed.

The synthetic propositions that make up the content of the sciences can be known only on the basis of experience; science depends ultimately, and in a fundamental way, on observation. This is the *empiricism* of analytic philosophy, central to the attack on traditional metaphysics, carried on, for instance, by Reichenbach. In his interpretation, metaphysicians like Kant took for granted the existence of synthetic *a priori* propositions—that is, propositions which can be known independently of experience, but which nevertheless are not mere tautologies. The task of the metaphysician was only to discover which they are, and to explain how it is that we can come to know them. It is this conception, Reichenbach argued, that gave philosophy a deservedly bad name among scientists, for the philosopher pretended that his armchair speculations, if sufficiently profound, could answer questions about the nature of things, while the scientist, asking much more modest questions, was constrained to go into his laboratory for experiment and observation. But there are no synthetic *a priori* propositions; the only propositions that can be known without a basis in experience are the analytic ones. And these we can know *a priori* because they do not say anything whatever about experience, and so we need not consult experience to see whether what they say is true.

Now analytic propositions can be known with certainty; we need not worry whether we have conclusive evidence for them, because our knowledge of them isn't a matter of evidence at all. But once we leave the domain of logic and pure mathematics, we have also left the domain of certitude. No synthetic proposition can be known to be true beyond any possibility of error. This is not just a matter of the fallibility of the human mind, for mathematicians and logicians have also been known to make mistakes, after all. It is a matter of probabilism in what is known rather than of fallibilism in the knower. When we know a synthetic proposition, the most we can say is that there attaches to it a high probability or degree of confirmation—that is, that there is considerable evidence for its truth. But in matters of experience there can be no such thing as *all* the evidence, for experience, at least in principle, is endless. Something might always happen tomorrow which would show that we have been mistaken. Accordingly, a great deal of the work of analytic philosophy has consisted in attempts to provide a clear logical foundation for such concepts as probability, evidence, degree of confirmation, and the like.

Because of the ultimate dependence on experience of the knowledge of all synthetic propositions, all science fundamentally is one, as all experience is one. This is the so-called thesis of *the unity of science* promulgated by Carnap and others. There are not two different sciences, one of nature and one of man—or, as the Germans used to say, *Naturwissenschaft* and *Geisteswissenschaft,* the one dealing with the physical world, and the other with the human spirit. All science has the same method: making logical inferences from the materials provided by observation. The terms used in the various sciences are also unified, in principle, for they can all be reduced to—analyzed on the basis of—terms referring to what can be directly observed in experience. As for the laws of the various sciences, much progress towards unity has already been made, for instance, in deriving the laws of chemistry from those of physics; and more unification can be looked for.

In particular, those analytic philosophers especially interested in the unity of science have subscribed to what they call the principle of *physicalism*—that all the sciences can in principle be reformulated in the language of physics. The claim is, for instance, that when the psychologist talks about guilt, anxiety, and such like, what he says can be confirmed or refuted by observations of behavior (including acts of speech); and from a logical point of view, such observations are of the same kind as those involved in the physicist's report that the pointer on his instrument coincides with a certain mark on the scale. But note how different this physicalism is from the metaphysics of old-fashioned materialism or of the more modern behaviorism. For the physicalist does not say that only matter exists, or that there are no such things as thoughts. He says nothing at all about what is to be found in the world, either natural or human; he talks only about the language which we use in our dealings with the world, and offers an analysis of how that language comes to have meaning.

And this, then, is the major task which analytic philosophy has set itself; to provide what it calls a "rational reconstruction of the language of science." In such a reconstruction, the content of science is not presented in the context of its discovery but rather in the context of its justification. There is no description of what actually was done to obtain the scientific knowledge, but a presentation, rather, of each proposition as a consequence of those other propositions on which it is logically dependent. Ultimately, then, we would have a set of basic propositions, whose terms provide meaning for all the other terms of science, and whose truth justifies all other scientific statements.

Now a number of different bases of this kind are possible. One may take as fundamental the propositions about objects of everyday life and their directly observable properties: "The liquid in the test-tube is transparent," "The pointer is somewhere between the '3' and the '4,'" and so on. This is the thing-basis of pragmatism—to be preferred, it seems to me, because it is formulated in the language by which all others are learned and in terms of which they must be understood. There is also the physicalist base, consisting of propositions about electrons, electro-magnetic fields, and the like. And most characteristic of analytic philosophy is the so-called phenomenological base, the propositions of which describe the perceptions held to be immediately given in experience: "There is a rectangular red patch here now." This line of reduction is called "positivistic," and runs from such nineteenth-century philosophers of science as Ernst Mach and Karl Pearson through the contemporary A. J. Ayer. The later developments are usually identified as "logical positivism," to emphasize the importance assigned to the new logic in this reconstruction.

An analysis of what constitutes a sufficient base for the language of science allows us to reduce to a minimum the ultimate furniture of the world. For whatever is not referred to in this base can be presumed not to be presupposed anywhere in the edifice of science. Traditional philosophers have postulated the existence of entities which seemed to them indispensable for any intelligible account of the world, but which the new logic shows to be superfluous. For instance, it was traditionally taken for granted that there must be substances to which attributes can "belong," even though experience, from the nature of the case, can reveal only the attributes; and in the same way that there must be selves to "have" experiences, even though they themselves obviously cannot be experienced (for there must then be another self to have *that* experience).

It was Russell who pointed out that, given a set of attributes and the laws governing their joint occurrence or succession, we need not postulate the existence of any entity outside the set to serve as their substratum. The set itself, as distinct from its individual members, will suffice. We imagine that things are substances to which attributes attach like hors d'oeuvres on toothpicks stuck into a cabbage which is never eaten. But the supposed cabbage is only a reification of the grammatical subject which is said to "have" the property designated by the predicate. In the material mode we may say, the thing *is* the set of its properties: to say that it has the property *Q* is only to say that *Q* is a member of that set, and not that a mysterious something outside the set stands in a correspondingly mysterious relation to *Q*.

Similarly, the self is not an entity over and above the psychic states or contents which it experiences, but simply the whole set of these states, as unified by the workings of memory and other such patterns formulated in the laws of psychology. Schematically, we may say that a self is the set of all and only those mental states which either remember or are remembered by a given state—with a sufficiently generous interpretation of the relation of remembering. I am justified in saying that a particular experience is one of mine and not one of yours, because I remember it and you only know of it secondhand; and that "I" remember it means only that it is related in a distinctive way to *this* experience—that is, to the one I can most conveniently, but not irreducibly, convey by referring to it as the experience of now standing before you. On these terms, the possibility presents itself of constructing the whole world out of the materials of only my experience. But the solipsism which this suggests must not be construed ontologically, as though I am claiming that only I exist—I can never hope that *you* would admit that claim! What is being said is, as always, something metalingual: that the only language I can understand is what can be related to my experience, and the same is equally true for each of you.

We are brought, then, to the question of what constitutes the truth of a proposition. The idealism prevailing in Britain and America around the turn of the century held that truth is essentially a matter of the coherence of the particular proposition in question with the whole rest of our knowledge. In that philosophy, that a proposition is true means fundamentally that it fits neatly into the logical system of our beliefs. For this reason idealists from Plato through Leibniz and beyond have been *rationalists;* the truth can be discovered through the exercise of reason in accord with the principles of logic, and the senses have only a subsidiary role to play. Ironically, the exponents of the new logic have insisted, on the contrary, that logic alone can never yield any save an empty truth. For synthetic propositions, truth is a matter of correspondence with something that, in general, lies outside logic and language. But the correspondence consists in a shared logical structure: a proposition is true when the structure of the proposition coincides with the structure of the fact to which it refers. A propositional form like "*x* is larger than *y*" becomes a true proposition when the variables are replaced by the names of two things which in fact stand to one another in the relation designated. The truth of more complex propositions can then be explicated in terms of their logical relation to simple propositions of this kind. Important work along this line has been carried out by Alfred Tarski; but, like most of the other achievements of analytic philosophy, it applies only to artificial languages whose structure is susceptible of exact analysis and description. In human terms, Pontius Pilate remains unanswered.

There remains one more area of concern—the realm of value. Many people might feel (and I think rightly) that this is as though I were to say that only one thing remains to be considered in *Hamlet* —the Prince of Denmark. For we are talking philosophy, and while unquestionably intellectual curiosity is a basic motivation for philosophizing, surely the pursuit of wisdom expresses a deep concern with the good that can be achieved in human life. Logic, philosophy of science, theory of knowledge—these deal only with questions of fact, with what is the case, or with the structure of the language by which we can describe what is the case. Questions of value are questions not of what is, but of what ought to be. They make up the material of the normative disciplines, as contrasted with what used to be called the "positive sciences" (it is an emphasis on these that is suggested by the name "positivism"). In every culture, philosophy has always been as much concerned with values as with facts; and in my opinion, its distinctive role is to assess the bearing of facts on cultural values.

The position taken by analytic philosophy, broadly speaking, is that there is a radical, logically fundamental difference between statements of what is the case and statements of what ought to be the case. The fullest elaboration of this difference was provided by C. L. Stevenson in a book characteristically entitled *Ethics and Language*. Statements of the first kind express beliefs about the world, while those of the second kind express attitudes towards the world. Now, when people disagree in beliefs, their disagreements can in principle be resolved, for there are certain underlying matters of fact with regard to which at least one of the parties to the dispute must be mistaken. But they can disagree in attitude, Stevenson argues, even when they share all their beliefs. Confronted with such disagreement, there is nothing a man can do but express his attitude, and try to induce others to share it. (Of course, he can try to force others to share it, if the use of force in such circumstances does not run counter to his other attitudes.) But there can be no such thing as a proof that he is right and the others wrong, in the way in which we can prove the correctness of a belief. For if the alleged proof begins with premises that express his attitude, then he is simply begging the question. But if the premises are confined entirely to matters of fact, there is no logical inference by which we can move from factual premises to value conclusions. Between "Such-and-such *is* the case" and "So-and-so *ought* to be the case" there cannot be any "therefore."

This position has come to be known as *emotivism,* though of course attitudes are not mere matters of emotion in any strict sense. The term is used to contrast with *cognitivism,* the view that value judgments are cognitions, embodying (when they are correct) knowledge, in just the way that other judgments of fact do. But the issues are by no means as clear-cut as the sharp distinction between the labels might suggest. Emotivists agree that many (apparent) value judgments relate means to ends, and so are thoroughly factual in character. Cognitivists agree that many (apparent) value judgments are sheer expression of delight or disgust, and so relate to subjective tastes rather than to objective matters of fact. There are more differences, in my opinion, in what they each regard as proper instances of value judgements than in the analyses they each make of specific cases. Nevertheless, the main push of the analytic movement has been in the direction of grounding values in personal choice rather than in reasoned examination of the facts.

But it is important to recognize that analytic philosophy does not thereby undermine the basis for moral, political, or any other sorts of values, as many critics of this movement have mistakenly argued (especially in the pulpit and the popular press). Neither in principle nor in practice does emotivism repudiate values or deprive them of a foundation. So far as principle is concerned, the position of analytic philosophy is only that "basis," "foundation," "ground," and so on, mean something very different when applied to judgments of value than when applied to propositions about matters of fact. When it is a question of beliefs, we can ask for the evidence, and test the logical validity of the inference drawn from the evidence. But when it is a question of attitudes, the basis can only be in the goals and standards by which each man makes his fundamental choices. Values, in short, are commitments rather than predictions; and I do not see that a commitment is weakened just by being recognized for what it is. If anything, rather the contrary is true; the strongest love is that which knows no reasons.

And as far as practice is concerned, it must certainly be admitted that the analytic philosophers have shown at least as much personal courage, and as much personal concern with the great moral issues of our time, as have their various philosophical opponents. Many of them, in fact (like Carnap and Reichenbach), fled the European dictatorships, at considerable risk and sacrifice, because they chose freedom. Others (like Bertrand Russell) have devoted much of their energies to the impassioned defense of human rights and the pursuit of happiness in a world at peace. The fear in some quarters that analytic philosophy undermines values is to my mind of a piece with the hostility that has always been expressed against any examination of established beliefs and attitudes. From Socrates to Spinoza and into our own day, men of even the highest moral stature and religious sensibility have been charged by their contemporaries with wickedness and atheism. I wish to dissociate myself as clearly as I can from this line of attack. My criticism of the value philosophy of the analytic movement is of quite another sort.

It is that the value commitments for which it allows, and even insists upon, have no organic connection with the philosophy. They belong to the personal life of the philosopher but are not integrated with his professional concerns. What he identifies as philosophy is not something that he lives by, but a purely intellectual pursuit, like the study of mathematics or physics with which it is so intimately associated. I am aware that contemporary professors of philosophy are all of them—myself included!—professors rather than philosophers, and I am not criticizing analytic philosophy for leading an academic life. But I believe that from the standpoint of society, rather than just of our profession, what is wanted is a philosophy to live by. Analytic philosophy unqestionably has a great deal to teach other philosophers, and perhaps scientists as well. But it has almost nothing to say to those who approach it in the perhaps old-fashioned but I believe still precious spirit of the search for wisdom.

In his *History of Western Philosophy,* Russell, with admirable objectivity, includes a chapter on the school of logical analysis of which he is such a distinguished member. The last paragraph of the book summarizes what he regards as the achievement of the school: "In the welter of conflicting fanaticisms, one of the few unifying forces is scientific truthfulness, by which I mean the habit of basing our beliefs upon observations and inferences as impersonal, and as much divested of local and temperamental bias, as is possible for human beings. To have insisted upon the introduction of this virtue into philosophy, and to have invented a powerful method by which it can be rendered fruitful, are the chief merits of the philosophical school of which I am a member." I think that is a fair appraisal, and even an overly modest one. But note how great is the preoccupation here with purely intellectual goals and standards—the emphasis is on science, truth, belief, observation, and inference. But art, beauty, morality, politics, and religion apparently lie outside the scope of this powerful method, if not outside the scope of philosophical interest altogether. In his deservedly famous essay on "A Free Man's Worship" Russell presents "the scientific picture" of the world and of man's place in it, and concludes that nothing remains for man but to be, in Russell's words, "proudly defiant of the irresistible forces that tolerate, for a moment, human knowledge." Knowledge remains central to the end, and this holds true throughout the movement of analytic philosophy, though not everyone shares Russell's youthful spirit of defiance.

Of course, the achievements of the human intellect can make us proud of being human; but for my part, I am proud, too, to belong to a species that creates art, aspires to brotherhood, and communes with God. Yet there is a certain clarity and vigor that its intellectualism gives to analytic philosophy, something clean and fresh, which allows us for once to breathe deep without being choked by the smog of so much Eruopean and Asian obscurantism. At the same time, I cannot help but feel that there is something seriously wrong with a philosophy, in the mid-twentieth century, that takes no notice of war, revolution, nationalism, nuclear energy, the exploration of space, or anything else distinctive of the life of our time save the magnificent sweep of the intellect in the achievements of pure science and mathematics. Goethe's Faust, too, was proud of his acquisition of knowledge; and was it not Goethe who said, "Gray, gray is all theory, but green the golden tree of life"?

If I had to express in one word the defect of character that I find in analytic philosophy, it would be *remoteness*—it simply is too withdrawn from so much that I feel to be so important. It is a bracing, antiseptic air, but too rarified to make my home in. When Aristotle formulated his conception of God, the question confronted him of what God could conceivably be engaged in doing. The only activity that Aristotle found worthy of deity was what he and other philosophers were engaged in—namely, thinking; and the only subject worthy for God to think about was, naturally, thought itself. So Aristotle's God was endlessly engaged in thinking about thinking. With very little paraphrase—only replacing "thought" by "language"—this might be said of analytic philosophy as well. It is a noble enterprise, and indeed, there is something divine about it. But most of us, I believe, want a philosophy which is more—human.

QUESTIONS

What is the difference between the logic of mathematical inferences and of inferences based on observation of matters of fact?

IT IS THE DIFFERENCE between induction and deduction, though these terms must be understood in a special way—what Sherlock

Holmes called "the science of deduction" is in the sense of modern logic purely inductive inference. Deduction is the logic of analytic entailment, that is, one in which conclusions follow with strict necessity from their premises. In inductive inference, the premises might be true and yet the conclusion false; it is only a reasonable conclusion to arrive at from these premises. But this does not guarantee its truth.

The development of an exact inductive logic is in some respects even more recent than the new deductive logic. Hans Reichenbach formulated it in terms of the mathematical theory of probability. While the connection between premises and conclusion for deductive inference is necessarily true, for inductive inference it is only probable. Now a probable event—as Aristotle already saw—is that which for the most part happens; in mathematical terms, a probability is the limit of a relative frequency. Which events are frequent, and how frequent they are, can be disclosed only by experience. For Carnap, inductive inference is a matter, rather, of purely logical relations between propositions, but of a kind which do not necessarily confer the truth of the premises on the conclusion. Roughly speaking, in deductive inference the content of the conclusion is already contained in the premises, and so it necessarily follows; in inductive inference, it is only partially contained in the premises. Hence the premises give only a certain degree of confirmation to the conclusion; and exactly how much depends on the relative measure of overlap in what they assert. You will not be surprised, I am sure, to hear that this logic has been worked out only for inferences in precisely formulated artificial languages, and as yet, very simple ones. But both approaches to inductive logic have already been brought into close connection with modern methods of statistical inference, which play such a fundamental part in scientific practice. Analytic philosophy has come a long way from the conception of scientific method in Francis Bacon and John Stuart Mill.

There is still great disagreement, however, concerning the classical problem of inductive inference formulated in the eighteenth century by David Hume. It appears that every induction depends on some assumption—whether as premise or as a rule of inference—concerning the simplicity, uniformity, or constancy of nature (just how this should be put is itself in dispute). We have only the past to guide us, but no way of knowing that the future will resemble the past; we know, of course, that past futures have resembled past pasts, but not whether future futures will. Now this inductive principle, Hume urged, is not analytic; but the proof of every synthetic proposition makes use of this principle, and so the principle itself cannot be established without arguing in a circle. Reichenbach's resolution of the difficulty is to show that the methods of inductive inference are sound if any methods are. If such a thing as knowledge is possible, induction will yield it, so we are justified in using it even if we can never know whether knowledge *is* indeed possible. Inductive inference is the successive appraisal of what Reichenbach calls "blind posits" which, when appraised, are replaced in turn by other "blind" ones. Logic itself does not rest on faith; but the use of logic does.

How does analytic philosophy conceive of the relation between philosophy of science and other parts of the subject?

AS I HAVE ALREADY POINTED OUT, analytic philosophy focuses on the task of formulating the conditions which a statement must satisfy in order to convey knowledge, and developing procedures by which to determine the meaning of any such statement. But any statement which conveys knowledge belongs to science, in the broad (though I believe misleading) sense of the term, which is customary here. For analytic philosophy, what cannot be said in the language of science cannot be said at all, and after all scientific truths have been uttered there is nothing more to be said. In a sense, then, philosophy of science is the whole of philosophy.

There are, of course, other functions which are performed by language. From the point of view of science, the business of language is to embody knowledge, to communicate to others what has been learned. But we use language also to express ourselves, to influence others, or even for no other reason than the intrinsic satisfaction which sometimes the use of language can afford, as in the case of poetry. Language has countless uses and effects; but analytic philosophy tends to assign all but its scientific uses to the psychologist, sociologist, literary critic, and so on. All these aspects of language tend to be subsumed under an omnibus category as "emotive" or "non-cognitive," and then tossed into the philosophical wastebasket. The British analysts, it must be said, have become increasingly sensitive to problems of meaning in other types of discourse than that of science. In particular, many of them have turned to the language of the law, and are making significant contributions, I believe, to the clarification of the foundations of jurisprudence. But in ethics and esthetics, for instance, the outcome of the whole logico-linguistic approach has been, to my mind—and put most charitably—disappointing.

Philosophers of other persuasions have insisted that it is the business of philosophy to make sense of everything that man undergoes and strives for. Cognition bears on all experience at the human level, but it is in turn affected by everything that makes us human. We cannot understand either science or any other aspect of culture if we look at science alone, as a set of propositions abstracted from their human context. I am not raising any objection here to conceiving of the task of philosophy as that of analyzing meanings, and leaving it to other pursuits to make something of what is meant. What I object to is prejudging the content of the various types of discourse by applying to them logico-linguistic categories arrived at by looking only at a highly abstracted system of pure science and mathematics. For this will not yield even the language of science, in any but a question-begging technical sense. Human language, Wittgenstein pointed out long ago, is no less complicated than the human being himself; and meanings, I may add, are as rich as all experience. Fundamentally, the shortcomings of analytic philosophy lie, I believe, not in its conception of the relation between philosophy and language, or even between philosophy and the language of science, but in its conception of language itself.

Is a question like "What is the origin of the universe?" a meaningless one for analytic philosophy because an answer to it lies outside the scope of scientific method?

WHAT IS BEING ASKED HERE gets at the heart of the whole matter. The illustrative question seems to be of just the sort that made up traditional philosophic speculation: the existence of God, immortality of the soul, freedom of the will, and so on. (These three are the ones taken by Kant as fundamental in his critique of transcendent metaphysics.) We find it hard to answer such questions, and if a philosopher propounds one answer, another philosopher offers a different one. What is worse, we do not know on what basis to choose among the various answers. At last, with some measure of scientific sophistication—this was typical of the late nineteenth century—we fall back on an agnostic position: "I just don't know whether there is a God or isn't one, whether man has a soul or is only a physical system, whether he is free to choose or is constrained everywhere by causal necessity. There can be no more evidence for one answer than for the other, and so, like a wise man, I suspend judgment."

Now the whole point of the logical positivist or scientific empiricist is that the agnostic position is no more tenable than either of the others, because it is equally confused as to the meaning of the questions raised. With the progress of science, the area of our ignorance constantly decreases. To be sure, the more we learn the more we discover there is yet to be learned; nevertheless, as knowledge grows, one after another of our questions finds an answer. But the philosophical questions are not of this sort. It is not that here the evidence is and remains evenly divided between the pro and con, or that, because of the limitations of the human mind (as Kant urged), we are not in a position to get at the evidence. The situation is rather that there can be no evidence only because nothing is really being asserted or denied. It is not that there is something in question which is too profound for science to grasp, but rather that we have been betrayed by our language into thinking we are asking a question when we are doing no such thing. It has the form of a question, the grammar of a question, but it does not have the logical structure of a question, so it makes no sense to talk of either knowing or not knowing the answer.

When we ask about an origin, for instance, what we mean is something like this: Here is a state of affairs, please describe for me the earliest state of affairs, related to this one by some sort of continuous transformation, which is still relevant to my present interests. This is very roughly what we mean by an "orgin." In this sense it makes no sense to ask about "the origin of the universe," for whatever earlier state you may describe is still a part of the history of the universe. The origin of man, say, is a fertilized ovum; or we may be interested in the biography of his ancestors. But there is nothing other than the universe to be specified as its origin, because "universe" just means all there is. (Of course, when astronomers talk—very meaningfully—about the origin of "the universe," they mean a particular constitution of things, galaxies and such like, and not what the philosopher is supposed to be asking about.) We have not left ourselves anything which could be understood to answer the question, and therefore have not asked a question. Whatever the problem, give me the data and I can hope someday to solve it, or at least to tell you what else I would need to be able to solve it. But a problem without data at all is simply no problem.

But there is something more to be added. May it not be that, though the question itself is meaningless, there is indeed something that I meant to ask by it? For it is just when we are most profoundly disturbed that we are least able to put our finger on just what it is that is disturbing us. There is *some* point in my asking the question even though it is not the point that my question purports to be raising. It may be that I ask about the origin of the universe when what I really wish to understand is my own destination. The diagnosis of a pathology of language is perhaps not without relevance. But when I have been cured of all diseases of language, what shall I say in the exuberance of my semantic health? This, I believe, remains the philosophic question, and analytic philosophy alone does not enable me to answer it. The position of the analytic philosopher was incomparably put by one of the godfathers of the movement, Lewis Carroll:

> What mean all these mysteries to me
> Whose life is full of indices and surds?
>
> $$x^2 + 7x + 53 = \frac{11}{3}$$

For my part, I freely admit that mathematics is endlessly fascinating; but if I am forced to choose one or the other, I will take the mysteries rather than the equation.

LECTURE THREE

Existentialism

WITH REGARD TO EXISTENTIALISM, as with regard to Zen, it is necessary to make a distinction between what has aptly been called the "beat" and the "square" varieties. All of my remarks will be confined to "square existentialism." Nevertheless, even if we exclude from our purview what is talked about in the coffee shops, we must acknowledge that existentialism has evoked a response so widespread as to be rare and possibly even unique among modern philosophies—at least among those which are not promulgated by systematic indoctrination. In continental Europe, to some extent in England and America, and quite markedly in Asia, existentialism has aroused the interest not merely of the beatniks in the various cultures but also of the professional philosophers and the serious students of ideas.

Part of the reason for this widespread interest in existentialism is directly traceable to certain chacteristics of the contemporary cultural situation. Existentialism owes its popularity not just to the shortcomings of other philosophies, but to failures in politics, economics, and social organization in general. It is not in the least accidental that existentialism should have taken hold of the public mind some hundred years after it might have done so: its basic ideas were already quite clearly expressed in the nineteenth century. For today large parts of the earth's population feel that they are confronted with a world they never made, a world too vast and complex to yield to human urging, and one which is indifferent—if not downright hostile—to human aspiration. If I were approaching our subject from the standpoint of the history of ideas, I would certainly have to devote a good deal of my time to an analysis of the situation of man in contemporary society, and of the ways in which existentialism seems to speak to a man in such a situation so as to allow him to come to terms with a life of almost unbearable anxiety or despair.

My interest, however, is not historical; I simply mention these social factors so that from the outset we can put the existentialist ideas in a perspective which will do justice to them. Whatever shortcomings we may find in these ideas when we view them in the light of their contribution to the philosophical problems to which they address themselves, we must also recognize that to evoke such an interested response on the part of so many people they must in some way or other bear on matters of very deep and widespread concern. To my mind, that is no small recommendation for any philosophy: when a philosopher speaks only to other philosophers, it is seldom that what he says is both philosophical and worth saying. Since this quality of relevance is perhaps the greatest virtue that I will ascribe to existentialism, I want to be sure that it is fully appreciated.

While abstracting it from its historical situation, we can still best approach existentialism by trying to uncover the reasons for the attention it has attracted in the contemporary world. Most prominent among these reasons, I think, is the fact that for the first time in rather a long time existentialism has provided us with a philosophy which is frankly hominocentric. It is a philosophy, that is to say, for which, in the words of Karl Jaspers, "man is everything." For some time, more and more people have come to feel that philosophy has been pushing the human being into a more and more peripheral position in its perspectives. In one direction, man has been pushed aside on behalf of a depersonalized Nature; in another, on behalf of a transcendent Deity; and in a third, on behalf of a State both depersonalized and transcendent. Confronting these other philosophies, most of us have come to feel that the philosopher is no longer addressing himself to the things that matter most to us as individual human beings. Existentialism comes before us with the avowed purposes of describing and evaluating the situation in which every man finds himself, and from which he looks out upon society, nature, and—if there be one—God. It aims at describing and evaluating what it calls "the human condition."

Existentialism, moreover, is a philosophy which does not content itself with a mere description and evaluation. It returns to the classical philosophical tradition in insisting that philosophy is quite different from other intellectual pursuits in a very fundamental way—namely, that its goal is not merely to arrive at a certain system of propositions, however logical the system and however true the propositions of which it is composed. A philosophy is not a body of propositions but a way of life. This is precisely what a great many people in this muddled world are searching for. We want to know, not just what propositions to accept, but what kind of life to live, and on what basis. Any philosophy which addresses itself to these questions begins with an enormous presumption in its favor: at least, it is talking about the things that people want to hear talked about.

Because of this conception of philosophy, existentialism sets itself quite firmly against any system or school—so much so, indeed, that existentialists don't like to be identified as "existentialists." Such an identification implies that they agree with other philosophers who share the label, but who, they may feel, are talking nonsense. More important is the danger that some shrewd critic might write down a series of propositions accepted by all or most "existentialists" and suppose that *that* is what it all comes to. Thereby, as has happened so often in modern philosophy, a way of life would become only a way of talking about life—a new way of talking, but still just talk.

But for the existentialist—and I think most of us would agree with him—life is more than just a figure of speech. And so he is determined to differentiate his philosophical enterprise from the more familiar sort which issues in the doctrines of a philosophical school.

On this point (as, in my opinion, on practically every other point in existentialism) the best observations were those made in the last century by Sören Kierkegaard and by a few others of his contemporaries. The situation, said Kierkegaard, is this. All the lessons we can learn at school are to be found in a textbook; and for all the problems with which we are confronted there, if we are sufficiently lacking in integrity, we can look up the answers in the back of the book. But human life has just this characteristic: it is impossible to cheat life. There are no answers to the problems of life in the back of the book. No philosopher worthy of his calling could write a book with an appendix of that kind to it. If you are able to look up the answers in the back of the book, then it is not an existentialist book, and what is in it is no better than the teachings of all the philosophies that existentialism criticizes.

Now on what grounds is existentialism criticizing other philosophies? To answer this question we must set it against its historical background—not to get at its psychology, but to put into relief something of its logic. Existentialism can only be seen clearly against the background of the failure of classical religious philosophies. I say this with full awareness that there is a religious as well as an atheistic wing of existentialism. Nevertheless, I think it would be helpful, for the purposes of this survey, if we were to recognize that all existentialists belong to the irreligious wing at least in this sense—that they are painfully aware of the inadequacies of traditional religious philosophies. Either they insist that no religious philosophy as such can be philosophically adequate, or else they maintain, at any rate, that the philosophies of institutionalized religion have become grossly inadequate to their own religious commitments. It is true, for instance, that Kierkegaard is a man of very great Christian faith, and that there are many Catholic existentialists. Nevertheless, for the religious, as for the atheistic existentialists, we can best appreciate that human condition which it is their task to describe, to evaluate—and to live in successfully—if we take as our point of departure the classic proclamation which Friedrich Nietzsche put into the mouth of his Zarathustra, who returned from the wilderness with the great message for mankind that God is dead.

This is really the starting point for contemporary existentialist thought, especially as Jean-Paul Sartre presents it. It is the sense that the human being is, in Martin Heidegger's words, "forlorn" and "abandoned"; he is thrown into the world, not set into a place fashioned for him beforehand by an all-seeing, all-powerful and benevolent Deity. The circumstances of human life have not been so arranged that man can discover what he is, what is expected of him, what he can hope for. He cannot discover these things because they have not been settled beforehand: he must invent them. Whether or not there is a God, existentialists agree that whatever gods there be have not defined the human condition in these most critical respects. For the questions posed by life we not only cannot look up the answers in the back of the book; there is not even an Author who has settled for all time what the right answers are.

Existentialism thus presents itself, as Sartre puts it, as "nothing else than an attempt to draw all the consequences of a coherent atheistic position." In *The Brothers Karamazov* Dostoevskii has two characters engage in one of his characteristically interminable yet endlessly fascinating discussions about the existence of God; and one of them—I think Ivan—concludes: "But you see, if there were no God, everything would be possible!" The existentialist is a philosopher who approaches the basic problem of human existence in just these terms, that indeed, everything *is* possible. The problem then becomes to decide which among the infinite possibilities is to be actualized by human choice. On what basis can such a choice be made?

Now, before addressing ourselves directly to this question we must first ask another—one which will appear only momentarily as a digression, but which in fact will lead us directly to the heart of the matter. Why the name "existentialism"? What is there about this point of view (I must not say "school of thought," of course) which suggests for it a label derived from the basic metaphysical category of existence? An answer to *this* question will go far toward explaining how the existentialist answers his own questions. For existentialism is very well named: in its view, existence is the most fundamental metaphysical category, not only from the standpoint of interpreting the nature of things, but more especially from the standpoint of interpreting human nature. Indeed, existentialism is best characterized by its distinctive conception of man's existence. In its simplest terms, that conception is the following.

When I entertain a concept about anything whatever—a concept of a chair or of an equilateral triangle or of an expanding universe in which entropy is constantly increasing—I have grasped or formulated a certain *essence*. It is an abstract character or complex of characters, a pattern of traits of such a kind that if anything exhibited that pattern then it would exist as a thing of that kind. An essence is a character almost in the sense in which novelists and playwrights deal with characters: it is a role to be filled by real actors, but which can be thought of whether or not anybody ever really plays that role. So I conceive, for instance, of an equilateral triangle; in doing so, I am thinking of the idea or form or pattern of a closed plane figure bounded by three straight lines, each of which is equal in length to the other two. Now this is the essence of an equilateral triangle. But there may or may not *exist* in this world of ours something exhibiting that essence, playing that role, as it were. If I were to encounter something that had these characteristics, then I would say that there does indeed exist an equilateral triangle; but if I had no reason to believe in such an encounter, by the same token I would have no reason to believe in the existence of anything having that essence.

So in conceiving of an equilateral triangle I was under no compulsion from existence; the question whether anything having a certain essence exists comes *after* my conceiving of that essence. With just as much freedom as I enjoyed in formulating the concept of the triangle I can formulate other concepts, corresponding to other essences—a concept of a unicorn, or of an atomic nucleus, or of a cancer-producing virus. In all these cases, experience may disclose whether there does or does not exist in this world of ours anything having the essence in question. And so with regard to anything and everything in the universe—with one exception, namely, man. With regard to anything else whatsoever, *its essence precedes its existence*. That is to say, I can conceive of a thing of a particular kind even if nothing of that kind in fact exists. If a thing of that kind comes into existence, it does so by being cast, as it were, into a predetermined role: it plays the part of a character which preceded the casting. Existence fills, so to speak, a position in logical space available before the particular existent came to be. In Los Angeles we might describe this as the view that the parking place is created before the car—for everything except man, that is; and trying to find a place to park is just the sort of thing that drives a man to existentialism.

Now in the case of the human being the situation is reversed: for man and man alone, his existence precedes his essence. First, a man *is;* and *what* he is is settled in the course of his existence and is not predetermined, not an antecedent condition of his existence. A man's existence is not exhausted by his exhibiting a particular essence, by his being just a man of whatever kind he is. He is more than just a type, a character defined by some role or other. People of this sort are sometimes met with in fiction, and then we say in fact that the character isn't "real" but only a personified type without human personality. The author has given him a name but has failed to breathe life into him; he is only an animated cliché. In short, his existence is determined by an essence, but in reality the situation is exactly the reverse. The human being, in his every action, defines his own essence.

This is the special sense that the existentialist gives to the category of existence. We may say that for him things just *are* while man *exists*. It is only man who, in Heidegger's phrase, stands in the *openness of being*. Only man exists in the sense that what he is is not limited, specified, determined beforehand—in a word, defined prior to his existence. We define things by giving their essence. (Modern semantics would insist that it is only words that are defined, and so only words that have essences—the word "man" no more and no less than any other.) Because man's existence precedes his essence, no definition of man is possible. This is the core of the existentialist's conception of human nature. If man is to be defined, it must be as the being which defies definition. If a philosopher were to define man as being of such and such a kind, man, on hearing the definition, would surely make something else of himself, if for no other reason than to spite the philosopher. The fact that man is capable of such an act of spite is just what constitutes his humanity. (You can see what a jaundiced view of mankind the existentialist has!)

The first principle of existentialism then, as Sartre formulates it, is this: "Man is nothing else but what he makes of himself." Everything else in the world is only what has been made of it by the rest of being. Everything else is subject to the law of identity: *A* is identical with *A; A* is *A,* was *A,* will be *A,* nothing but *A*. Every thing but man is just the thing that it is and absolutely nothing else. Only man is not subject to the law of identity. Man is the one existent of which we cannot say he is only this and nothing more. In the very act of becoming aware of the particular "this" that he is—whatever is may be—the human being has already transcended it. Man is the being whose existence consists in continuously transcending itself. Man's existence is constituted by this fact: that he is continuously becoming what he was not. If I dare say so, here we have the essence of existentialism, the reason why existentialism is properly so called. It is by working out the implications of this conception of man's existence that existentialism tries to answer the philosophical questions about what we are, what we can hope for, and what we ought to do.

Now to conceive of man as the existent which determines its own essence is to recognize that the most fundamental attribute of the human being is his capacity for choice. From this viewpoint, we are most wholly and most truly human in our acts of choice. For it is these acts which express the fact that for us existence precedes essence. But this is not to say that we become human by virtue of choosing good rather than evil. There is a subtle but extremely important point to be made here. The sort of act which is in question is not a choice between a predetermined good and evil. What makes us fully and distinctively human is not choosing between willing good on the one hand and willing evil on the other, but consists rather just in choosing to will. It consists in the bare fact that we genuinely *make* a choice. This is the significance of Kierkegaard's famous "either/or." What makes us human is that life has a meaning for us, that is, that we determine for ourselves a perspective on life in which there is embedded a difference between good and evil. To say that it is all one is to say that life makes no sense at all. The meaning of life lies in the values which we can find in it, and values are the product of choice.

The humanity of man, therefore, does not consist in the virtue of his choices but in their genuineness, in the fact that he has made choices. It is decision, Jaspers says, that makes existence real. A man that makes no decisions has no existence. Of course, there may be such a thing, but his being is precisely the being of a thing, not the existence of a human being. We cannot ascribe personality to him, for this belongs only to the human. He has no personality because what he is is determined for him from without. We can say of him only *what* he is, not *who* he is—for he is nobody. In short, his essence precedes his existence. To exist as a human being he must reverse this relationship; he must, that is to say, decide for himself what his life is to be.

But the words "for himself" are, strictly speaking, redundant. The point is simply that *he* must decide: the choices he makes must be genuinely his or he is not making them. Sartre puts it this way: the human being *invents* values. Ordinarily we would prefer to say that he "creates" values. But this locution might tempt us into the mistake of supposing that the essence of the value—what makes it a value—is something already there. It may have been provided for us by God, or by our forefathers, or by the State, or by the process of Evolution, or by what you will; the mistake lies in supposing that it has already been provided, and that man creates values only in the sense that he creates things which exhibit that pre-existent essence. But all this is just what the existentialist denies. He is saying something very different, and much more fundamental. He is saying that it is we who create the values themselves and not just the things that belong to value-categories; this is what he means by the assertion that man *invents* values. If we ask, "What is the good of going on living? What meaning is there in life? What value is to be found in man's existence?" the existentialist replies, "Only what man himself puts into it." There is no a priori meaning of life, no value which, beforehand and in its own nature, *is* a value. Whatever meaning and value man can find in his life must be the outcome of his own choices, his own inventions. It is a projection onto the cosmic plane, so to say, of his personal freedom.

Thus, the existentialist moves from the concept of existence to the concept of choice, and from choice, in turn, to the concept of freedom. Plainly, in the existentialist conception it is not merely true that man is free, as though this happened to be one of his attributes among others; man *is* freedom. Freedom comes as close to constituting the essence of man as his existence makes possible. Whatever a man may be, he is free to be something else if he chooses; but he is not free to choose to give up his freedom. For in choosing to do that he would betray the fact that he has already lost what he pretends to give up: it is no longer his to give. Only one who is already in bondage can choose to accept slavery, for the slavishness lies in the acceptance.

What man most truly wants, in his capacity as a human being, is simply the right to an independent choice. (This idea, like so many others in existentialism, is already explicit in Dostoevskii.) We may think that a man wants *A* rather than *B,* and *C* rather than *D;* and so we come to him and say, "Behold! I have this day set before you *A* and *C,* and secured you forever against *B* and *D!*" But alas, we shortly find that he shows not the least signs of gratitude. For it is not the difference between *A* and *B,* or between *C* and *D,* that really matters to him—if he exists as a person and not as a thing.

What matters is the difference between his freely choosing something and his being forced upon even that very thing. What counts for a human being is not what he has, but whether it is the outcome of his own choice or the choice of another. Nothing can compensate a man for the loss of his humanity in the subjugation of his will to the will of another. What we get out of life depends upon what *we* get, not upon what someone else gives.

In this fundamental respect, Sartre points out, morality is like art. What counts in art is precisely the act of free creativity. The important thing for the artist is that there are no rules formulated beforehand and by someone else to which he must subject himself. Whenever the critic does formulate such rules, the artist, with his creative genius, sets them aside, and in spite of them achieves a thing of beauty. Only with hindsight can we see that everything that he did was exactly what should have been done. And even then, what we see convinces everyone except the creative genius of the new generation. Values in general express just this sort of creative freedom. The freedom, indeed, is inseparable from the creativity.

But man's freedom is also inseparably linked with responsibility. The significance of a choice is not exhausted by the act of choosing but extends also to what is chosen: it lies, that is, in the consequences of the act and not just in the act itself. Responsibility is only the measure of the farthest reaches of freedom. In the existentialist account, each man is plainly responsible, to start with, for his own individuality. What we are, each of us, is determined by one thing and by one thing only—ourselves. For we have already seen that in this conception a man really is only what he himself has made of himself. No one and nothing else can make anything of him as a human being: whatever a man does not make of himself does not belong to his existence as human. It belongs to him only as a thing and not as a man. In just this respect and to just this degree he falls short of actualizing the potentialities of his humanity. Now this is to say that for what a man is as a human being no one else can be responsible. The limitless freedom of choice in which man's existence consists is thus at the same time a boundless responsibility for what he makes of himself.

As the existentialist sees it, we are responsible for more than what becomes of us; we are also responsible for what becomes of others. When we make a choice we are choosing, not merely for ourselves, but for all men. In the act of choice we are saying not merely "This is what *I* choose," but also "This is what is *to be* chosen." By my existence, by what I become through my choice, I am determining what all mankind everywhere is forever to become. My act defines not just my essence, but the essence of mankind. It is my choice that makes me human, and thereby it makes something of humanity. My individuality is constituted by my choice and does not stand antecedent to it. In the choice itself I am acting as a representative of mankind, as though any man, existing as I am and so circumstanced, would make the same choice. This is what it means to choose: to deliberate, to reflect, to weigh and analyze—that is, to put all mankind in my place. I define my subjectivity only in the process of objectifying it, become a person in the depersonalization of responsible choice. Thus existentialists universalize individual choice after the manner of the Kantian categorical imperative: You must never will what you cannot consistently will should be willed by all other rational beings. It is wrong to lie, for in willing to lie you cannot consistently will that everyone else should always lie, or your own lie would also be disbelieved; truth can do without falsehood, but the lie cannot live without truth. If I choose to lie I bear the responsibility of making all men dumb. In every choice I am responsible for the fate of all mankind.

Now this is an enormous responsibility, to be sure. The existentialist, indeed, insists that it is a crushing responsibility; and the awareness of this condition he calls "anguish." Existential anguish is what a man feels in bearing the burden of responsibility for all men. It is the realization that in making a choice for himself he is thereby choosing the course to be pursued by mankind. This is why Kierkegaard says we choose only "in fear and trembling," why he speaks of the "dizziness of freedom," why Sartre says that man is "condemned" to be free. Such freedom is a dreadful thing. It is already hard for a man to bear if he thinks of it only as imposing on him the responsibility for his own fate. But if he realizes that because he is free he alone bears the responsibility for the fate of mankind, then his freedom is truly dreadful, and he must live in anguish.

Naturally we try to evade this responsibility. We may seek an escape from it by pretending—not just to others, but above all to ourselves—that we are not really free: I have no choice and live, not as I would, but as I must. My actions result from the force of circumstance. I am a powerless victim of fate, of my heredity, of society, of conditioning and complexes, of what you will—provided only you agree that I myself had nothing to do with it. "Have pity on me, O my friends, for the hand of God has been laid upon me!" This is one alternative; the other is to admit the freedom but deny the responsibility. It is true that I chose; I made my bed, but why must *you* lie in it? How am *I* to blame for *your* misfortune? The bell does not toll for me, and you need not weep at my funeral. In short, my brother, you are your own keeper, not I. And so, Sartre says, there are (besides existentialists) only two kinds of people in the world: those who try to escape from freedom and those who try to deny responsibility—cowards and stinkers. Apart from these, there exist only we unhappy few, we existentialists. We and we alone recognize that "there are no excuses behind us, no justifications before us."

And now let us ask of these few, to what end are their choices directed? What are the values for which the existentialist, being neither coward nor stinker, is willing freely to assume responsibility? The answer has, I think, a curiously old-fashioned ring. It is at bottom the same one which was proclaimed over and over again by the nineteenth-century romantics. The values are those of so-called "individualism"; the ideal, what the nineteenth century called the "hero" and the twentieth translates as the "existentialist." This is what Kierkegaard would have chosen as his own epitaph, if he were privileged to write it: THE INDIVIDUAL. Not this kind of individual or that one; not the individual standing in this or that relationship to others, or to Nature, or to God; not the individual of this or that achievement, or who strove for one goal or another; but simply—the individual. For having said that, the existentialist feels, one has said all that can be said about a human being, and all that a man fully existing as human would wish to have said about him.

The thing is to understand myself, said Kierkegaard. There are always people for whom that is quite the thing, as indeed it must be for all of us at some time or other. It is not surprising that existentialism has aroused such wide interest: it invites us all to play the role of Narcissus while costumed as a brooding Hamlet. How fascinating each of us is—to himself! One might suppose that maturity comes only when the fascination has worn off, or rather, when we become capable of finding it outside ourselves—but of this, more later. For the moment what is interesting is that the self which the existentialist is trying to understand is characteristically seen by him as something about which *we* might feel—at least, at first blush!—that the less we see of it the better. This is what Dostoevskii expresses in almost all his writings: that individuality is really revolting, but it is the highest good. Simultaneously to have both these feelings about the self—this is what nineteenth-century romantics called "the Russian soul"; the twentieth century provides a more realistic analysis of ambivalence and inner conflict. At any rate, Dostoevskii asks over and over again, "Can a man of perception and sensitivity have any self-respect whatever?" The present-day existentialist echoes the question; and his metaphysics is intended chiefly to make possible an affirmative answer.

On the existentialist view, the basis of such an answer must lie in individuality as such, not in its particular contents or traits. For our being human, our distinctive existence, lies, you will remember, only in our making a choice, not in choosing this rather than that. The supreme virtue is to be one who chooses, that is to say, to be as we have chosen. To choose freely and to assume responsibility for the choice—that is what it means really to be what we have chosen to be. The supreme virtue, in a word, is integrity. Correspondingly, self-deception is the greatest vice. Life, Jaspers says, is a drive towards honesty, toward really being what we are. Mere things, as you recall, are wholly subject to the law of identity; for man, identity is something to be achieved. A man who is identical with himself—with his human self, the self which he has made by his free and responsible choices—such a man existentialism calls "authentic." Existence, in the special sense which the existentialist gives to this term, is, as Jaspers puts it, the will to be authentic. Only the authentic man really is what he is, because only of him is it true that *who* he is has made him *what* he is rather than the other way around. The man who lacks authenticity is indeed playing a role: his existence has yielded to an essence which defines what he is. In a sense, self-deception is impossible: he who lives in deception no longer has a self to deceive.

We can, however, deceive others; and in a way, we must. For the more authentic we are, the greater the gulf which divides us from other authentic individuals. When one man is close to another, the individuality of each comes into question. For there is the possibility —and even the temptation—for each to act out the image of himself which he sees reflected in the eyes of the other. To be authentic is to choose for yourself what you are to be, regardless of what others expect, demand, or invite you to be. It is a mistake, of course, to conclude that being authentically an individual requires that you be like no one else on earth, that you choose what no one else would conceivably choose. This is the beatnik blunder, and does not belong to square existentialism: as has often been remarked, to be different as a matter of principle is also a kind of conformity, and negates freedom, responsibility, and authenticity.

Yet because the authentic individual, as existentialism conceives him, is so completely self-contained, he experiences himself as completely isolated from others. And so the existentialist echoes, in what strikes me as a very anachronistic key, the agonized cries of the nineteenth-century romantics about how lonely they are, how they are misunderstood, how little of their true selves appears to others. On the peaks, Nietzsche proclaims, one is always alone; and the modern existentialist might add, every authentic individual stands on his own peak. Note that it is not a question here of the social structure, or of the patterns of a depersonalized culture; loneliness is a metaphysical category, not a historical one; it is derived from the existentialist analysis of the human condition, not of contemporary society.

The derivation is a simple one. If man's existence consists in what he freely and responsibly chooses for himself, it must follow that no one can ever do anything really important for another. Because if what we do for another has some importance for him, to just that degree we have lessened his existence; just that much have we taken from his humanity, his individuality, his authentic being. As Kierkegaard put it—always, I think, better than any of the others—it is impossible for one man to be anything at all to another, except in his way. Or, in positive terms, the highest relationship which can obtain between one man and another is that which was manifested in the life (and not just the doctrines) of Socrates. One can be a midwife to others, helping them give birth to themselves. A man cannot help others to achieve predetermined ends, and certainly not ends which he himself has predetermined, if those he would help are to exist as authentically human.

Among contemporary existentialists, Jaspers is especially concerned with the possibility of acting together on behalf of an objective whose worth is not negated by the mere fact of togetherness. "The thesis of my philosophizing," he has said, "is that an individual cannot become human by himself." Philosophy he regards as "a faith in communication," in the possibility of reaching out to others and thereby establishing a common ground for individual existence. "The only reality one can ally oneself with in reliability and understanding," he insists, "is one's fellow man." But it is not clear to me how this conclusion can be consistently reached from existentialist premises.

And now I suspect that for some time you have been wondering why all this is called a philosophy, and why the existentialist does not frankly admit that at bottom he is really a kind of amateur literary psychologist. In fact, he does admit it; he even insists on it. This is what gives his philosophy such a human content, such a relevance to the things that trouble people just because they are people, not cosmologists or logicians. If what we want to understand is the human psyche, there is no help for it—we must be psychologists. But existentialism does not pursue psychology as a branch of science for which human behavior is a part of nature to be analyzed and explained as other natural phenomena are. Its psychology has more kinship with literature and the stage than with scholarship and the laboratory. But I do not say this with overtones of contempt; it is not my purpose to draw an invidious distinction between the literary mind and the scientific one. On the contrary, for my part, I have found the existentialists most worth reading precisely when they turn their talents straightforwardly to psychological questions. For instance, I think Sartre is very much more rewarding when he writes about self-deception or anti-semitism than when he plunges into the depths of ontology and logic, just as Kierkegaard was a better psychologist than theologian, and so for the rest. Existentialist psychology is none the worse because it has not subjected itself to the conventional division of labor in the intellectual community, or because it has not availed itself of the brassy costumes in which the academician supposes that scientific truth must be clothed.

What I find unpalatable is not the form of the existentialist psychology but its content. That novelists, poets, and playwrights have had deeper insights into human nature than we have yet been able to bring into the laboratory is a truth of which, in this age of psychoanalysis, no one needs to be reminded—except perhaps the professors of psychology. And just as Freud must be honored for his pioneering attempts to bring such insights into the purview of the scientific study of human behavior, so also, surely, existentialists deserve our approbation for trying to bring them also within the purview of philosophy.

But for the existentialist, how limited those insights are!—

measureless in depth, perhaps, but extraordinarily lacking in breadth and wholeness. It is impossible to escape the impression that for him man's existence is nothing but vexation of spirit. What he is prepared to accept as fundamental for the human being is not joy, but sorrow; not passion, but boredom; not understanding, but self-consciousness; not reason, but rationalization. What existentialism deals with is not so much a psychology as a psychopathology. Man is conceived as suffering from what Kierkegaard called a "sickness unto death," and Heidegger a "being toward death." The existentialist is forever gazing into the void; and what is unmistakable is that he enjoys the giddiness. We need not go so far, perhaps, as to make the diagnosis of a Freudian death-wish. But it is remarkable that the existentialist insistence on facing the facts of life ends so often in despair over the fact of death. The existentialist categories so often have overtones of misery: their writings are full of words like "anguish," "nausea," and "care," "enduring" life, being able "to stand it." What Jaspers said of Nietzsche—that he didn't think his problems but suffered them—seems to me an apt characterization of existentialists as a whole: they are the philosophers who suffer their problems, who agonize over them.

For this, they have all my sympathy, both personal and professional. But like everyone else confronted with another human being's despair, I find it hard sometimes to resist saying simply, "Cheer up, old boy! It can't be *that* bad!" It's perfectly true that we begin to die from the moment of our birth; but does this controvert the fact that we also begin to live from that moment? This is too much of a truism, I suppose, to sound philosophical, but it is no less true for all that, and, I venture to say, no less profound than its opposite. The despair of which Sartre and the others speak derives from this: that since what we are is determined only by our own free and responsible choices, there is nothing in the world we can count on except our own wills. But why should this state of affairs drive us to despair? The Stoics started from the same premise and drew from it quite the contrary conclusion, that it provides an unshakable basis for the cheerfulness and equanimity of a rational self. Spinoza made that premise the starting point of a logical progression to the blessedness of the intellectual love of God. Gautama Buddha, repudiating the metaphysics of both Self and God, found repose in the will to master the will, and from his deathbed charged his disciples, "Be ye lamps unto yourselves!" If cheerfulness, blessedness, and repose seem so foreign to existentialism, it is because the existentialists have treated them as aliens, and not because they are not as native to the human spirit as are anguish, nausea, and despair.

Kierkegaard says somewhere that the important thing is not to cultivate the mind but to mature the personality. The criticism I am making of existentialism amounts to this—that Kierkegaard was quite right! And I cannot feel that existentialism expresses the philosophy of a mature personality. It seems to articulate, rather, the travail of childhood and adolesence in learning the facts of life—what we then felt to be bitter truths, but what maturity accepts without inner torment as simple matters of fact. And yet I suppose that, just as different philosophies are suited to different temperaments, so we must also have philosophies fitted for the different stages on life's way. There is a time for each of us when we *should* view life through a haze of romanticism, and a time, too, for being blinded by the tears of metaphysical anguish. But eventually the pathos of adolescence must give way in maturity to the tragic sense of life—and to the comic spirit as well—so that, like the great Greek realists, we can see life steadily and see it whole. At best, existentialism teaches us only how to be good losers. But even that is a great deal, and makes it deserving of careful attention. A philosophy which expresses defeat—or better, which struggles for a mature acceptance of defeat—has something to say to everyone: to this favor we must all come.

But it would be manifestly unjust to leave the matter at this point. However true it may be that existentialism has confused philosophical with psychological questions—and from a rather jaundiced view of psychology at that—it remains true that the task it has set itself *is* properly and profoundly philosophical, in the best sense of that word. The aim of describing and evaluating the human condition is one which has been almost completely lost sight of in Anglo-American philosophy—in my opinion, to our very great loss. Existentialism is unceasingly preoccupied with the human condition: with the constraints to which a man is subject, not because he happens to be alive at a particular time, in a particular society, and in a particular place in that society, but simply because he is a human being. Surely, if there are any such things as philosophical problems, distinct from the problems of theoretical science and of practical affairs, they must relate to such constraints.

And it is beyond question that these constraints are real and of vital significance. A man works hard all week, Dostoevskii says, in a meaningless and empty life; Saturday night he gets drunk, sleeps it off in jail, and so returns to work. But where can man go out of this world? "The foxes have holes, and the birds of the air have nests; but the son of man has not where to lay his head." In authentic existence, there is no tavern in which we can overcome anxiety, no jail in which we can expiate guilt. Man is encompassed by his existence, and as Sartre says simply, there is no exit. He cannot escape his fate, precisely because his fate is of his own making. He must live by values of his own invention. Man is the measure of all things; but of all measures, man alone cannot be calibrated.

This is the situation that the existentialist describes as "absurd." What this rather badly chosen word is intended to convey is not simply that life is full of the unexpected, the incongruous, pointless accidents and meaningless routines. It is rather that existence cannot possibly be explained, for any explanation would have to be made in terms of even more fundamental categories. And nothing is more fundamental than the sheer fact of a man's existence as just the person that he is. He might be in another situation, rich instead of poor, healthy instead of sick, born in a time of peace rather than in an age of wars and revolutions. But all these differences, to the existentialist, are trivial compared with the sameness of the human condition for all men everywhere. I think we can agree that such sameness is of vital importance in coming to understand both our own lives and the lives of other men. But I would not wish to say that it is of "overwhelming" importance. The existentialists, I am afraid, tend to be overwhelmed by it.

There is one last observation that I must make. Existentialism emphasizes not only constraints but also possibilities. There must be alternative possibilities of action, or choice would be meaningless; and there must be alternative possibilities of existence, or it would be predetermined by essence. This manifold of possibility gives rise to the final basic existentialist category: *ambiguity,* what Jaspers calls "the endless ambiguity of all existence and all action." We live, he says, "in a seething cauldron of possibilities." No single choice defines once and for all the nature of man and thereby of the world significant for human existence. Choice is continuous as we go through life, and with each choice some possibilities vanish forever while new ones emerge for the next choice. We are continuously making something of life, but we can never make it out: life is inescapably ambiguous.

This is why existentialism turns so characteristically to literature to express its philosophy. For poetry and myth—indeed, art in general—is ambiguous in just this way. The existentialist believes that only the riches of the artistic consciousness can be adequate to the rich ambiguity of life itself. The masks which all things wear belong to the truth, they are a part of the truth; just as the poetic symbol reveals by the very fact of concealing, and reveals a deeper truth than the naked prose. To know things is not to strip off their masks and see them as they are, for their actuality consists in what clothes them as much as in the nakedness beneath. All knowledge is a process of interpretation, of reading symbols, all science a paraphrase, all action a struggle with the strands of ambiguity in which man's existence is enmeshed.

I take refuge finally, then, in this doctrine. For existentialism, too, shares in this ambiguity, and all that I have been saying about it is no more than my struggle for an interpretation. It is a choice that I have made; and I suppose that I have no choice but to assume responsibility for it.

QUESTIONS

Doesn't the view that choice involves responsibility for all *men contradict the position that each man determines his own essence, his own authentic being?*

I THINK this would indeed be a contradiction if the individual could be analyzed apart from the social matrix in which his individuality is embedded. For responsibility surely implies power. And if the individual is conceived as being so effectively isolated from society that no other individual can affect his authentic being, by the same token no other can be responsible for him. As I pointed out in the course of my exposition, this does, in my opinion, constitute a problem for existentialism. But it is by no means a problem of which the existentialists are unaware, or to the solution of which they have not directed very serious efforts. If we start out by postulating a gulf separating each man from his fellows, I doubt if any philosophy can build a bridge to re-unite them.

But the existentialist, so far as I can see, need not make his individualism so absolute. He may say that the individual, in choosing for himself, determines what man is to be, for the reason that each of us contains within himself a reflection, as it were, of a whole society. It is not merely the pre-existent society in and by which we have become what we are. More to the point is the society which we are prepared to bring into being by the choice that we have made. When I choose, I do not say, "This is what *I* shall be, and the rest of the world go hang!" For this would contradict the fact of my *involvement* with the rest of the world. The "I" whose being I am determining in making my choice in turn contains determinants of what the rest of the world is to be, acting through the relationships in which I stand to the rest. In making myself a particular sort of person, I am making my family a particular sort of family, my community a particular sort of community, my state a particular sort of state. Indeed, insofar as the limits of my influence allow, I am making of man a particular sort of being.

Among contemporary existentialists, Jaspers is especially interested in the implications for authentic individuality of the fact of interpersonal relatedness. Such relatedness is undeniably a part of the human condition, as fundamental as the isolation and loneliness so much emphasized by the romantic individualists. But fundamentally, the "estrangement" of which the existentialist speaks refers to man's alienation from the world rather than from his fellows. The question is whether the fact of sociality suffices to overcome the more fundamental estrangement. In my opinion, it does. In the religious idiom, if you would love God, love your fellow man; and God's love, in turn, finds expression in the love bestowed upon us by other human beings. But the experience of love—whether we give it or receive it—has nothing to do with anguish, dread, and despair.

In insisting that the individual is responsible for every choice he makes, isn't the existentialist denying the freedom to be irresponsible, and so imposing prior constraints on man's essence?

THE ANSWER TO THIS QUESTION involves an important point about existentialism which the beatnik has never understood. It is the mistaken identification of existentialist freedom with immature irresponsibility. This is what lies behind coffee-house existentialism, whether in Paris or Los Angeles. Existentialism is vulgarized with the superficial interpretation that if we do exactly as we like, without regard to consequences, we are expressing authentic individuality. It is like the vulgarization of psychoanalysis which mistakenly identifies the removal of unconscious repression with the removal of rational restraint. In both cases, just the contrary is true. Neither the philosophy nor the psychology provides a justification for doing the sorts of things that would otherwise make us feel guilty. In both cases, it is primarily a matter of understanding the guilt—explaining it, not explaining it away. For some existentialists, indeed, guilt is implicated in the very fact of man's existence.

Less metaphysically, we might say that authenticity must be achieved before it can be expressed. And its achievement consists in becoming responsible: we cannot be both authentic and irresponsible. The refusal to accept responsibility for a choice shows that it was not, in fact, freely chosen. It is in itself a denial of precisely that freedom which it pretends to express. The insistence on responsibility does not limit freedom any more than setting up a target imposes limits on marksmanship. The one simply doesn't make sense without the other. Suppose you say to the existentialist, "Look here, if you argue that my existence consists in perfect freedom to choose, how can you deny me the alternative of choosing to be irresponsible?" The existentialist can reply quite simply, "You're absolutely right: that alternative is as open to you as any other. Only, if that is what you *choose,* you are as responsible for that choice as for any other."

Does existentialism offer any guidance on how to choose with regard to any specific moral or political alternatives?

SARTRE FACES THIS QUESTION in one of his lectures on existentialism, and discusses it in terms of a concrete moral problem. A young man comes to him for advice concerning the following alternatives: should he escape from France and join the Resistance forces abroad, or should he remain to take care of his old and invalid mother? Which moral obligation takes precedence—political or personal? Which love does morality enjoin to be greater—for family or for the larger community? Now Sartre goes into this problem at great length; but what he says in the end to the young man amounts to this: "Don't worry, you'll make up your mind. You'll look into yourself very carefully, examine your situation, see what alternatives are available to you, realize what sort of person you will become if you act on one alternative or another, what sort of men we will all become, and then—you will choose." The young man may reply, "Yes, I knew all along that I would think it over and make a choice, but what I am asking is, which choice do you think I should make?" But from Sartre's point of view, there is nothing more to be said; even if we are given advice, there is no escaping the fact that it is we ourselves who must still choose whether or not to act on it. Existentialism contents itself with calling attention to this fact. It emphasizes the necessity of choosing, but has nothing to say to make the necessity less painful.

Now this is a serious criticism of existentialism. Even though a philosophy cannot make our choices for us, it is not unreasonable to expect that the philosophy will help us choose, at least show us how to go about making a sensible choice. As we have seen, pragmatism also insists that the specific content of moral values cannot be predetermined, is not to be deduced from abstract and general philosophical principles apart from the particularities of the concrete context of action; but pragmatism *does* have a great deal to say about the method of resolving moral issues. Existentialism is silent even about the method of arriving at a choice.

Yet I feel that there is something important to be said in defense of the existentialist position. Even those moral and religious philosophies which insist on an absolute difference between good and bad may also recognize that the morality of a particular choice lies precisely in its being made freely by the moral agent himself. It is no good giving him the answer to his moral problems, for it is not the right answer unless it is *his* answer. Otherwise, what sense is there in saying that he made a moral choice? If he acts only in the sense of following a party line, so to speak, in accord with ideological, metaphysical or religious dogma, he may perhaps escape moral censure ("The poor fellow only did as he was told; it's not *his* responsibility!"). But he can never in this way achieve moral stature, for it was precisely his responsibility *not* just to do as he was told, but to come to a decision for himself. The predetermined act is of itself neither right nor wrong, morally speaking; for the actor was not a moral agent. From the existentialist point of view, he was in fact something less than human. The contestant who is coached on the answers demonstrates only that he knows the right people, not his subject-matter; and in accepting the coaching demonstrates also, perhaps, that he does not know even himself.

On this point, as on so many other questions of this kind, there is a striking parallel in psychoanalysis. The psychoanalyst also refuses to advise his patients; when the patient asks "What shall I do?" the therapist does not give him an answer but analyzes the question. The help that he gives lies in making clear to the questioner the nature of the conflicts that induced him to ask the question to start with. What is hoped for is that when we understand ourselves, and the situation in which we find ourselves, we will be able to come to a decision for ourselves. If someone comes to us wearing a blindfold, we do not take him by the arm so as to lead him, but try to undo the bandage so that he can see for himself. We are all of us inclined to ask others to take us by the arm; the existentialist is right to refuse us this favor. His moral philosophy may not be of much help; but it is to its credit that it will not help us to escape from freedom.

Is the existentialist's despair a consequence of his belief that man's existence lies in his freedom, while in the world today there are so many forces that limit and even destroy freedom?

IF WE WERE LOOKING at existentialism from the standpoint of history, as I suggested at the beginning of my lecture, we would probably be inclined to answer this question in the affirmative. In what historical circumstances did existentialism begin to move into the focus of public attention? When did it begin to arouse popular interest, and to secure widespread acceptance? In a France laid low by the Occupation, in a Europe shattered by the most destructive war in history, throughout the world in a time of unprecedented perplexity and insecurity. The workings of such motivations might even be traced, perhaps, in the life histories of the individual existentialist philosophers. But all this, I am afraid, would do a serious injustice to the philosophy. It is one thing to uncover the *causes* of a belief, but quite another to lay bare the reasons for the belief. The causes belong to psychology, sociology, and history; but it is the reasons which must provide the substance of a philosophical appraisal.

From the philosophical point of view, then, I think the question must be answered in the negative. Existentialism is not—in its own conception, at any rate—simply a formulation in abstract metaphysical terms of the meaninglessness and anguish of modern life. The violence of twentieth-century despotisms has claimed more victims than ever before in human history. But for existentialism, there are no innocent victims, as Sartre has put it. We are familiar with the idea that every people has the government that it deserves. The existentialist generalizes this idea: nobody is merely a victim of circumstances; whatever happens to a man, he has it coming to him. Now this is a hard saying, to be sure. What sense does it make as applied to the Jews of Hitler's Europe, to the Negroes of South Africa or South Carolina, to the millions throughout the world crushed by poverty or power?

But what the existentialist is getting at is rather more subtle than this suggests. His point is that the things that merely happen to a man just don't count when he is brought up against the ultimate ground of his existence. What gives meaning to life, in the most fundamental sense, is not what happens to us but what we ourselves do. When life itself is in the balance, the things that count are not those that come from without, but those rather that are rooted in the self. And these, in the very nature of the case, are not subject to external circumstances. This is what the Stoics held, Spinoza, and perhaps Socrates. It is a point of view that is prominent in Buddhism, and plays a part, I think, in all the major world religions. It is in this perspective that the martyrs of our own time, as well as of the distant past, were able to face death with the hymn, "The Lord is with me, I shall not fear!" If Thy will is truly mine, what is done can never victimize me. Only a man himself can be the instrument of his own damnation.

The condition of man with which the existentialist is occupied is thus not to be confused with the conditions of society. Existential anguish is not a response to the existence of dictatorships and hydrogen bombs. The existentialist is not in despair because society has become too large and complex for the individual to be able to shape the course of his own destiny. On the contrary, the existentialist might find even more ground for despair if there were fewer constraints on action. The fewer such constraints, the more we are forced to recognize how completely the responsibility is our own. It was precisely in Paradise that Adam behaved like a coward and stinker, hiding from his own freedom and displacing on Eve his own responsibility.

The existentialist analysis thus transcends historical circumstance in the way in which the religious outlook is a timeless one. But, though strengthened by this accord with religious insight, existentialism also betrays a weakness, I think, in just this determination to rise above history. For modern despotisms do not act on man merely from without; they have learned also to penetrate to the very core of his humanity. Epictetus was able to say, "What! You will put me in jail? My body, you mean!" But history has brought us at last to a capacity for imprisoning men's minds as well. From a moral point of view, it is this power, not that of the atom, which is the most significant invention of the twentieth century. The existentialist analysis may disregard Hiroshima and dictatorship, but on its own principles it cannot overlook Dachau and brain washing; for here it is precisely the humanity of man, his authentic existence, which is destroyed. A philosophy which rises above the problems of war, hunger, and disease has, I must confess, a certain sublimity about it; but under the conditions of modern-life philosophy is inexorably pulled back down to earth. The tyrant to whom the philosopher is so sublimely indifferent is not so indifferent to *him,* and alas, can subvert the philosophy itself to his own tyrannical purposes. Metaphysical freedom may be breath-taking; but only provided that we can breathe the air of freedom in our actual historical situation.

If according to existentialism man's purposes are only what he himself decides they are to be, on what basis can existentialism criticize other philosophies, since they are also products of human decision?

AN IMPORTANT PROBLEM that every philosophy must face sooner or later is how to account for the mistakes in all other philosophies. I think I may say, speaking without cynicism, that this is not too bad a measure of the effectiveness of a philosophy—how much justice it can do to the mistakes of others. It is not sufficiently appreciated, in my opinion, how important this is even for a scientific theory. Among the facts which a new theory is called on to explain, first place must be assigned to those which the older theories accommodated. The hypothesis that the earth is round also explains why it seems to be flat: a sufficiently small portion of the surface of a sphere differs from the geometry of the plane by an amount too small to be noticeable. For such reasons, the Marxist invokes the conception of "ideology" to explain philosophies of history at variance with his own; the psychoanalyst speaks of repression or resistance in similar contexts; and every philosophy which postulates a reality radically different from the world of appearance must rely on some theory of illusion to explain the difference—like the Maya of the Indian thinkers, the transcendental dialectic of Kant, or the pitfalls of language of the contemporary analytic philosophers. In one way or another, we must "save the appearances."

In this respect I think that existentialism is in an embarrassing situation. Its account of the human condition may explain how we got into this mess, but not why so few people realize that they're in it. It is so occupied with truth that it does not have a workable explanation of error. Of the two, I think the second is the more important, for both philosophy and science. Confronted with the mystery of sleep, the existentialist asks instead, "On the contrary, why do we ever wake up?" The religious philosophies account for metaphysical sleep and the nightmare of existence with a doctrine of original sin, a falling away from divine grace. But for many of us, such doctrines raise more serious difficulties than the ones they dispose of.

The best answer that is available to existentialism in general is perhaps its conception of knowledge as a species of interpretation of the endless ambiguity of existence. On this view, it is not so much that other philosophies are mistaken as that they are other interpretations, expressions of other meanings being read into life. It is as though the work of art is created by the reader rather than the poet; or rather, we are each of us poets, and the book that we hold in our hands is blank. "This is now my way," said Nietzsche, "what is yours? As for *the* way—it does not exist!" There are, to be sure, good poems and bad ones; but the better the poet, the worse he is as a critic (or so the existentialist must say). No one individual can set himself up as arbiter for the choices to be made by others, for such an attempt would consist in nothing else than making *his* choice.

In criticizing other philosophies, then, the existentialist is in an impregnable position only because he never really sallies forth to engage the enemy. "Did I say that you were mistaken? Of course, I didn't really mean it! All I meant to say was that *I,* on the other hand, am an existentialist." Now this has some charm, especially when it is expressed with the literary gifts that so many of the existentialists enjoy; I often wish that there were more of this spirit (and more felicity of its expression) in contemporary philosophical polemic. Yet it seems to me that it also leaves something to be desired. I confess that, for my part, when I hold a philosophical view, I find it hard to resist the conviction that it's my view because it's right, and not that it's right because it's mine. Paradoxical though it may be, I think it is the existentialist who is presumptuous. At bottom, he is putting himself in the place of God; for mortal man, it is God's world that is the locus of truth, and not the world that I create when *I* say, "Let there be light!" It may seem gracious to acknowledge that the other fellow is also quite right; but it is only a seeming if what it expresses is the philosophy that I myself am never wrong.

Does the existentialist believe that each generation has to start over inventing values with no inheritance from past generations?

OF COURSE, EACH GENERATION MUST MAKE ITS CHOICES for itself. But this is not to say that it must make them without any inheritance from earlier generations. What is essential is that the choice is made—that freedom is exercised and responsibility assumed. But it does not follow that in making the choice we do not have access to materials deriving from tradition as well as from our own creative imaginations. The point is only that tradition itself cannot constitute a choice. The man who lives in a particular way because that is the way in which life has been lived is not really living his life. He is not existing in the sense of the existentialist. He is not an individual: there is no authenticity in him. But he might *choose* to live in just the way in which others have lived before him. What differentiates his life from the life of the man who has authenticity is not that he does one thing and the other man another. What they do may be the same; it is the *meaning* of what each does that is so different. Looked at from without—which is to say, superficially—it is the same behavior. But as human conduct the two patterns may be worlds apart. Both we and the Russians vote—that is, we mark ballots; but the significance of what is being done depends on the perspectives of freedom and responsibility in which the action is being performed.

And so it is with regard to the uses of the past. The existentialist is here, I think, on quite sound ground. We may use the past without dependency, act independently without denying ourselves the fruits of others' experience. Whether one conforms to pre-established patterns or rebels against them, psychologically it is all one. In both cases, there is no act of choice—the conformist is enslaved and the rebel irresponsible. Maturity does not set its face against either the past or the future.

What the existentialist is urging is that we recognize the full range of possibilities in the future, as the past has shaped these possibilities. We must confront the possible worlds in the making, the various sorts of humanity that could inhabit them, and assume on our own frail shoulders the fearful burden of choosing one world or another and fashioning man in the image we have chosen. In doing so we are defining our own humanity, giving meaning to the world in which we ourselves exist. But to do it takes unimaginable courage, and where are we to find such courage? This is the question which confronts modern man. It is the merit of existentialism that it will not let us rest until we have faced that question. And perhaps even more, its merit is that it insists on replacing that hopeless abstraction "modern man" by the homely concreteness that each of us finds within himself.

LECTURE FOUR

Freud and Modern Philosophy

WHATEVER ELSE PSYCHOANALYSIS HAS BEEN CALLED, nobody, I think, has accused it of being a philosophy. However much it may be given to speculation, in a sense in which this is contrasted with hard-core scientific inquiry, it aims at an understanding of human behavior in a scientific spirit. Yet both its subject matter and its insights are so closely involved in the characteristic concerns of philosophy that it is not unreasonable to talk of a Freudian outlook on life. This is why I venture to include a discussion of psychoanalysis among conventionally recognized philosophies. But there is another and more important reason.

Philosophy is culture become self-conscious; the business of philosophy is to rationalize revolutions in culture. The practices of religion, politics, art, and science may be carried on with greater or lesser awareness of their presuppositions and principles. To bring them into awareness is to begin to philosophize about them; the end of philosophy is to make them intelligible and acceptable. From time to time, in one or another area of culture, changes occur too great and sudden to be assimilated to established patterns of understanding and action. These are the cultural revolutions.

Now the products of every revolution—in science, art, or whatever—are hard to understand, for understanding is by way of the concepts and categories of the old dispensation. So these revolutions provide a challenge for philosophy—as Greek geometry did for Plato, modern physics for Descartes and Locke, the Reformation for Kant, and Darwinism for Bergson and Dewey. Such a revolution was brought about by Sigmund Freud. The juxtaposition of Freud and philosophy in this essay does not mark a historical connection, therefore, but one which may yet become a matter of history. My aim here is to assess only the implications, not the influence, of Freudian thought on the main lines of contemporary philosophy—in epistemology, esthetics, ethics, social philosophy, and philosophy of religion.

First, epistemology. The goal of epistemology is to provide a theory of knowledge which accounts for the origin, content, and validity of knowledge, in whatever forms it occurs. This aim has traditionally been conceived as a matter of logic rather than psychology, of abstract norms rather than concrete facts. But between the conception and the creation of such a logic falls the shadow of a presupposed psychology. Whether based upon the psychology or only commingled with it, every epistemology is shaped by underlying conceptions of the mind and conduct of which cognition is a product. Thus, Locke and Hume theorized about knowledge in the perspectives of associationist psychology, as in our own day Russell made use of behaviorism, Dewey of a functionalist psychology, and the phenomenonologists of Gestalt. An epistemology which takes account of the depth psychology of Freud and his successors is yet to be written.

Psychoanalysis shares with philosophy the point of view which poses the problem of the theory of knowledge: a distrust of what people think they know. Much of what presents itself as known is projected onto the object from the depths of subjectivity. But an important element even of what is sound in knowledge is contributed by the knower. Freud provides an empirical refutation of Locke's *tabula rasa* and Baconian induction. His account of the growth and development of the reality-testing functions of the ego renders absurdly superficial any conception of knowledge as resulting from the cumulative force of "objective" facts acting on an empty mind. Knowledge grows by what it feeds on: not "pure" sensation but experiences made significant by present needs and learned patterns of behavior for their future satisfaction. What Nietzsche called the dogma of immaculate perception must now be recognized as psychological heresy. The difference between what is "observed" and what is "inferred" or "explained" is no longer a matter of abstract logic but of the concreta of personality and culture.

That knowledge is impossible without a significant contribution from the knowing mind was, of course, already explicit in Kant. But in the place of Kant's pure Reason with its transcendental categories Freud puts a mind with a determinate history, rooted in the biology of the organism and flowering in the sublimations of culture. Dewey has observed that the classical empiricists were empirical about everything save the concept of "experience" itself, making of it an all-embracing abstraction which miraculously gives birth to both knowledge and existence. But experience is something that happens, an event among other natural events, different for the infant and the mature adult, for the psychotic, the neurotic, and the mind that knows itself, varying in all of these with the constraints imposed by nature and society.

And if empiricists have been unempirical about "experience," rationalists have been equally guilty of irrationality in their conception of "reason." Epistemologies of this type made the senses suspect but accepted intellect without question. Knowledge was held to be genuine and compelling in proportion to the workings of reason in its production. For psychoanalysis, both as clinical practice and as theory, the misuse of reason is as characteristic of the human animal as is its proper employment. Far from being the avenue to truth, reason may serve as a powerful defense against the recognition of truth, masking anxiety by a quest for certainty, perpetuating illusion by elaborate rationalization. Both Hume and Spinoza saw in reason the slave of the passions. It was left to Freud to document this insight with detailed clinical observations. But Hume's scepticism condemned reason to cognitive impotence, while Spinoza's rationalism made it the sole source of truth. Both misconceived the workings of reason by setting it against emotion in its very nature. Not "reason" and "emotion" but rational and irrational emotion are the elements which enter into cognition. Freud's psychology calls for a more subtle appraisal than epistemology has yet made of the passion for truth.

It calls also for a re-examination of the range of cognitive experience. Contemporary analytic philosophy is inclined to restrict knowledge to the highest psychic levels, to what is fully conscious and wholly controlled by logic and the reality principle. In this conception, the paradigm of knowledge is science, but science rationally reconstructed as a product of pure intellectuality. Imagination is denied epistemic significance, and its work is identified as "poetry." Thus scientism peoples the mind with children of light and children of darkness, and considers only the first to be wise in their generation.

Romanticism acknowledged this image of the poet as being, like the lunatic and the lover, a creature of the night. But the philosophers of romanticism insisted on the epistemic importance of the mythopoeic faculty. Though he be of imagination all compact, the poet nevertheless arrives at truth. Poetry is not merely a matter of clothing with feeling a nakedly prosaic cognition. Truth is the very stuff of poetry; fact and fancy are but one. Such a romantic epistemology obviously courts the danger of obscurantism. When the litterateur preempts the domain of truth, both science and letters are likely to suffer.

Yet the problem for epistemology is a real one. An adequate theory of knowledge must be comprehensive enough to do justice to the whole range of cognitive experience—in art and religion, in myth and mysticism, as well as in science. The faculty of imagination which Kant bequeathed to romanticism was, he said, "an art concealed in the depths of the human soul, which nature is unlikely ever to lay open to our gaze." Freud's theory of symbolism and of the workings of fantasy brings this "art" within the purview of science. And in doing so, it provides a challenge for philosophy.

As yet, philosophy has responded to this challenge only by reinstating, in a more subtle form, the classical doctrine of "two truths." What the medievals distinguished as the domains of philosophy and theology, and the moderns as the realms of reason and faith, is formulated today in the dualism of "referential" and "emotive" meaning. Knowledge is in these terms narrowly conceived as "referential" only; and the content of art, religion, and morality excluded from the province of epistemology as non-cognitive. But recognition of unconscious processes allows us to trace the affects with which symbols are charged to underlying cognitions, and to see these, in turn, as canalizations of impulse. The possibility thus emerges of a new epistemology, which neither limits reason to make room for faith nor emasculates it to counter the threats against its potency.

Even as an instrument of knowledge, to say nothing of its role in conduct, reason becomes effective only when it draws upon energies not themselves abstractly intellectual and shapes materials not of its own substance. Psychoanalytic therapy, as well as theory, makes central such an employment of reason, called "insight." It has a quality of irresistible immediacy which contrasts with the psychic distance of the purely discursive intellect. Modern philosophy has also distinguished two modes of cognition: James, between "knowledge by acquaintance" and "knowledge about"; Russell, between "acquaintance" and "knowledge by description"; Bergson, between "intuition" and "intellect." But in all of these, reason reaches out in vain for direct experience, and the deliverances of sense or intuition become ineffable. Bergson's romantic pragmatism, indeed, defines metaphysics, the area of what is truly cognitive, as the science which dispenses with symbols; and the early Wittgenstein's logical positivism terminates in the silence of the mystic.

Freud thus poses for epistemology the romantic's problem while suggesting a solution for it within the realist's framework. Knowledge is not the product of Augustine's light of grace, nor yet does it presuppose Santayana's animal faith. It can be accounted for without appeal either to the supernatural or to the subhuman. The resources of the human mind itself will suffice, but only if the mind is seen in its full depth and complexity.

It is in esthetics that Freud's thought has probably had the greatest, if not the most direct, influence on academic philosophy. But some of the implications of psychoanalysis for esthetics appear to me to have been often misconceived. And others have scarcely yet established themselves in philosophizing about the arts.

Freud gives art, like mind, a concrete history in the human organism. Art owes its origin neither to the artistic "soul" nor to a transcendent form of Beauty. Dewey's insistence on the continuity of art with non-esthetic experience, on bringing "ethereal things" into connection with "the live creature," accords wholly with Freud's perspectives. Psychoanalysis is at odds with the idealistic esthetics which conceives of a work of art as an ideal essence produced and contemplated by a correspondingly abstract Mind. Art is created and enjoyed by real people in their concrete individuality, with biological needs and socialized aspirations, acting on materials subject to physical constraints.

To such a naturalistic esthetics Freud makes an important though as yet sketchy contribution: his analysis of creativity provides a beginning for the serious task of dissipating the mystique of inspiration. The Muses are no more than a myth—and no less. That inspiration is as fundamental to art as are the skills of craftsmanship is unexceptionable. But the truism does not imply for the well of inspiration a source outside the psychic life of the artist, only outside his conscious life. The discovery of the unconscious brings within the domain of nature and science much of what traditional esthetics assigned to a transcendent metaphysics.

That psychoanalysis finds the same "primary process" at the core both of the dream and of art has led some to a wholly mistaken identification of art and dream. But surrealism and dada, and the "theories" they have generated, are no closer to Freud than is the purest classicism. For fantasy becomes art only when it is externalized and controlled by the responsible, realistic, and logical ego. The same "primary process" is at work also in the production of science, philosophy, and even mathematics—in short, wherever creative imagination must submit its work to the scrutiny of the critical faculties. The artistry lies in the care and judgment with which the critical task is performed, as much as in the richness of the creative materials available for criticism. Without both, the work is either as formless and unintelligible as the so-called art of the insane, or as mechanical and superficial as the formulas of the skillful hack.

Because the process of creative imagination issues in symbols while the symptoms of neurosis are also symbolic, many literary critics and others have concluded that art is the product of neurosis. The depth meanings of art have been construed out of hand as latent meanings born of the artist's illness. But I cannot see that this conclusion is in any way warranted by psychoanalytic theory. That theory, to be sure, was developed largely from a study of psychopathology. On the contrary, Freud's theory of neurosis sees illness as impeding the creative impulse. The energies of the neurotic are deflected from realistic problems to cope with inner conflict. If he is unable to master his own emotions he cannot control the affect with which the symbols of his art are to be charged. If he does not understand himself, he cannot attain that understanding of the human condition which his art is to communicate. True, great works of art have been created by neurotic artists. But their achievement testifies to the force of genius triumphing over disease, not to a reward for the endurance of pain and suffering.

Indeed, psychoanalytic theory not only contradicts the conclusion that art springs from neurosis, but even contributes insights into the origin of this mistaken belief. It is not that art is thought to be the reward of neurosis but that neurosis is viewed as a punishment for art. The artist is guilty of the sin of *hubris,* taking unto himself the prerogatives of the divine. The arrogance of his passion to create makes him rival the Creator. What God hath put together he tears asunder, to remold it in his own image, nearer to *his* heart's desire. If his efforts succeed, it is only with God's help; inspiration is the touch of God's hand by which the artist becomes empowered to create. But to look upon God's glory is to be smitten with blindness; and he that wrestles with the angel of the Lord becomes lame. The myth of the blind artist long antedates Freud; but it need not long survive him.

For the blindness of the artist symbolizes only the inwardness of his vision. In enjoying access to his own unconscious he can make manifest to others their common humanity. This approach to art preserves the core of truth in the conception of art as self-expression, while freeing that conception from the infantilisms of romantic individualism. Not Narcissus but Pygmalion is the true artist. He is in love, not with his own image, but with a creation having a form, movement, and substance—in a word, a life—of its own. Only in these terms can art come to have importance for anyone other than the artist and his psychoanalyst. Throughout human history art has developed in intimate association with the most basic concerns of culture—in the institutions of religion, war, food-gathering, the family, and community life. The dehumanization to which art has been subjected in our own time—not least by artists themselves—cannot be made the basis for esthetics. By implication, if not in explicit detail, Freud allows to art a role far more important than a passing release for the artist and a way of passing time for the onlooker. Art brings to artist and audience alike a pulsing awareness both of human desires and of the realities which frustrate and fulfill them.

It is in this sense that art is the fulfillment of a wish: it creates a microcosm in which everything has significance, everything is of value. And it does so by an objective transformation of materials which everyday experience finds recalcitrant. The masterpiece is the work of one who has mastered his materials, forcing them to yield to his will, and who has mastered his impulses, to accord with the real possibilities lying before him. Art is the triumph of the pleasure principle and the reality principle acting in concert. The former lies at the root of Plato's esthetics, for whom the form of Beauty and of the Good are one. The latter is the insight contained in Nietzsche's analysis of art as an expression of the will to power. For contemporary philosophy, Freud poses the challenge of providing an esthetics which does equal justice to both inspiration and skill, inner idea and outer expression, latent content and manifest form—in short, to both wish and reality.

And Freud suggests also the unifying conception which binds together these two moments of the esthetic; it is the symbol. Art as symbol is the distinctive contribution of modern esthetics, from Croce onward. The work of art does not answer to a mysterious "sense of form" nor yet merely to the desire for the delectation of sense: it *makes* sense. Yet its meanings are not to be literalized; the most abstract shapes and sounds can be as rich in content as the most faithful representations. Art, whatever its medium, depends on what is symbolically expressed, not on what is literally represented. An esthetic response to a work is a re-creation of the symbol, an imaginative interpretation in which the audience shares with the artist the shifts in psychic level and in psychic distance through which the work was created. Here, as Croce saw, all the resources of linguistics—or as we would say today, of semantics—can be brought to bear on the problems of esthetics. And the resources of psychoanalysis as well.

Ethics as a branch of philosophy is an abstract theory, not to be confused with the morality embodied in concrete behavior. It is a theory *about* such behavior, which attempts to lay bare the presuppositions and principles of moral conduct. Freud's thought has important bearings on both ethics and morals.

A perennial concern of traditional ethics was the problem of free will. The determinism presupposed and discovered by science was thought to be incompatible with the genuine acts of choice required by morality. Metaphysicians ranged themselves into two camps, one excluding man from the domain of science, the other excluding objective morality from the domain of action. Kant's resolution of the issue culminates the classical development: free will falls outside the realm of scientific reality, but is a necessary postulate for the kingdom of ends to which man by his moral nature owes allegiance. Freud's conception of human freedom bypasses these metaphysical controversies altogether.

As a scientist, Freud adheres unswervingly to a deterministic viewpoint. Indeed, the determinism espoused by scientific philosophies in the past went far beyond the actual scientific achievements of their day. Psychoanalysis contributed significantly to an experiential basis for the speculative conviction that causal law was as much at work in the realm of the spirit as in the rest of nature. Not just significant choices, but even the apparently meaningless, trivial, and "accidental" features of psychic life were brought by Freud into determinate connection with events of personal history. There is method in all madness, a meaning derived from causal connection with earlier patterns of impulse and action. The position Spinoza was brought to by his rationalism Freud arrived at empirically: what we call uncaused marks only our ignorance of causes.

But freedom, as Spinoza also insisted, can rest only on knowledge, not on ignorance. Slavery to an unknown master is slavery still; and not to know even that we are in bondage is only to deepen it. Metaphysical free will either puts ethics into irreconcilable conflict with science or can only identify freedom with an illusion. Either we must believe that the human psyche is too subtle to be caught in the coarse net of scientific causality, or else we must analyze freedom in terms of causal agency, not in contradistinction to it.

Such a causal analysis of freedom is at the core of the psychoanalytic theory of its own therapeutic method and aim. Its method is self-knowledge, its aim is self-mastery. Man is free when his choices are the product of full awareness of operative needs and actual constraints. Such needs and constraints, so far as they lie in the self, owe their being to a history of fulfillments and frustrations. But it is a history buried in the unconscious, and what irrationlities it engenders remain invulnerable behind masks of rationality. To remove their masks is not thereby to destroy them but only to reveal them for what they are. To know what he truly wants and what he can truly have—this truth does not make man free, but makes freedom possible. Self-mastery is not antecedently guaranteed, but is something to be achieved.

This conception of freedom accords well with the Stoic's formula of "recognition of necessity," Spinoza's "determination by Reason," and Dewey's "reflective choice." For such perspectives Freud provides a greater purchase on the concreta of human behavior. Whether and how far man is free need no longer remain a matter for dialectical dispute; it is to be settled by the empirical study of man. And in the course of such study, what freedom we find may be broadened in scope and strengthened in action. Psychoanalysis allots man less freedom than he thought was his, but makes possible more freedom than in fact he had.

Deterministic freedom, however, seems incompatible with moral responsibility. How can we hold a man responsible for what he "could not help doing"? But the question is ill-conceived. Responsibility is not retrospective but prospective. The question to be asked is rather, "Will he act differently for being held responsible?" Causally, the entire prehistory of the universe is "responsible" for every event; ethically, he alone is responsible who can respond to the duties the event calls forth. It is being *held* responsible which is primary; "responsibility" is but a name for that quality of character of which duty takes hold.

What psychoanalysis brings to this viewpoint is the insight that only the self can hold itself morally responsible. Obligations can only be accepted, not imposed. This, indeed, is what binds freedom and responsibility together. So long as a man's duty has another's voice, he is not yet free, and *therefore* not yet responsible. Here again Freud and Kant are at one. Kant's principle of the autonomy of the will is precisely that the moral law is given to the self *by* the self. But Kant grounds his principle on the pure rationality of an abstract noumenal self, while it is, alas, the all too human phenomenal self which appears on the scene of action. From Plato to the utilitarians morality appealed to "reason"; Freud addresses himself to the problem of the conditions under which the appeal can be made effective.

What is at issue is the conception of the relations between the self which promulgates the moral law, the self which assumes the moral obligations so defined, and the self whose impulses defy those obligations. Traditional ethics was unaware of the depth and complexity of these relations. It failed to recognize that moral integrity—the integration of these diverse selves, indeed, their very acknowledgment—cannot be presupposed. Rationality lies in the realistic unification of this diversity; it is not itself the moral agent which ethics postulates. That morality rests on the injunction "Know thyself" has been acknowledged since Socrates. But only since Freud has ethics been in a position to follow out its implications.

And if the appeal to reason requires revaluation, even more is this true of the appeal to conscience. Freud shares Kant's awe and wonder at the starry heavens above; but as for the moral law within, here, Freud says, God has been guilty of "an uneven and careless piece of work." The critique of conscience as the ground of morality is perhaps the most notable contribution of psychoanalysis to ethics. This critique is not simply a matter of tracing the development of a moral sense to the introjection of parental standards. To disregard conscience because of its origins is to be guilty of the most arrant genetic fallacy. The rational ego also has its history; it does not thereby stand condemned. Such reductionism is a recurrent charge against Freud. In my opinion it is a charge which finds its target only in the vulgarizations of psychoanalytic theory.

What Freud contributes to the critique of conscience is a recognition of its destructive potentialities. A man may be driven by duty as much as by desire, be in bondage to his "principles" as much as to his passions. And under such compulsion he is likely to bring others to perdition and not only himself; more blood has been shed by moral zeal than in the pursuit of pleasure. When the self is brutalized, brutality to others follows quickly. If a man is his own first victim, he is seldom the last.

Thus, while traditional ethics was content to castigate the passions, Freud invites the attention of the moral philosopher to the immoralities hidden in the castigation itself. Ethics must follow psychology in its exploration of the dark regions that lie beyond the pleasure principle.

All this is not to say that established morality must now go by the board. Psychoanalysis has often been attacked—and not alone by the Pharisees—for weakening moral principles. In part this stems from the detachment of the analyst, as theorist and in therapy. The amorality of objective inquiry is mistaken for the immorality of tacit approval. And the therapeutic aim of achieving "normality" is misconceived as a substitute for moral standards, rather than as a condition for the relevance of moral categories. But only those of little faith fear the outcome of an objective appraisal of their values. Freud is continuing the classical philosophic tradition in holding with Socrates that a life which cannot withstand examination is not worth living.

In part, the fears for morality also stem from another vulgarization of Freud, that the aim of analysis is to encourage the libido to express itself in libertinism. In fact, analysis aims at the resolution of unconscious conflict; and it is explicit in the theory that such conflict is not resolved by supporting one side or the other. Freud does, indeed, criticize conventional morality—and even more, conventional moralization—as futile and dishonest. For the moralizer relies heavily on repression, anxiety, guilt, and the magic of the word, rather than on mature moral insight and conviction. Though it may deplore the sickness, philosophy can only be grateful for the diagnosis: the prevailing moral code is largely a tyranny tempered by hypocrisy.

In short, Freud offers for philosophical consideration a perspective in which morality is seen to be no less complex than is the moral agent himself. Various ethical theories have focused on one or another element of this complexity—as, say, Kant did on the superego, Nietzsche on the id, and Dewey on the ego. But no ethical theory can be adequate which does not do justice to all these elements, in their relations to one another and to the cultures which provide both setting and significance for moral action. The primary task for a philosophical ethics, as for psychoanalysis, is to understand morality before judging it. Thirty years ago Santayana, writing of the modern conflict of ideals, observed that the "age of controversy" is past, and has been succeeded by the "age of interpretation." In this transition Freud has played a significant role. But it is in the nature of things that we should be better aware of what has already been lost than of what is yet to be won.

Social thought is shaped by its conception of the individual as well as of society. Accordingly, psychoanalytic psychology has profound implications for social science and social philosophy.

As a scientist, Freud posits a human nature sufficiently stable and invariant to make possible scientific generalization beyond individual case histories. Some such posit is presupposed in every study of man, and indeed in every science for its own subject matter. The kind of order and regularity Newton discerned in the physical world Kant thought Rousseau discovered beneath the varying forms of human personality. Contemporary philosophy can find in Freud a more empirical basis for the belief in such regularity.

Now the "deeply concealed essence of man" of which Kant speaks in this connection need not be understood in Aristotelian terms as a fixed and immutable "nature." Psychoanalysis postulates constancy, not fixity—a regularity of pattern, not recurrence of the elements composing the pattern from case to case. For Freud the constancy of human nature is biologically based. But this basis does not preclude —on the contrary, it produces—enormous variation in actual conduct. The plasticity of impulse and the range of its socially conditioned expressions is central to psychoanalytic theory. What is insisted upon is only that the variability is not endless. It occurs within limits, and it is these, rather than a fixed "essence," that make for discernible regularities.

To be sure, the location of the limits cannot be prejudged, but is itself the object of scientific inquiry. Undoubtedly some social philosophers have drawn them too narrowly, in order to rationalize a status quo as all that is humanly possible. But because "human nature" has been ideologically appealed to in defense of privilege, it does not follow that such a concept can be given no scientific standing.

How human nature is conceived obviously affects the formation of broad social policy. In particular, social philosophy has been especially influenced by a belief in a native moral disposition, good or bad. Classically, this belief is embodied in the fiction of the "state of nature"—man considered apart from the institutions of social control. For Locke it was a state of "good-nature"; for Hobbes, life without agencies of socialization would be "nasty, brutish, and short." On this issue Freud stands squarely with Hobbes: the belief in the innate goodness of man he regards as "disastrous." The fictitious "state of nature" can be given empirical anchorage in childhood, if anywhere. And the picture of an innocent childhood corrupted by society is a romanticist myth. Its being so is not simply a matter of infantile sexuality. Far more to the point in psychoanalytic theory are the aggressive impulses which from the outset play so important a role in patterning behavior.

But neither does Freud endorse the myth of the innate depravity of man. The condition of childhood departs from Hobbes' "war of each against all" because as yet the "each" is unformed—the self becomes socialized in the very process of its growth and maturation. And while it is true that Freud reveals the evil impulses in human nature, it is no less true—though less widely remarked upon—that he also reveals the powerful forces within the personality making for their censorship, suppression, or sublimation. In short, human nature for Freud is morally neutral. It is rich in potentialities for good and evil alike. Which is actualized, and to what degree, is not predestined, but depends—within limits—on the wisdom with which society nurtures its human resources.

Such wisdom can be grounded only in knowledge: rational social policy must be based upon the achievement of empirical social science. And social science, for Freud, is nothing other than the study of human nature. Social phenomena are paralleled in individual history, and can be explained by reference to that history. The culture pattern of taboo he interprets in terms of a compulsion neurosis; war, in terms of individual aggression; religion, by reference to father-fixation. The thesis of Plato and Hobbes that the state is "the individual writ large" Freud generalizes to all social institutions. The several social sciences are not autonomous but are all reducible to psychology.

Many critics of Freud have addressed themselves to this generalization, and with some justice. Inferences based on dynamic insights and checked by clinical observations are here too often replaced by sheer speculation, warranted only by extended analogies. Yet even here Freud's scientific genius did not entirely desert him. For indeed, the various social sciences cannot easily be distinguished from one another save, perhaps, as several points of anchorage to which the study of man moors floating anxieties about its scientific status. No institution—political, economic, or "social"—can be understood wholly in its own terms. This does not presuppose an organismic philosophy of culture, but marks only the recognition of empirical interconnections and dependencies among elements which have been abstracted to start with from what is given as unitary.

And what is given are the actions of concrete individuals; it is these on which all the abstractions of social science are ultimately grounded, and to which all observation in social science is at last directed. Empiricism is committed to individualism—as a methodology, not as a social philosophy. It is the rationalists like Hegel who gave primacy to the group over its members, to wholes over parts, to History over discrete events. In Freud's perspective, Marx has not stood Hegel back on his feet at all: to account for individual behavior in terms of social classes and social forces is exactly to reverse the order of explanation. It is for this reason that psychoanalysis is often so much more sympathetic to literature than to contemporary "scientific" sociology. Because the novelist, at any rate, presents determinate individuals, and may do so with a consummate sense of psychological realities. It is the student of "movements," "forces," "classes," and "institutions" who runs the risk of writing fiction.

Yet the individual may in turn be analyzed socially: not even psychology is autonomous. And such a social analysis is explicit in Freud's own psychology, though its methodological implications are not explicitly assessed. For repression is imposed by man; and surely Freud yields to no one in the importance he assigns to the role of the family as a determinant of the character and action of its individual members. Psychoanalysis thus not only accommodates but requires the distinctively social processes insisted on by Durkheim and Weber. The methodologist is here confronted with a tangle of important questions concerning the interrelations among the human sciences.

But social philosophy is concerned with more than the methodology of social science. It aims at nothing less than an interpretation and appraisal of culture as a whole. Here again Freud raises possibilities for the replacement of speculative by empirical considerations. For to deal with the nature of culture as such is not necessarily to make of it a transcendent reality, but only to detach what is essential in it from the accidents of time and circumstance. But the essence of a thing is only the shadow it casts in the light of some purpose or other; the accidental is what our interests make irrelevant. Social philosophy is interested in social policy. For the philosopher, the essence of culture includes whatever bears upon the realization of human values.

In its full generality, this interest lies beyond the scope of psychoanalytic theory. Yet so far as it goes, that theory has a claim on philosophic attention. For it holds that inner conflict is a product of society as such and not of historical accident. Repression and a heightened sense of guilt is for Freud the price of civilization itself. It is on this basis that he condemns as futile both the cynical denunciations of "modern culture" and the romantic efforts to escape from it. What differentiates man from other species is precisely his capacity for culture, which is to say, his capacity for neurosis. Man is not the rational animal but the repressed animal, and repression and socialization are the same reality viewed from within and without. As in so much nineteenth-century thought, here conflict becomes the creative principle. The competition of species, the opposition of thesis and antithesis, and the class struggle are now joined by the antagonisms of id and superego and Eros and Thanatos as providing the dynamics of progress and growth. Through the workings of culture, libido is sublimated into social benevolence, aggression into mastery over nature. And in this transformation culture itself is created.

In his conception of man's place in nature, at bottom Freud belongs to the Age of Enlightenment. But in his view of man's relation to man his sober empiricism sometimes gives way to the dialectic of Romanticism. Freud says somewhere that he proposes to replace metaphysics by metapsychology. For philosophy this may not be an altogether favorable exchange. But the offer must be carefully weighed.

Man's place in nature—this is the preoccupation of the religious philosophies; and it is here that Freud's naturalistic temper is most marked. There is no need to make room for faith conceived as a relation to the supernatural. Lacking an object, faith is not a relation at all, but a condition in the faithful. The psychological understanding of religious belief is to replace the logical analysis of religious truth. Not the semantics but the pragmatics of theology is the proper province of the philosophy of religion.

Freud agrees with James in discerning certain uniformities beneath the variety of religious experience, but differs from him in their interpretation. For Freud they are traceable, not to the presumed identity of the object experienced, but to the shared humanity of the experiencing subjects. The genesis of religious belief is, in Ernest Jones' phrase, the dramatization on a cosmic plane of the child's relations to his parents. Infantile dependency is a cross-cultural invariant under changing patterns of family relationships; and it is this invariant which is abstracted and projected as universal religious truth. The force of this analysis cannot be met by the easy charge of a genetic fallacy. It is not a question of the genesis of religious belief but of its latent content. Genetic propositions are instruments for interpretation, not premises for demonstrative syllogisms. Freud suggests more than once that scientific interests originate in curiosity about the facts of life; science is not thereby reduced to a state of mind. For science is a matter precisely of curiosity about the *facts;* the scientific interest can develop only with the maturity of a mind capable of sustaining the weight of the reality principle. The question is whether religious belief similarly accords with the norms of maturity. However that question be answered in its generality, religious philosophy cannot overlook the elements of infantilism so often expressed in what is conventionally identified as the religious life.

The psychoanalytic condemnation of religious belief properly extends only so far as faith substitutes for psychotherapy. The peace of mind or soul recurrently promised is not the peace which passeth understanding but one which can very well be understood in psychoanalytic terms. It is the rootless security found in an external source of morality and personal integrity. Such a sense of security is without ground either in a real self or in an external reality. In Freud's perspectives, it is the outlook of a child for whom the world is still a nursery. James' "will to believe" is the imperious claim of a neurotic dependency for its own preservation in the face of what James himself called the robust sense of reality.

Such a condemnation is shared, I am convinced, by the religious spirit. A faith justified by psychological rewards is subtly dependent on a sickness of soul, in which prayer can be only petition, worship only the awe of omnipotence. Not: to be loved though unworthy, but: to find the world worthy of our love—this is surely the religious quest. Security, integrity, and self-respect are its conditions, not its promise.

The mysticism which is the core of the religious experience is thus, to my mind, untouched by Freud's corrosive analysis of its external corruption. Of Bergson's two sources of the religious life, psychoanalysis challenges only the Law, not the Prophets. Perhaps it points to the need even for purification of prophecy—as speaking, not for the god, but out of the fullness of an encompassing self. Such an experience of boundless identification, what Freud calls the "oceanic feeling," he relates to early stages of ego development. Whether such an account of its genesis also exhausts its content remains problematic. What is beyond doubt is that the philosophy of religion cannot adequately deal with the problem without the fullest exploitation of psychoanalytic insights.

I cannot conclude this survey of the significance of Freud for philosophy without brief attention to Freud's own philosophy—the *Weltanschauung* grounded in character and temperament, more or less independent of the formulas in which academic philosophy finds expression.

From this standpoint, Freud is a rationalist, following in the Jewish tradition of Maimonides, Spinoza, and Einstein, closer perhaps to the intellectualism of the first than to the rational mysticism of the other two. With Spinoza's "intellectual love of God" Freud shares the attitude, if not the object. Reason itself is for him emotionally charged, and from its own nature, he is convinced, must give the emotions the place they are entitled to. His best hope for the future is that "the intellect—the scientific spirit, reason—should in time establish a dictatorship over the human mind." On his banner is inscribed "Where id was, there shall ego be."

This rational ideal Freud holds out for everyone, not just for Plato's caste of intellectuals. Its attainment is a mark of maturity rather than of philosophical achievement. In an era when political suppression from without reinforces the psychic repression within, Freud remains confident that the voice of intellect, though it speak softly, will persist till it is heard, and heard by all.

Such a conviction is scarcely the credo of the pessimism with which he has been charged. Freud is not so much a pessimist as a realist, possibly the most thoroughgoing realist in Western thought. The noblest enterprise of philosophic antiquity Kant saw in the attempt to distinguish appearance from reality. At bottom, this remains the philosophical task. Freud was occupied with its most basic part: to dispel man's illusions about himself. The rejection of his work he traces to the blow which he delivered to human pride, like those struck by Copernicus and Darwin; and indeed, in that achievement he himself takes pardonable pride.

What is remarkable is that he dispelled illusion without falling into cynicism or groping for new illusions to replace the old. In his own words, he bows to the reproach that he has no consolation to offer. But he is not himself inconsolable; he remains always a yea-sayer to life. The apostle of reason among contemporary academic philosophers is unquestionably Bertrand Russell, whose *Free Man's Worship* hurls defiance at a universe to which human meaning and value is foreign. Freud's rationalism is more resigned: his aim is only "to transform neurotic despair into the general unhappiness which is the usual lot of mankind."

Whether such an appraisal is true of the human condition or only of the life of man in the century since Freud's birth, it is surely impossible to say now. But if in time to come man is secure in a freer, more creative, and more rational existence, not just philosophy and psychology, but human culture as a whole, will owe a debt to Freud's achievement.

QUESTIONS

How can psychoanalysis claim any scientific status if it always explains away any facts that count against it?

IT DOES CERTAINLY SEEM as if psychoanalysis is impervious to any criticism based on contrary evidence. Objections to the theory are explained as manifesting "resistance" to disclosure of the contents of the objector's own unconscious, and the more vigorous the objections the more insistent the psychoanalyst is on this interpretation. Behavior exactly contrary to what the theory calls for—like a son's active dislike of his mother instead of an Oedipal attachment to her—is explained as a "reaction-formation," a disguise of the true feeling, or else as showing only that the feeling must be ambivalent, combining both love and hate. A dream putting the dreamer in a painful or embarrassing situation is still claimed to be a wish-fulfillment, only the wish is to punish or humiliate oneself. And so on.

In this way it appears that the claims of psychoanalysis can never be falsified. If the evidence is favorable, good; and if it is unfavorable, it is interpreted to mean its opposite—good once more. But a proposition which is proved true no matter what happens has no content. As Karl Popper has especially emphasized, the content of a scientific statement consists essentially in what it excludes, in the things which it says do not happen. A statement that excludes nothing tells us nothing, for it does not narrow our expectations: as far as such a statement is concerned, anything at all might happen. And in that case, the statement may just as well be ignored, from a scientific point of view. (Of course, I exclude mathematics, which also cannot be falsified by any experience, but which serves in quite a different way, as an instrument for extracting the content of empirical statements which *can* be refuted by the evidence.)

In my opinion, however, the logic of the situation with regard to psychoanalysis is quite different. Its interpretations do not convert things to their opposites except in a special sense which still allows the theory to be falsified. Specifically, logicians distinguish two sorts of "opposites"—contradictories and contraries. Two propositions are *contradictories* of one another if, whenever either of them is true, the other must be false, and vice versa. They are *contraries* if they cannot both be true, but might both be false. The contradictory of "white" is "not white": everything must be one or the other. But "black" is only the contrary of "white": many things are neither one nor the other, but gray or purple. Now, it is only the transformation of unfavorable evidence to its contradictory which makes it favorable; transformed to its contrary, it may be just as unfavorable as before.

The propositions of psychoanalysis often have the form that something is either white or black, where the black is interpreted, say, as a reaction-formation against the white. But this could very well be false, if the real color were an intermediate shade or some other hue altogether. The theory of the Oedipus complex is not falsified, it may be, by the case of a son who hates his mother; but it would be falsified if he had no particularly strong feelings about her one way or the other, if she played no significant role in his emotional life. It seems strange to say that the atheist who spits at the church door is testifying to his faith; but after all, he could just pass it by. There is plenty of room for falsification of psychoanalytic hypotheses. The point is that all observations in science need interpretation before they become data for or against some hypothesis. So long as the interpretation leaves open the possibility that the data may be less favorable to the hypothesis than to its contradictory, the logical requirement of which we have been speaking is met.

Of course, the question whether the data do in fact support psychoanalytic hypotheses is an entirely different matter. It can only be decided by empirical considerations, not by purely logical ones. You are entirely free to repudiate Freud's claims; but I do not think you are free to appeal to logic alone to justify your repudiation.

Is the implication of psychoanalysis for the theory of knowledge that the difference between fact and fantasy depends, after all, on who is differentiating them?

DEFINITELY NOT. It is true, I think, that a certain psychological relativism has sprung up which often appeals to psychoanalysis for justification; but I believe that this is a mistake. While much of what we think we see is a projection from our own psyche, in ways that psychoanalysis has elaborated, this does not destroy altogether the objectivity of our perceptions. Psychosis is not just a matter of cultural definition, and even neurosis is more than just a deviation from a social norm. Mental illness expresses itself, and may even consist essentially, in a failure to deal appropriately with the reality situation. What is "appropriate" may vary from person to person and group to group; but the reality is not subject to the same sort of variance. The neurotic is not just out of tune with his society, but with himself, and therefore fails, in the world as it is, to achieve even his own ends. In the psychotic it is precisely the reality-testing functions of the ego that are severely impaired or destroyed.

What psychoanalysis implies for epistemology in this connection is the enormous importance in knowledge of meanings, the interpretations made by the knower of the materials of perception. As pragmatists, too, have ceaselessly emphasized, the facts of experience are not "data"—what is given—but rather what is taken: a "fact" is etymologically something made. The perceptual experience from which knowledge issues is more like reading the expression in a face than it is like solving a cryptogram or a crossword puzzle. What is at work is not a process of sheer ratiocination, but processes of identification, introjection, projection and other such mechanisms, largely unconscious and preconscious. The model of the knowing mind as a computing machine equipped with sensory receptors will serve at best only for a correspondingly eviscerated model of knowledge. It is human beings that know, and their full humanity—with its hopes, fears, desires, and hates—permeates the whole of knowledge, in both substance and form. No other conception, it seems to me, can make sense of the actual history of science. If the psychology of the human mind is to be dismissed by epistemologists as a corruption of its logic, we shall have to conclude that the only true scientist is, say, a fully automatic anti-aircraft battery, which locates targets and computes trajectories with perfect rationality. But it has no imagination, so that its hypotheses, however verified by its hits, never rise to the level of a scientific theory.

None of this should obscure the fact that, though it is we who make interpretations, it is not within our power to make them fit, save by altering them in accord with objective requirements. The symptoms of a neurosis have a meaning, and in terms of that meaning the neurotic behavior solves certain problems for the personality. But the solution is an inadequate one, from the very nature of the case. It is inadequate, first of all, because it takes the symbol for the reality itself, so that the needs which pose the problem are only symbolically satisfied, but not really: a starving man may dream of food, but he cannot feed on dreams. And it is inadequate, secondly, because it can satisfy some needs only by thwarting others—conflict remains at the core of every neurosis. The objective conditions which must be met by rational behavior are as fundamental for psychoanalysis as are the elements of subjectivity which make for irrationality. It is only when our preoccupation with the role of fantasy in psychoanalytic theory causes us to overlook the equally basic role of fact that we imagine that the theory leads to subjectivism. But in that case the mistake is ours, not Freud's.

In the psychoanalytic approach to art, isn't the meaning to be found in a work of art a matter of subjective interpretation?

Psychoanalysis does emphasize the importance of imagination in the response to a work of art, as well as in its creation. What is called for on the part of the reader or viewer is a creative interpretation, not a predetermined assignment of meanings on the principle of a dictionary or code book. The response to a work of art, if it is to constitute an esthetic experience, cannot be a purely intellectual reconstruction of a fixed content which the art object unambiguously conveys. On the contrary, it must be in some measure a re-creation of the artist's achievement, sharing with him something of the process of inspiration by which it was produced. The reader of a poem must become in the reading something of a poet himself, or he will get the message but not the poetry. In this sense art does call for an investment of subjectivity: a work of art speaks only to those who make it their own.

There is, therefore, a certain ambiguity in every work of art, for if its content were unequivocally predetermined it could not provide an occasion for an imaginative and creative response. Such ambiguity —or richness of meaning, if you prefer—has been central in the ideas of many art critics and estheticians, and is not just postulated to fit the requirements of psychoanalytic theory. It is this that gives point to the question just posed. Modern psychologists have developed a number of projective tests in which the response that is made to highly indeterminate stimuli reveals something about the mind or personality of the respondent. What he sees is a projection from within, not a reflection of what is objectively present. But a work of art is not a Rorschach ink blot. The problem is to distinguish imaginative responses grounded in esthetic sensitivity from purely projective interpretations that are largely irrelevant to the work of art itself.

I believe that such a distinction can be made, though I freely admit that in particular cases it may not be all easy. If interpretations, whether of art or of any symbol, cannot be made on a dictionary principle, with a code book providing a mechanical translation of manifest meanings into latent content, it does not follow that in that case anything goes. There are still standards to be met for an interpretation to be something more than projective. There may be knowledge about the artist (or the patient, as the case may be) which gives more weight to one interpretation rather than another—biography may not be decisive, but it is surely not always irrelevant. There is the natural expressiveness of materials or subject matters, as well as the workings of conventions in an artistic tradition or a whole culture. Interpretations will differ in the comprehensiveness of what they take into account and also in the coherence which they can give to the various elements of manifest meaning. And a concatenation of evidence derived from a variety of sources—myth, folklore, ritual, dreams, and so on—may give to an interpretation a weight much greater than any single line of inference could provide.

Ultimately, however, the justification for any particular interpretation lies in what is to be done with it when it has been made: to enhance an esthetic experience, promote therapy, or open new lines of scientific inquiry. Whether or how well an interpretation will serve the purpose, whatever it is, is surely not just a matter of the interpreter's think-so. Here as elsewhere, objective constraints can be recognized in the gap that lies between a wish and its fulfillment. In closing the gap, we transcend subjectivity.

What room does the Freudian ethic have for any standards beyond those actually prevailing in society?

It is curious that psychoanalysis has been attacked, in terms of its bearings on morality, both for libertinism and for conventionality. On the one hand, there are objections that it gives sexuality altogether too much importance, making for a self-indulgence which weakens the moral fiber, if it is not itself downright immoral. On the other hand, there are objections that the outcome of psychoanalytic therapy is only to "adjust" the individual to a society whose moral achievement, whatever its standards, may leave a great deal to be desired. Both these sorts of objections, I think, come to the same thing: they suppose that psychoanalysis identifies the normative with what is normal, and so encourages and even justifies the immorality that is already so widespread in our culture. It aims at making the neurotic, who is abnormally conventional, normally unconventional—that is, no better than he should be, which is to say, as bad as the rest.

I think that this objection is sound in itself, but I believe it to be misdirected. There can be no question that the mere fact that a certain behavior pattern is widespread does not in itself make it right. Reviewers of Kinsey have often pointed out—but apparently, not often enough—that even if ninety-eight percent of the population suffered from a cold every winter, it would not thereby cease to be an illness. The normality which enters into the therapeutic goal just cannot be interpreted in a statistical sense, or at least, not in the simple and direct fashion that has become so common. Similarly, if adjustment is a passive conformity to prevailing practices, the adjusted individual has in effect abandoned moral aspiration. For his morality cannot rise any higher than its source—an inevitably corrupt society. Where all is rotten, it is a man's duty to say so. Peer Gynt was the great apostle of adjustment, in the hall of the Mountain King as in the madhouse; and in the end, he had no self left to adjust.

But psychoanalysis, in my opinion, is not committed to any specific moral doctrine, conventional or otherwise. Its aim is to make the individual capable of morality—that is, capable of free and responsible choice; but it does not predetermine what that choice is to be. I am not unaware of the difficulty, in psychoanalytic practice, of avoiding the imposition of the therapist's own values on the patient. This is not the only branch of medicine in which the cure involves a risk of infection with a new disease. But to acknowledge danger is not the same as predicting disaster; on the contrary, the more we are aware of the risk, the more we can do to minimize it. In fact, the psychoanalyst cannot ignore the risk in the converse direction—he himself may be unduly influenced by those he is treating: counter-transference may be as morally corrosive for the therapist as transference sometimes is for the patient.

Thus psychoanalysis, insofar as it succeeds in acting on its own principles, produces neither conformists nor rebels. Whether a man keeps a wife or a mistress, writes poetry or advertising copy, votes with the party or espouses anarchism, is in itself of no significance for his mental health. Psychoanalysis will wean him away from conventional patterns of behavior if in his psyche they are infantilisms which call, indeed, for weaning. Unconventional behavior will give way to more "normal" patterns if it is rooted in adolescent rebelliousness rather than expressing mature choice. Either pattern can be strengthened as the personality achieves more integration and awareness. The process of education in general does not consist in replacing one set of beliefs by another, but rather in transforming our reasons for believing. Cured of his neurosis, a man may espouse the same values as before; only now, he knows what he is doing, he is prepared to accept the consequences, and above all, he accepts himself as the man he now knows himself to be. Adjustment, in short, means the resolution of inner conflict and not the surrender to the demands of society, whatever the morality which these demands express.

I must add, however, that psychoanalysis does not leave the content of morality as completely undetermined as all this might suggest. For its therapeutic goal is not limited to the capacity for free and responsible choice; it consists also in the capacity for love and for work. More accurately, its theory is that these capacities are interdependent. No one can love another who hates himself, nor be creative in a life of self-destruction. The war within, like all others, replaces freedom by compulsion, and awareness by strategic deception. In the continuing neurotic conflict the victorious end never comes to justify these means: the emergency measures adopted in crisis become a way of life. Psychoanalysis is committed to a repudiation of this politics of personality, and it thereby commits itself to the positive values in freedom and creativity. There is no doubt of the moral relevance of these ideas. But at the level of abstraction at which they function in the theory, they leave open an enormous range of possibilities for specific moral choice.

What justification can there be for applying a psychology of the individual to social issues?

Of course, the easy answer is that society consists of individuals, so that applying psychoanalysis to, say, politics is like using atomic physics to explain the behavior of the stars. In point of fact, political psychology is at least as old as Machiavelli; in our times, Graham Wallis, H. D. Lasswell, and Erich Fromm, among many others, have made significant contributions, in my opinion, by focusing on the role of human nature in politics. Parties and governments are made up of men, after all, who cannot abandon their humanity as easily as their political principles. Much of political life is, in Lasswell's phrase, the displacement of private affects onto public objects.

Yet groups of men can behave in ways that are unknown to its members—sometimes, indeed, being downright inhuman. Bodies may remain motionless even though the atoms swarming within them rush about at breath-taking speeds. The transformation of individual to social psychology requires great care, and probably more knowledge of both individual and society than anyone can yet lay claim to. I cannot see, for instance, that a premise which endows each citizen with an aggressive instinct warrants the conclusion that wars among states are inevitable Citizens also have sexual impulses, but I am not aware of a corresponding passion for world union. William James once urged the cultivation of what he called a moral equivalent of war, a discharge of hostilities in relatively nondestructive channels. No doubt, many worthy ends are served by the Olympic Games; but I beg leave to doubt whether an American victory over the Soviet track or swimming team will lessen the chances of conflict between us on land or sea.

The problem can be brought to a focus, I think, by considering in what sense, if any, we can attribute to societies traits and behavior patterns which apply literally to individuals. So far as I can see, there are three possibilities. One is statistical: to say that a society is neurotic, for instance, might mean that some significant number of individuals in the society are neurotic. There are no particular difficulties here, but on the other hand, the question remains unanswered how groups and institutions are affected by having members with a certain individual psychology. A second approach is analogical: here to say that a society is neurotic is to imply that the behavior of the society as such—not necessarily the behavior of the individuals in it—exhibits the irrationalities and other failings characteristic of a neurotic personality. On this basis, whatever we have learned about the neurotic personality has an immediate relevance to social problems. Unfortunately, the ground for the analogy seems to me extremely shaky. What similarities are being assumed, and what evidence supports the assumption? Can a society be neurotic without an unconscious? Is it economic interest that serves in place of the libido? Is there an ego with defense mechanisms, and a symbolism at work in symptom formation? I am aware that any analogy can be pressed to absurdity, but there are surely some that need not be pushed very far.

There is a third approach, neither statistical nor analogical but causative. To say that a society is neurotic may mean that institutions and practices characteristic of the society contribute significantly to the development of neurosis in its individuals, and that their behavior, in turn, reinforces those very practices. A society which ceaselessly stimulates sexuality while condemning its gratification, that rewards competitiveness while extolling benevolence, that values ends for which it denies the means—such a society might be expected to generate conflicts, guilt, and anxiety in its members. And we can also expect that they, in turn, will seek out and support those institutional patterns which answer to their neurotic needs. I believe that Freud's social psychology can be reconstructed in some such framework as this, rather than analogically. The problem is how to carry out the reconstruction in a way which benefits both from the empirical soundness of the statistical approach and the speculative richness of the analogical one.

Here the social philosopher must wait upon the achievement of the social scientist. But there is one point on which I must insist. In my opinion, the Freudian outlook is not as gloomy as has often been made out. There are those who see the individual and society as caught up in a vicious circle: a sick society cannot nurture the growth of a healthy personality, nor can sick minds create and sustain healthy institutions. But we need only read the circle in reverse, and it is no longer vicious. Mature individuals, rational and realistic, can make some contribution to social sanity; and as social patterns improve, we can look to the growth of freer and more creative personalities. Which end of the stick you pick up—the individual or social institutions—doesn't much matter, if only you take hold, and lay it on. It may be that we do not have enough time or enough strength to ward off the madness that threatens. But we would be mad to quit before we have really begun.

LECTURE FIVE

Communism

IT IS WITH SOME TREPIDATION that I undertake to lecture on a subject of such frequent concern as this one. But it strikes me that the situation with communism, just the contrary of the weather, is that everyone is doing something about it but nobody talks about it. That is, we talk a great deal, but usually about its objectives in some specific region of the political arena, or about the achievements and failings of specific communist institutions. Above all, we talk constantly of the threat posed by communism to our own objectives and institutions. We do not talk nearly enough, in my opinion, about underlying principles and how they are organized into a world view which for so many people holds out a promise rather than a threat. In short, I want to discuss communism as a philosophy, rather than as a political program or regime.

I think one of the reasons why communism is not more often discussed from this point of view is because of the widespread notion that to understand everything is to forgive everything. It is a notion that I don't accept; I'm sure we've all known people of whom we have found that the better we understand them the less we're inclined to forgive them. I have no fears that a better understanding of communism will in any way weaken our devotion to our own values. Ironically, many of the people who have such fears are also fearful of examining the foundations of democracy; they think that anyone who embarks on such an examination is only preparing an obituary, as I think Harold Lasswell remarked. It seems to me that understanding—whatever it is that is being understood—does not imply either acceptance or rejection. It implies rather that we have provided ourselves with a more rational basis for deciding what to accept and what to reject, and with more effective ways to translate our attitudes into action.

So then, I have come neither to bury Khrushchev nor to praise him, but only to try to understand him. Not as a person, of course, nor as a representative of a particular social system, but as an embodiment of the philosophy by which that system is explained and justified in the eyes of those who are devoted to it. It is another irony that I feel impelled to add that there really are such people, many millions of them. The idea that communism is loathed by all or even a significant part of those who live under it is, I'm afraid, not much more than a wish-fulfilling fantasy, and not a harmless one either. Whatever force the dictatorships employ, they do not rule by naked power alone, but in the perspectives of legitimacy. What I want to do is to examine these perspectives.

It is true, however, that we are not dealing with a philosophy in the sense of the movements of thought surveyed in the preceding lectures. Yet the situation in the intellectual world today is not merely that there are many philosophies competing for the loyalty of the inquiring mind. It is that almost every one of them differs from the others in its conception of what philosophy is all about, what it is getting at, what it can even hope to achieve. Positivism, existentialism, and Zen—to take only three—don't just differ in the way in which, say, Plato, Aristotle, and Lucretius did. Each of the ancients would have recognized the others as a member of his own calling, pursuing essentially the same ends. I believe this is not true today. The members of the American Philosophical Association are all, to be sure, united on a concrete professional basis: they all teach in what is everywhere called a department of "philosophy." But even on the American scene, to say nothing of a world philosophical congress, almost all of us experience grave doubts as to whether we can really acknowledge some of the others to be our colleagues in a shared enterprise; and there is a large, though largely futile, polemic in which these doubts are given vigorous expression. I suppose that something of this kind also goes on elsewhere in the arts and sciences—think of the attitude of behavioral and psychoanalytic psychologists towards one another. But you will not begrudge me, I am sure, the feeling that nobody else's troubles compare with my own.

Communism, then, is usually said to be an ideology rather than a philosophy. Of course, there is an official communist philosophy in the standard nineteenth-century European sense, called, as you know, dialectical materialism. I must tell you at once that I will have very little to say here on that subject, narrowly conceived. As a metaphysics, I think it is largely an anachronistic irrelevancy even from the standpoint of communism itself. The materialism has been pretty well outdated by the developments in the physical sciences in the twentieth century, and the dialectic outdated by the developments in logic and mathematics. Nor are the communists at all unaware of these developments; it is just that the new ideas are not considered in what is officially labeled "philosophy." Dialectical materialism provides little more than an orthodox vocabulary and phrasing for the ideas that really make up the philosophy of communism. In itself it is for the most part a loosely knit tissue of logical trivialities and of empirical generalizations so sweeping as to be almost surely false.

For instance, the "law" that quantity is transformed into quality amounts, so far as I can see, to the tautology that when things are sufficiently different from one another, we think of them as different things. Every quantitative difference is by the same token a qualitative one if we choose to take it as such. There are as many colors in the spectrum as we care to give names to, and any difference in wave length can thereby be made a "qualitative" one. The "law" that every thesis generates an antithesis which leads, in turn, to a new synthesis is an example of the loose generalizations that are miscalled a metaphysics. For clearly, not all differences between things imply that there is an opposition between them as well, but only that they are distinct; and not all oppositions generate a new system of organization, unless mutual annihilation is also going to be called "synthesis." Whenever we conceive of something, we mark it off from what it is not; it does not follow that we have thereby conceived of it as being in conflict with anything, no matter how "dialectical" we get. When conflicts do occur, they are sometimes creative; but there are destructive conflicts as well. In short, the philosophy of communism has incomparably more substance than is to be found in the clichés of its orthodox metaphysics. We must look elsewhere if we are interested in understanding the communist world-view, and not just the sloganizing of the official ideologues.

If you prefer to restrict the word "philosophy" to its narrowest and most unflattering sense, then let me say that I am discussing communism as an ideology rather than as a philosophy. But we must be careful not to condemn it out of hand by just the label. In all fairness we must recognize that it is to communism itself that we owe the critique of ideology. What they used to call "ideology" in a bitterly critical vein is what today we call propaganda in the case of groups and rationalization in the case of individuals. But there is another sense of the term "ideology" in which no such disparagement is implied. In this sense, ideology is not restricted to the opponents of democracy, nor to the opponents of communism either, but is, rather, a universal feature of every system of social organization. Naked power everywhere clothes itself in the robes of authority. An ideology is just that set of ideas and perspectives which confers legitimacy, which makes the social system it is defending or promulgating intelligible and worthy of acceptance or support. Communism, then, is not a dead metaphysics but a living ideology.

You could say, if you like, that it is a social philosophy; the logic, ethics, esthetics, and so on are in communism only derivations from the social philosophy, transpositions of it and even analogies to it—perhaps in the way in which the core of positivism is its logic or of existentialism its theology. What is confusing is that communism is not only social philosophy but also social science. However far our own political convictions may lie from those of Marx and his successors, any objective appraisal must acknowledge the enormous contributions to social science which they made. As we proceed, I hope to direct your attention to some of these contributions. For the present, I want only to point out that if we reject the doctrine, we need not repudiate all the facts and principles which the ideology marshalls in its support; and if we recognize the significance of such empirical materials, we are not thereby committing ourselves to the social philosophy into which they are woven.

I want to begin now by examining some of the fundamental presuppositions of the communist world view, how it goes about its thinking, what emerges as the distinctive traits of the communist perspective. And first, the communist position on the nature of values, their content and their justification.

One of the most widespread misconceptions of communist philosophy, in my opinion, has been encouraged or at least sustained by a piece of bad semantics; I refer to the misinterpretation, if not willful misunderstanding, of the word "materialism." In the sense in which that word is commonly used in press and pulpit, communism just is not materialistic, as I see it. To attack it on that score is not only futile, but also dangerous, in that it overlooks one of the most important elements in the appeal that communism can and does have for other peoples. In the sense in question, materialism is the view that the Good for man has its locus in the stomach, or even lower, that it is definable in terms of physical well-being, and that it can be measured by the acquisition of material goods; this view is more clearly labeled "moral materialism." It is this that is meant when communists are forever being excoriated as "atheists" and "materialists." It is this that arouses moral indignation—I cannot imagine that many Americans are exercised about a metaphysical theory as to the relation, say, of mind and matter. Indeed, throughout the history of philosophy, materialism of all sorts evoked hostility just in so far as it was felt to imply, or to be associated with, moral materialism; the attack concerned itself, not with the nature of the world substance, but with the nature of values.

Now the point is that, just as Epicurus was not an epicurean, Marx was definitely not a moral materialist. The values which he held out—especially in his earlier writings, but still important in the appeal which communism makes today—were not materialistic, but just the contrary. What communism aims at, in its own perspectives, is not filling the stomach, but emancipating the spirit from what it calls "wage slavery"; not the acquisition of goods, but the creation of a society in which man himself does not become merely a commodity. Basically, in fact, the value system of the communist philosophy—insofar as we can speak of such a system at all (a point to which I shall return shortly)—these values, I say, are virtually indistinguishable from those of our own democratic tradition. They are the values usually identified as characteristic of European social democracy, from which, of course, Marx derived them.

I think it is a blunder, not just of historical scholarship but of political action, to pose our issue with communism as that between idealism and materialism. For to millions of people, even in the uncommitted countries, it seems that it is communism which espouses noble ideals: independence of colonial peoples, equality of the races, promotion of the arts and sciences, and so on; and all this with an apparently completely unselfish dedication to high purpose. Moreover, some Americans, in their anxiety to differentiate our own institutions from the communists', in condemning as "communistic" any far-reaching programs for social justice and equality, in effect surrender these democratic values to them. The outcome is that it is we who appear to be the materialists.

The fundamental difference between the values of communism and those of our own democratic tradition does not lie in what they are in themselves, but in what they amount to in the context of political and social action. And in the realm of values the context becomes the content. In communist practice, the social democratic values which we share are no longer working *ideals,* helping to shape and define specific political objectives. They are, rather, *utopias*—symbols of an indeterminate future lacking any concrete linkage with the problems of the present. As such, they are central to the ideology and provide a focus for loyalties and identifications. But they play no part in the choices actually made from day to day; and it is these that make the future. The utopia is the withering away of the state; the reality of the continuing present is the dictatorship of the proletariat. The utopia is the independence of all peoples; the reality, the subjugation of satellite states to the Soviet imperium. And so for the rest.

Abstracted from the context which alone can give substance to it, communism wears a mask reminiscent of early Christianity, aspiring only to the kingdom of heaven. As a matter of fact, there are many sincere Christians who find in the Marxist ideology an expression of their own deeply moral convictions. Nothing is gained by arguing that materialism has no place for such convictions; it does. What it has no place for is the concrete action by which the kingdom of heaven can be brought down to earth. Behind the mask of Christian aspiration there stands Caesar.

The working ideals of democracy serve in communism as utopias for reasons that are intrinsic to the ideology itself. What makes them utopias is not just that they are unattainable, that perfection is not of this earth. Ideals too, after all, are continuously receding horizons, or they could not serve to draw us onward. A utopia is an end of action that is not defined in terms of the means by which we can move toward that end. It is unattainable, not because we cannot take the last step to get to it, but because we cannot take the *next* step. In communism, ends are dissociated from means because its values are taken to be *absolute:* the objective of bringing about the revolution and establishing world communism is unqualified and unquestioned. This is the end, and any means which serves it is justified by it, and by nothing else. But this is to say that the nature of the means is irrelevant to the content of the end, that peace and freedom can be attained by violence and slavery. What the absolutist fails to realize is that the child *is* father to the man, and I am a part of all that I have met. The means do not merely lead to the end, they *become* the end. To make values absolute is to destroy the present in the name of a future that never comes.

Thus the absolutist ethics of communist ideology, by its own dialectic, becomes a nihilistic one. For ethics, in that ideology, is no more than an expression of class interest. A system of morality, together with the ethical theory which is put forward to explain and justify it, is no more than a weapon in the class struggle. What becomes, then, of the values for which the struggle is being carried on? If moral standards are only an expression of class interest, there is nothing by which they can themselves be calibrated; and if the salt has lost its savor, wherewith shall it be salted? To subordinate morality to the absolute end of the revolution is to deny it any ground in which it can be rooted. Moral values can only be defended in terms of a political commitment which must be made apart from those values; and in that case, what is the good of the commitment? The logic is the same as that which vitiates the communist notion of class science: if science is also only an expression of class interest, what becomes of the truth of the theory of class struggle? When goodness and truth are subordinated to the absolute ends set up in the ideology, the ideology itself cannot claim to be either true or good. Communism becomes only a more militant nihilism, and the communist finds himself at last a rebel without a cause.

Yet the critique of what he calls "bourgeois morality" does have some justice in it. Nietzsche, too, attacked this ethic as a slave morality, a system of values serving to maintain a division in society between masters and slaves. What I think must, in all fairness, be acknowledged is that there is much hypocrisy in our conventional morality, and that it is most often insisted upon just where it will interfere least with what we really want. And when we do yield to its demands, this is likely to be a result of weakness and fear, rather than the expression of courage and strength in our convictions. But the moral to be drawn is not that morality is only a hollow sham, but that it is we ourselves who are the hollow men. It is not absolute ends that will give substance to our lives, not the apocalyptic moment of the revolution, but the unending struggle for the relative good which alone provides meaning and direction for present action on behalf of a good that is yet to come.

The irony is that communism prides itself on being realistic. Pernicious consequences are not excused by benevolent intentions: "Consciously or unconsciously, Comrade *X* has betrayed . . ." and so on and so forth. All that matters is the pay-off; in the assessment of policy, all that counts is what forces can be set in motion to bring about its successful implementation. This is the point in the anecdote widely told about Stalin: cautioned during the war that a certain measure would evoke the bitter opposition of the Vatican, he is said to have replied, "Well, and how many divisions has the Pope got?" This is *Realpolitik* all right, but it is not realism. It is unrealistic because in its pursuit of power it has transformed a means to an end, and then made the end absolute. It is so caught up in the struggle that it no longer knows or cares what the struggle is for. Ruthlessness is identical with realism only for the devil: human aspiration stems always from an imagined good. But when the effort to achieve an imagined good makes the good wholly imaginary, then action is only self-defeating.

Communism, in short, espouses a kind of vulgar pragmatism, as Sidney Hook has often argued. Not virtue is its own reward, but success, and success itself defines what is virtuous. What succeeds is revolution, and what fails is political adventurism. The strength of the Soviet Union in itself justifies the policies adopted to give it strength; every other consideration is irrelevant, if not downright counterrevolutionary. These are the perspectives of what Richard Hofstadter has aptly called Social Darwinism. The political arena is the scene of a bitter struggle for survival; and the sheer fact of survival is the necessary and sufficient criterion—the only possible criterion—of fitness to survive. All meaning and value is siphoned off into the utopian future; the present is the domain of brute fact.

Consider, for instance, the concept of truth in the perspectives of communism. Truth is what serves the cause of communism and must not be confused with the bourgeois notion of the outcome of detached and objective inquiry. No one can be detached, for no one stands apart from the class struggle: whoever is not with us is against us. Thus history *must* be rewritten, in accord with the changing patterns of the struggle. It is not that the communist historian replaces history by fable; the fable is the only meaning that history has for him. "In effect," the thinking runs, "Trotsky really had nothing to do with the Bolshevik revolution; for consider how he subsequently undid all his own efforts!" Or again, "Of course, the United States practiced germ warfare in Korea; what it did there amounted to just that; and *this* is the truth of the matter, the only truth that has a meaning." The communist is not just lying in a good cause; the cause wipes out the distinction between falsehood and truth, or rather, defines that distinction for itself. Thus a sheer expediency is transformed into a matter of principle; realism becomes opportunism; and opportunism in turn degenerates to the cynicism of, say, the Nazi-Soviet pact, or the betrayal of Hungary.

This criticism that I am making of the communist philosophy of value extends also to its conception of the relation between values and facts. Marx and Engels made much of the claim that theirs was not a "utopian socialism" but a "scientific" one. Their socialism, they argued, depended only on recognizing certain historical facts, not on responding to the appeal of certain moral values. But in my opinion, this "scientific" posture is a masquerade, which can be maintained only by first projecting values onto the facts, then afterwards triumphantly rediscovering them in the facts.

For example, I would say that the communist idea of *exploitation* is quite flatly a moral category—not in just the connotation of the word, but in the content of the idea. In saying so, I don't mean to disparage it; rather the contrary. I see nothing wrong with approaching social problems in terms of moral conceptions of what is just and unjust, like a "fair profit" and a "just return for one's labors." But communism purports to derive its conception of exploitation from a scientific theory of economics and, in particular, what it calls the labor theory of value. Now the substance of this theory—in the respects in which it is relevant here—is not peculiar to communism, but can also be identified in the democratic tradition. John Locke, for instance, held similar views: ownership of property is justified only insofar as the owner has "mixed the labor of his hands" in it. But note that in Locke this is a matter of social doctrine, not of scientific fact; the question is what is right and proper, not what happens as a matter of fact. Communism, as I will explain in more detail shortly, pretends to be doing no more than to describe and explain the facts of economic behavior and historical change, though of course it wants to *use* its theorizing to facilitate the change.

It is here that the "dialectic"—what the communist substitutes for logic—becomes so important for the theorist: it enables him to fit the facts to the requirements of the ideology. Skillfully employed, the dialectic has the resourcefulness of George Orwell's "doublethink," by which anything can be made into its opposite. And when, besides, it is always possible for the ideologue to warn against applying the dialectic "mechanically," no facts whatever need to stand in the way of the claim that the whole doctrine is only a recognition of fact. In short, the ideology simultaneously presents itself as the expression of the interests of the proletariat, and so a matter of values, and as a scientific rather than utopian socialism, and so a matter of fact. But doublethink destroys the basis for facts and values alike.

There is something about this pattern of thought which suggests to me the so-called logicality of the paranoid. It is a closed system in which everything has its place, and everything is meaningful. Communists are always saying, "It is no accident that *X* did so-and-so, and *Y* said such-and-such." Whatever happens is interpretable within the framework of the theory, and everything supports the theory. Every piece of contrary evidence is fitted in with the help of the dialectic, or dismissed as a fabrication of Trotskyites or the ravings of bourgeois objectivists. And the syndrome of paranoia is completed with delusions of grandeur in Russian inventions and delusions of persecution in American intentions. But political psychopathology has its own dangers. For that matter, if the Russians feel that they are constantly being watched and talked about, it would be a poor psychiatrist who did not recognize that this is no more than the truth. These are murky waters all in all, and I will feel more comfortable with a sounder footing.

Let me leave, then, the presuppositions of the communist world-view, and turn to questions of content; and first of all, those concerning the communist philosophy of history.

History is the central theme running through the whole of the ideology. Many important philosophies have been shaped by some one or another discipline or area of culture, which gives to the philosophy its basic orientation, and often a good deal of its substance as well. In this way Plato leaned heavily on geometry, Aristotle on biology, the modern existentialist on psychology, positivism on mathematical physics, and so on. For communism, history is the most philosophical of the arts and sciences. Communist metaphysics is largely a projection onto the cosmic scene of patterns and processes which it finds in human history.

Most characteristic of communist thought is a certain strand of propheticism, a constant appeal to the wave of the future. Over and over again the communist talks of the shape of things to come, and insists that it is futile to try to forestall the destiny that the course of history assigns to us. Such predictions, we know, sometimes have a way of fulfilling themselves, that is, of being fulfilled largely because the prediction was made in just such a way under just such circumstances. A political party unceasingly predicts its own electoral success, not merely to comfort itself, but also as a campaign tactic. If you were to say to a friend, "You're going to be annoyed with me!" and say it persistently enough, no doubt you will sooner or later turn out to be right.

Communism uses history in this self-fulfilling way. But the ideology claims to be essentially predictive. It is on this basis that it presents itself as scientific rather than utopian socialism. Its being scientific is not a matter of dissociating socialism from moral values, for on the contrary, Marx urges over and over that only under socialism can such values actually be achieved. Nor is it a matter of the efficiency with which socialism can attain these human ends, as though the capitalist world is only blindly groping for the path which the communist, with his science, has discovered. What makes his viewpoint scientific—so he claims—is that he, and he alone, can explain and, what is more, predict the course of human history. It is just a matter of how things are, how they must be, how they *will* be.

I believe that the easiest way to understand the communist appeal to history is to see it as a secularized myth of the Fall and the Redemption, another version of the religious ideology so important in Western civilization. This secularization was already quite developed in nineteenth-century romanticism. In my opinion, both communism and fascism, as ideologies, can be regarded as the heirs of the romantic movement. But I don't want to be misunderstood. It is often said that communism is a new religion, with its own scriptures and saints, dogmas and rituals. I think this view has some merit; but it is not the view I am putting before you here. I am not saying here that communism is a religion, but that the philosophy of communism is in substance a religious philosophy couched in secular terms.

The communist myth of human history begins with the Eden of what they call primitive communism; man is then cursed with class differences and the class struggle, moves through the trials of a feudal and bourgeois period, enters the purgatory of socialism, and is redeemed at last in the heaven of communism. Production takes the place of Providence, property is sin, and revolution is redemption. I will not argue for the details of my interpretation. There is no point in constructing a dictionary in which the secular ideas are to stand in strict correspondence with the religious vocabulary. But if I may borrow a communist expression, it is no accident that the thought of such a dictionary should occur to us. Communism speaks a new and barbarous language, but what it is saying is not so very foreign to us after all.

There is one point, however, at which the communist myth differs in a most critical way from the Judaeo-Christian conception. It is that in the religious tradition, the hero of the drama is the individual soul, his is the sin and his the salvation. The secular version replaces the individual by some corporate entity—the race, the nation, the state, or for communism, the class. It is the class with whose fate communism is concerned, and it is class consciousness which opens the way to redemption. Communist disregard for individual freedom is thus deeply rooted in its philosophy. Basically, such disregard is not a necessary evil, a purely temporary expedient; it is simply not seen for what it is. Freedom is defined institutionally, not in personal terms, for the person himself has only a derivative reality: he is a prop carried by the hero of the drama, essential to the business on the stage, but not one of the characters. I shall return later to this question of individualism.

What is fundamental in the whole historicist outlook is the idea that history follows a predetermined course. Communism seems to me to show some striking similarities here to the theologies of predestination, and perhaps even to the doctrine of innate depravity. History is the unfolding of a preëstablished pattern. For communism, this pattern is a spiral: there is a movement back and forth—the dialectic—but a constant course upwards toward a predetermined end. In these terms we can also neatly characterize a number of other historicist philosophies—maybe a little too neatly! The "progressive" conceives of history in a linear pattern, and movement along the line is what he calls progress. The "reactionary" (in a nonpejorative sense of the term) sees history as cyclic, and longs for the swing of the pendulum back to the Golden Age which it has left. The "conservative" conceives of history as a fixed point, subject to small oscillations, but remaining essentially immovable. A democratic social philosophy, as I see it, differs from all of these historicisms. It refuses to acknowledge any pre-existent pattern of history: we create the path on which we move as we go forward on it.

The content of the historical process communism explains on the basis of the doctrine of what it calls "historical materialism." This is the position that the political system, and indeed the whole pattern of culture of any society, is a superstructure erected on the foundation of the system of production characteristic of that society. It is a reflection or expression of the material basis of social organization. In what I might call its doctrinaire form, the thesis of historical materialism reduces every culture product to elements of the economy—styles in literature, religion, art, and philosophy are no more than traits of the system of production. Shakespeare really was a great playwright, but his greatness lay in the vigor of his expression of the bourgeois revolution in England. Empiricism is really a type of idealism, serving to conceal from the masses the social realities of the world in which they live; and so on. This kind of thing is its own *reductio ad absurdum,* and I leave it without further comment.

But historical materialism can be conceived in a much more responsible way as, in fact, Marx and Engels for the most part did conceive it. In this sense, it is an insistence on the importance of treating economics as the independent variable in society, on which the other aspects of culture are dependent. Probably the most important application of this line of thought is Lenin's theory of the state, and his analysis of it as what he calls "the executive committee of the ruling class." What the uninitiated sees as a purely political issue is in fact a transposed economic struggle. It is economic interests with which politics is concerned; political forms and programs have the primary significance of sustaining or overthrowing economic patterns.

Undoubtedly, there is a good deal to be said for this point of view. Politics *is* often a transposition of conflicts in economic interests. But there is also a good deal to be said for the converse point of view: economic issues may only be expressing political differences, conflicts over the distribution of power. If our political patterns serve basically to perpetuate an economic system in which the rulers enjoy economic privilege, the Russian economic patterns may be serving basically to perpetuate a political system in which the rulers enjoy political privilege. Wealth may serve the purposes of power, just as power may serve for the acquisition of wealth.

Nevertheless it must be conceded that the economic factor in history has an enormous importance, far more than was generally recognized before Marx and his followers. To recognize this factor, and to trace its workings in specific historical contexts, does not mean that scholarship has been abandoned for subversive propaganda. I need only remind you of such great social scientists as Charles A. Beard and Thorstein Veblen in America, or Richard Tawney and Max Weber in Europe, all of whom owe a debt to Marx in this connection. Yet I think that everyone but a doctrinaire communist also recognizes the existence and importance of non-economic factors as well—economics alone, for instance, just won't explain, in my opinion, the resurgence of nationalism in Asia and Africa today. And I think that everyone but a doctrinaire communist would recognize that the relationship among these several factors is not uni-directional. Economics is not always the independent variable but may profitably be considered (if the word "profitably" doesn't give my case away!) as dependent on other elements of the culture. The Jews, for example, were not exploited colonials; but the State of Israel is at least as nationalistic as, say, India. And the raising of swine, which is particularly suited to the soil and climate of the country, is flatly prohibited, in spite of the desperate need of the economy for sources of protein. Historical materialism is perhaps no worse than most of the other broad historical generalizations that have been promulgated: Marx can easily hold his own on this score with the Spenglers and Toynbees. As a generalization it is no worse, but I suspect it is not a great deal better.

In itself, historical materialism is a static principle; a dynamic element must also be introduced. For the materialism tells us how to view a particular stage of society—a political and cultural superstructure on an economic base—but it does not tell us how or why one stage of society gives way to another. This part is played in the ideology by the thesis of *economic determinism:* what happens in a later stage of society is determined by the system of production characteristic of the earlier stage. (The expressions "economic determinism" and "historical materialism" are often used as synonyms, or with other meanings than I have given them here. But there are two ideas here which should be distinguished, and I find it useful to differentiate the two with these labels.)

In his materialism Marx, of course, departs from Hegel; but in introducing the dynamic element, the determinism, he makes clear that it is, after all, Hegel that he is taking his departure from. Aristotle's logic postulates a fixed order of nature, a system of genera and species in which every individual finds—and keeps—his place. Feudal society is, as it were, an institutionalization of this outlook, and the collapse of feudalism is also marked by a repudiation of Aristotle. By the nineteenth century, process had replaced substance as the fundamental category, and change is equated with growth. With Hegel, history comes into its own; with Marx, it becomes everything.

Through the instrumentality of economic determinism, the system of production plays the part of Providence in the secularized myth. It provides impetus and direction to the movement of history towards redemption. Because of the workings of the dialectic, history does not move smoothly in a uniform direction, but in great spurts, as productive energies are released by successive revolutions. What happens in history is the outcome of clashes between thesis and antithesis, yielding a higher synthesis, which in turn generates an antithesis, and so on. Every society contains within itself the seeds of its own destruction, and the throes of its death are the birth pangs of the new order. Even this idea is not without its religious roots. History is a dramatic conflict, between the forces of good and evil; and out of this conflict, through sin and repentance and the ultimate conquest of temptation, man is redeemed. Against this background, the communists see themselves as the Children of Light, fighting against the forces of Darkness; and with Providence on their side, they are sure to triumph.

In short, what Marx did was to take the concept of natural law developed in the Enlightenment as constitutive of a rational order of nature—both in physics and in economics—make this law historical, then give it the compulsive force characteristic of the old religious philosophy of history. Something of this sort is conveyed by the ambiguity of the word "law" itself. On the one hand it refers to a scientific generalization and on the other hand to a statutory enactment, as though the laws of nature are the statutes which God has laid down for its behavior. The necessity of natural law is thus both a moral and a physical compulsion, and just this is the character of determinism in communist ideology. It is not the scientific conception, that whatever happens must be explicable as following invariably from some antecedent condition. In science this is at most a methodological principle—abandoned, indeed, in the opinion of many philosophers of science, since the advent of quantum mechanics. In the communist ideology, economic determinism is not a principle of explanation, but the explanation itself. And more to the point, it is a guide, not to understanding, but to action.

Yet paradoxically, it deprives action of meaning. For the only freedom that the determinism of history allows is to delay or to ease the birth pangs of the new order; but that coming is inevitable. The irony is that it is the revolutionist who turns his face to the past, for in his ideology it is the past that gives us our future, whether it is a future that we will to have or not. What I find irresistible is only the conclusion that the communist's so-called logic of history is no logic at all, but the projection onto human affairs of his fantasy of fulfilled aspirations. Of course, there is no gainsaying the fact that the past exerts an enormous pressure; but I see no justification for the dogma that its working is essentially outside control. It is true that the historical situation always limits the alternatives among which we can choose: in every situation only certain possibilities are open to us. But it is no less true that among these we have a genuine choice to make. That the sequence of events has been so determined—whether by the forces of history or by the will of Providence—as ultimately and inevitably to make man free, is, to my mind, not even a pious hope. For freedom is not a heritage but an achievement. The communist is busy with preparations for the triumph that history has in store for him; but it is the preparations themselves that make the triumph, when it comes, an empty one.

We must now examine more closely the economic foundations of this historicist philosophy. Just as Marxist materialism is often misunderstood, there are widespread misconceptions as well of the role assigned in communist ideology to economic motivations. It is too often supposed that this ideology assigns primacy among the springs of human action to some sort of acquisitive instinct, or at any rate, to the desire to maximize economic advantage. The communist theory of history, and its analysis of current social problems, is thought of as trying to explain everything in terms of each individual's pursuit of his economic interests. This is a vulgarization of Marx quite comparable to the one which attributes to Freud an attempt to explain all human behavior by reference to sex. The communist obviously could not explain even his own behavior in terms of personal economic advantage. He carries on the struggle, not for himself, but for the proletariat; and in order to secure for them, not a greater share of material goods (hence his contempt for the labor movement), but a freer, fuller life—as he sees it. This misinterpretation of communist ideology is of a piece with the attribution to it of moral materialism that I discussed earlier.

The vulgarization goes further. Just as Freud, in the popular mind, is thought to support what has been called the "bedroom theory of history" (as presented in too many "historical" movies), Marx is thought to support a "conspiratorial theory of history." The image is of a group of capitalists—bankers and munitions makers—meeting secretly to plot the continued exploitation of the masses in order to satisfy their boundless greed. And the same image is then projected onto the communists themselves, meeting in the Kremlin to plot for *their* aggrandizement. Influential men do meet to make important decisions, and they do sometimes meet secretly. But however accurate the image may be for the conduct of communist affairs, it definitely is not the image of society put forward in the communist ideology itself.

The point is that the image in question postulates a rational, calculating economic man, and there is no such animal. Even if we were to grant that economic motives are the primary ones, human beings are not that skilled in anticipating the consequences of alternative choices, and in weighing them in the balance of their own interests. It is seldom that even the most rational of us actually behaves on the basis of any elaborate calculation of what would be to his own greatest advantage. Even where there are no powerful emotions at work, we rarely decide on such a rational basis; and the greater the emotional investment, the less our decision-making fits this economic model. And, of course, in the most important cases we hardly begin to have the data and knowledge on which to base our calculations, even if we were rational enough to carry them out. Communism does not hold that individuals do what they do because they are impelled to it by their economic interests.

In fact, an important part of the ideology involves an explicit repudiation of this view—in the communist critique of the profit motive. And in my opinion, this critique has much merit, not in condemning the motive, but in condemning the theory that it is the sole or at least the primary motive even of only economic behavior. We take our place in the economy, not just for profit, but also for the self-respect that is based on what we can produce, on what we can contribute with our work; for the satisfaction of doing something for others with whom we identify—our family, group, or nation; for the gratification of what Veblen has called the "instinct of workmanship," which makes us want to use the skills we have regardless of what we are paid for them. More and more it has come to be recognized that, beyond a minimum subsistence level, goods and services are valued not as ends but as means: people want to make money largely because they suppose that it will bring them affection and status, love and respect. Even the robber barons of nineteenth-century capitalism found fulfillment only in giving the stuff away. Self-esteem depended on making, not the biggest profits, but the biggest endowment. At best, the theory that the economic enterprise, even in capitalism, is actuated by the profit motive is only a first approximation; and more and more economists, so far as I am aware, are coming to view it as rather a poor approximation at that.

To be sure, the word "profit" can be interpreted so broadly that the view that it is the sole motive, not only for economic behavior but also for everything else that men do, becomes necessarily true; but in that case, it is also necessarily emptied of meaning. Of course, whatever we do on purpose we do *for* a purpose—which is to say, in the expectation of some enhancement of our situation, the achievement of something we value. And if this is to be called "profit," we never act for anything else. But this is a far cry from the vulgarization of economic determinism. When the Gospels ask, "For what shall it profit a man if he gain the whole world . . . ?" it is not economics that is in question.

Now the communist ideology is very insightful in its criticism of this conception of individual motivation. But it preserves the centrality of economics in another way, by introducing another agent of action whose motives *are* economic. For the fiction of economic man communism substitutes the fiction of the economic class. The class is the entity whose behavior is to be understood solely in terms of economic interests. And the class is not merely a statistical generalization from individuals. If we do not find economic motives in individuals taken singly, we will not find them by considering the individuals collectively. The class is an entity which has its own independent existence; it has the reality of a Platonic Idea, but with the concreteness and inner dynamism given to it in the philosophy of Hegel.

Communists speak constantly about classes, in the expectation that using the term will help bring about the reality alleged already to exist. The concept itself is a political instrument as well as a part of the ideological apparatus. Many people in the democracies are correspondingly fearful of both the word and the idea of classes, as though our silence will help destroy their reality. If the class is not brought into being through class-consciousness, at least it thereby becomes politically significant, so the word will be used or not according to our political objectives. The word "class," in short, suffers from what has been called normative ambiguity: it is sometimes used in propositions of fact, and sometimes in judgments of value, and it is often unclear which use is operative. The question,

"Are there classes in society?" may be interpreted as an invitation to a political commitment, and most of us, I suppose, would answer "No." But it may be interpreted also as a query in social science, when the answer must be "Of course there are!"

The idea that a society can best be understood as made up of distinct social classes is neither distinctive nor original with Marx. You will find it in Aristotle and, as a matter of fact, in connection with his theory of revolution, which he explains in terms of the division of society into the rich and the poor. The communist conception of a class is really an extension of Aristotle's notion of fixed species—and this is just the trouble with it, in my opinion. Communists talk as though there exist in any society only just so many classes, distinguished from one another in just such and such ways. But the usefulness of the concept of classes for the purposes of social science depends on the recognition of a multiplicity of classes, and, even more important, on the recognition of a great many different sorts of indicators of class membership than the economic roles which communism makes fundamental. A "bourgeois" may mean a shopkeeper, as contrasted with the landed gentry; it may mean a citizen or burgher as contrasted with a feudal noble; it may mean a commoner, as contrasted with the aristocrat of high social standing. In short, economic, political, social, and other dimensions may be singled out, and each of them analyzed in turn into a multiplicity of variables. When the concept is generalized so as to include them all, I don't know what generalizations can be made that are true without being trivial.

Marx, for instance, made the prediction—and it is a cardinal tenet of communist theory—that as time went on the middle class would progressively disappear, and the lot of the proletariat would become increasingly miserable. I should think that only the most hardened doctrinaire could pretend that this forecast has not been dramatically falsified, so far as America is concerned at any rate. This line of thought was very much in the air in the nineteenth century, and in ways which didn't necessarily have anything to do with the class analysis of society. Malthus, for instance, made gloomy predictions not altogether unlike this one, but in entirely different terms and with incomparably better confirmation in the subsequent course of events. The communist theory of social classes suffers from the same combination of rigidity in its concepts and looseness in its generalizations that I have called attention to in other parts of the ideology.

To be sure, democratic thought also recognizes the existence of classes, though in another form. Where communism holds out the utopia of a classless society, democracy formulates certain ideals of social organization: equality of opportunity; participation in government; security against unemployment, old age, and disease; and so on. Where these are absent, or present in a sharply stratified distribution, we may speak of the existence of classes, which are in this sense as repugnant to democracy as to communism.

Now the theory of classes in communist ideology is not just concerned with the existence of classes. It deals, not just with the structure of society, but with the social process; and specifically, the theory is that the process is essentially one of class conflict. The whole idea of conflict was enormously important in nineteenth-century thought: take biology, for example, with the concept of a struggle for survival, or the Malthusian doctrine of competition over a diminishing per capita food supply. Even the physics and economics of the period focused on systems in which equilibrium is arrived at through the continued action and interaction of opposing tendencies, like gravitational and centrifugal forces arriving at a planetary orbit, a buyer and seller arriving at a price, or an employer and worker arriving at a wage. To be sure, classical economics postulated a kind of pre-established harmony in human affairs, whereby, when every member of society seeks to maximize his individual good, the good of society as a whole is maximized. But the conflict persists, and indeed is essential, in the economic relations of the individuals to one another. What Marxism did was to shift the locus of the conflict from the individual to the class, and to replace the pre-established harmony of the bourgeois philosophies by an equally pre-established dissonance of the dialectic. The competition that the ideology repudiates in the market place it embraces in the political arena. For it is only through the class struggle that society achieves a higher stage of development.

There is no doubt, I suppose, that conflicts between classes do occur and are important. But though class conflict is a genuine phenomenon, it is an intermittent one, and by no means constitutes the whole of the relations among classes. But notice what his dialectic allows the communist to do when he is confronted with an indisputable case of coöperation rather than conflict between classes. He does not modify the theory, but condemns the coöperating parties for class collaboration, charges them with lacking class consciousness and so betraying their own class interests. That is to say, he moves from social science to social doctrine, preserving inviolate the proposition that class conflict is basic in society by the device of making it instead a value judgment, an expression of his own wishes for society. And when the value in turn is challenged, he takes refuge by returning to his allegation of historical fact. Thereby the system of his thought remains intact—and out of touch with any reality save that of his own making.

The history of all hitherto existing society is the history of class struggles, says the *Communist Manifesto*. But it is also a history of racial struggles, of national struggles, of religious struggles—a history of all sorts of struggles among all sorts of human groups. There are class conflicts; but there are also conflicts within classes, and conflicts that cut across class lines. As much history, surely, concerns the efforts of rival elites to displace one another as it does the efforts of the subjugated masses to overthrow the elite. And perhaps more to the point, history also exhibits coöperation as well as conflict: alliances, coalitions, partnerships, and integration. The communist sees the past only through his own vision of the future. But if conflict is to be the central fact of human history, this civilization may abruptly become only a hitherto existing one.

There remains one other feature of the economic foundations of the ideology to which I want to draw attention: its conception of socialism. What is fundamental in this conception is not just a certain mode of organization of the instruments of production. The important thing is that the agent and beneficiary of the system is conceived of as a corporate entity. It is in this sense that communism is a collectivist ideology. There is a great deal of confusion nowadays about the idea of collectivism, for it is sometimes thought of in relation to social ends and sometimes in relation to the means by which such ends are to be attained. I say that *values* are *collectivist* when they are conceived of as localized in some corporate entity, enjoyed by individuals only derivatively; they are *individualist* when it is the group—class or state or whatever—which is derivative. When we speak of a nation as rich, for instance, we may mean that its citizens enjoy a high standard of living—these are individualist values; or we may mean that it has a favorable balance of trade, a surplus in its treasury, and so on—the collectivist sense.

Now collectivism, as I see it, is an emphasis upon collectivist values. It is the perspective in which the power, wealth, and achievement of a society is localized in the society as such, and not in its individual members. The citizen serves the state, rather than the state its citizens. The point I want to make is that collectivism in this sense must be carefully distinguished from the use of collective *means* to secure social ends, whatever these are. Individualist means may be adopted for collectivist ends, like physical training undertaken in the spirit of making oneself fit for military service. And conversely, collective means may be serving individualist ends. This is exemplified, I think, by the very situation in which these lectures are being given. We are in a state university, a collective enterprise of the citizens of California. But it is in the service largely of individualist values—the educational enterprise is directed, not to making California rich or strong or anything else, save derivatively; it aims at developing the cultural resources, the skills and capacities of the individuals who make up our community. A state university is a socialist enterprise, if you will, but it is not a collectivist one. The T.V.A. and other such developments may be a step toward socialism, as their critics never tire of denouncing, but it is crucial to understand that this is not the socialism which appears in communist ideology.

I believe this to be so crucial because the communist strategy is precisely to identify the two, and thereby to present its ideology as the only one which can accomodate joint action on behalf of a common good. The result of such an identification—or confusion—is a dangerous polarization of political life. The Radical Right supports the communist in his claim that any movement toward the use of collective means is a movement toward communism. And this implies that we must either leave all social and economic arrangements just as they are, or accept communism. In this way communists can pose as the party of protest, and exploit for their own purposes any democratic aspiration towards a greater social good. Correspondingly, whoever opposes communism is thereby condemned to the support of the status quo, against any change whatever.

This is the same illogicality that often appears in what is thought of as a defense of property rights. Whatever role the collectivity plays at any particular time in defining and protecting those rights becomes, as it were, the zero point from which all departures are measured. It is imagined that property rights are essentially individualistic and that the introduction of collective instrumentalities is necessarily a destruction of those rights. The fact is, however, that property is not a relation of things to men—it is a relation among men. The title to property, the corporation that owns it, the contract specifying its use or transfer—all these are legal entities, entities, that is, constituted by collective action and not merely individual effort. No property right is absolute; it is always hedged about with restrictions on its enjoyment and use. But we take for granted the restrictions operative at a given moment, and then suppose that any changes mark the entering wedge of collectivism. In fact, greater restrictions may be called for precisely by our individualistic values, just as more traffic regulations may be needed to enhance individual freedom of movement.

What remains fundamental is the difference between collectivist ends and collective means. Only the first moves towards communism; the second may be the most effective defense against it. Economic planning, for instance, has nothing to do with a communist ideology. Indeed, the basic elements of an economy may be altogether socialistic, yet entirely within the frame of a democratic ideology. Such democratic socialism is more than an abstract possibility, but is actually to be found, in varying degrees, in a number of countries, such as England, Sweden, and Israel. In our own country, many people—and I among them—believe that more vigorous collective action must be undertaken to deal with our economic and social problems, that their solution cannot be left entirely to the workings of individual or so-called private enterprise. Whether these people are in a majority may be doubtful; but I take it that there can be no question of their commitment to the democratic ideology. Competition is no more central to the world-view of democracy than is coöperation. On the contrary, it is communism that expects good things to come out of conflict—not, perhaps, in the domestic economy, but, what is even more important, in the international political arena.

I turn then, finally, to the communist political philosophy. The main theme of this philosophy derives from communist historicism and its economic doctrine. It is that there is a historical mission to be fulfilled, the mission of instituting and maintaining a certain system of economic organization—socialism, in the collectivist sense I have just discussed. The communists who hold power, or who are struggling to obtain it, are justified in what they do by the part they play in fulfilling this mission. The communist ideology thus reinstates the traditional political philosophy of the divine right of kings, only in a secularized version, just as its historicism secularized the myth of the Fall and the Redemption. The communist rulers are the vicars of History on earth.

In these terms, politics becomes a calling. It is not an opportunity for personal aggrandizement or the fulfillment of personal aspirations of whatever kind; it may even call for the martyrdom of false confession, exile, or death. The lives of the old Bolsheviks testify almost without exception to their view of politics as a calling. They were markedly self-denying, and even ascetic—as was Hitler, for that matter, and some of his closest associates. He also thought of himself as fulfilling a historic mission, as answering to a call. The communist elite justifies its rule on the principle that history—to paraphrase Bacon's aphorism about nature—to be commanded must be obeyed. They are the ones who obey history, who are responsive to the will of the secularized deity embodied in the working of the dialectic.

The Communist Party thus becomes, in effect, a priesthood, cloaked in the mystique of the True Church, with its faithful and heretics, its prophets and satanic adversaries. Its leader, as Carlyle said of the hero, is distinguished by his ability to penetrate beneath appearance to underlying realities, to grasp the essence of every historical situation. It was in such perspectives that Stalin was able, for instance, to negotiate a pact with the Nazis, and that the Party is able to retain its following (or a large part of it) through a bewildering series of changes in line and leadership. We are not to be deceived by the talk of "collective leadership" in the post-Stalin era. So far as the mystique is concerned, the *Führer-prinzip* is still operative. Whether you have one leader, three, or three dozen, the principle of legitimacy remains the same. It is a question of fulfilling a mission, not of representing their subjects or governing by their consent. The rule may be despotic, but it is a benevolent despotism—so the ideology maintains. It is a dictatorship of the proletariat, not *by* the proletariat, that is to say, but in the interests of the proletariat. The Communist Party is their vanguard, treating those marching behind them like a Big Brother would who knows what is good for them and is determined that they shall have it.

Once the mission has been fulfilled, there is no more role for the communist ruler to play, and the ideology then calls for the withering away of the state. What an irony that it was a Russian who so dramatically portrayed the human tragedy of this delusion! I mean Dostoevskii, and his immortal story of the Grand Inquisitor in *The Brothers Karamazov.* You remember that in the story Jesus returns to earth at the time of the Inquisition, and, of course, is promptly denounced as a heretic and sentenced to death. The Grand Inquisitor visits Him in His cell the night before the scheduled execution and admits that he knows who his Prisoner is. But what is he to do? Christ Himself established the Church and gave it its mission; and now, when there is so much for the Church to do, His coming only gets in the way. The execution will have to proceed. In the politics of the absolute there is no alternative. He who says "Let justice be done, though the heavens fall!" is brought at last to war against God, and—supreme irony—in God's own name. And this is his damnation.

It is not that Stalin's reign of terror corrupted the teaching, or that Lenin's political ruthlessness distorted Marx. The communist ideology carried within itself—to borrow its own phrasing once more—the seeds of its own destruction. The politics of the absolute may be traced all the way back from Marx, through Hegel, to Rousseau. Rousseau distinguished between what he called the "common will," the aggregate wills of the people, and the "general will," the will of the people in the aggregate. One is what they want, and the other what they would want if they knew what was good for them—that is what it amounts to. The good society can only be founded on the general will; but the trouble is that somebody has to figure out what the general will is. The voice of the people may be the voice of God, but it is oracular, it needs interpretation. Now only the communist is privy to the secrets of history; only he knows what is truly the will of the people. To challenge his interpretation is to replace their will by your own, to disregard history—ultimately, to put yourself in the place of God. And for this sin, there can be no forgiveness.

To bring communist rule within the frame of political democracy is to compromise with sin, with Satan himself. The heroic Soviet Union is the polar antithesis of the demonic bourgeois world. If the visitation is not from God, it is of the devil, and if the false prophet is to be stoned, the true prophet must be followed without question. Communism, in a word, demands *faith*, and he that believes shall be saved. This is why many thousands of Nazis became communists after the war, just as many German communists became Nazis in the early 'thirties, and many American communists turned to authoritarian religion in the 'forties and 'fifties. These various philosophies were for them psychological equivalents, pathways for escape from freedom, as Erich Fromm has pointed out.

It is intrinsic to the communist ideology that its mission can only be carried out dictatorially. It must be expressed in dogma or it cuts itself off from its own foundation. To allow for channels of protest or even of criticism is to admit to a merely human fallibility which cannot ensure an ultimate triumph. The sign in which ye shall conquer must be written in the heavens, or it is no sign at all. Mao Tse Tung was being a good communist when he invited a hundred flowers to flourish, then cut them down one by one. The Communist Party is not, and cannot be, a party. It is a political order, in the sense in which we are acquainted with religious orders. Its leaders are the Elect, rather than the elected. The history of all hitherto existing communist parties is a history of power struggles; changes in policy can be determined in no other way, within the framework of their own political philosophy. Political defeat must be a mark of moral degeneration to be punished by death or disgrace, because political success is the sign and substance of moral justification.

But this is not to say that communism knows only the reign of terror. Too many Americans, in my opinion, make the serious mistake of supposing—do they really believe it?—that the communist rulers are secretly as detested in their own countries as they are in ours; and "liberation of the satellites," however that is to be achieved, is casually equated with their emancipation from communism. I believe on the contrary that communism, like every other established regime, governs by consent. Only, it is not a freely given consent, but what some of our own manipulators of public opinion and attitudes are coming to refer to as "engineered consent." Quite distinct from the rape of the masses through violence and terror is their seduction through ideology. And as I have elsewhere had occasion to remark, I leave it to you to judge whether virtue is not more often lost to seduction than to rape.

We often fail to realize that the famous democracies of antiquity, like Athens, were democratic only so far as the small core of citizens were concerned; the vast population of slaves simply didn't count.

Something of this kind is characteristic of communism as well. I mean more than the fact that those who aspire to freedom are read out of the community as "unsocial elements," be they formalist composers, abstract painters, or Nobel-laureate poets. I mean more even than the entrenchment of privilege for a bureaucratic elite. I mean that in the perspectives of communism the masses are regarded fundamentally as tools and materials to bring about and maintain the social revolution. They are manipulated for the achievement of ends which are not for them, save through the symbols of a utopia by which they are assured that they shall inherit the earth. For the actors in the communist drama are not real people but ideological abstractions; and so long as "the proletariat" triumphs, the fate of Ivan is of no concern to anyone else—and at last, not even to Ivan himself. We in America need not be unreconstructed individualists to insist that the individual human beings that make up America are the ends, and not merely the means, of social reconstruction.

Some years ago a group of writers published a collective volume of autobiographical essays recounting their experiences with communism under the title *The God That Failed*. The title is an apt one in referring both to divinity and to failure. The history of communism as a movement is, I think, a deeply tragic one—tragic in its failures, and even more tragic in its successes. The dedicated and sincere communist—and most of them have been that—presents to us the tragic spectacle of a man destroying himself and his own most cherished values under the illusion that he is a creator. Each man kills the thing he loves, the poet says. I find it hard sometimes to resist the feeling that the history of communism, and maybe the history of the whole modern age, is a testimony to human stupidity. But I feel too that, by the same token, it is a testimony to the greatness of human aspiration.

What we all want to know, of course, is what is to be done: how can we strive to fulfill our high aspirations without yielding to the instrumentalities which will instead destroy them? I will not pretend that I have the answer for you; in any case, our concern here is not with politics but with philosophy. But there is one remark that I want to make. In Aristotle's account, tragedy is a spectacle that evokes pity and fear. The tragedy of communism has done quite well enough as to fear; I feel there is room for pity too. And most of all, I believe there is room for more rational policy, in which informed intelligence triumphs over blind emotion of whatever kind.

QUESTIONS

What is the basic difference between the communist and the fascist ideologies?

I THINK THERE ARE TWO. The first has to do with the agent of the historical process. In fascism, it is the race or nation, or some mysterious combination of the two. (During the time of the Berlin-Tokyo Axis, Japanese were somehow Aryans; but for that matter, today the Russians refer to themselves among the Asians and Africans as also a "colored" people.) In the communist ideology itself, however, as distinct from the phrasings of export propaganda, it is the class, and the class alone, which is the agent of history. It is absolutely essential to the theory that classes be recognized to cut across racial and national lines. Nationalism has always presented a difficult problem for communist ideology, to the solution of which Stalin particularly addressed himself. The ideological adequacy of his solution is currently a matter of debate in Moscow, Warsaw, Belgrade, and Peiping.

There is a second basic point of difference between communism and fascism. There is a sense in which communism subscribes, as I have pointed out, to the fundamental values of social democracy. But the dialectic allows it to distinguish what it calls the genuine values from those of "bourgeois idealism." Thus communism shares in the Nazi denunciation of *verstunkene Demokratie*, with its false and empty moral principles. But it insists that what is wrong with these principles is only that in the democracies they remain abstract and verbal, while under communism they are concretely realized. However, since the Soviet Union and its satellites are still surrounded by powerful capitalist states, their communism is as yet in a transitional stage—in which, for instance, the state cannot yet wither away. Thus what the fascists accept as a virtue both now and in the future, communism justifies as only a temporary expedient, which will eventually be done away with. It is with regard to the long run that the two ideologies differ most sharply from one another, not with regard to the here and now. But as Keynes is so often quoted to have said, in the long run we shall all be dead.

Is the working philosophy of the communists in the Soviet Union a distortion of Marxism?

I AM STRUCK by the fact that here in America we can discuss this question, as well as the corresponding ones about Jefferson or Lincoln, without any fear of the consequences.

But to turn to the ideological problem. I have already pointed out that it is the role of the communist elite to interpret history; and from their own point of view, the same must also be said with regard to the task of interpreting Marx. Marx wrote voluminously, over a long period of time; he said many different things, and by no means always unequivocally. The question of what he "really" meant can profitably be dealt with only in concrete biographical terms. "Marxism," however, is not the creation of Marx alone, but also of Engels, Lenin, Stalin, and many others. What is important for the understanding of the communist perspective is, I believe, not so much the scholarly question whether the latest pronouncement of the Central Committee of the Party departs or not from what appears on certain pages of the Sacred Texts. It is, rather, whether the latest policy or practice distorts the image which communism projects of itself.

Let me be specific, with a single illustration. If there is one objective which Marxism explicitly formulates, it is to free mankind from wage slavery. The communist therefore excoriates the ethics of competition by which this slavery, as he argues, is perpetuated. But he himself reinstates this slavery on another basis, on what I might call the ethics of efficiency—Stakhanovism, piece-work payment, politically enforced production quotas, and such like. I just noticed a report (but I confess that I saw it only in the bourgeois press) that the Soviet Union has adopted regulations by which the academic degree of a teacher may be revoked if a certain proportion of his students fail to achieve what is expected of them. I don't know whether this could properly be called wage slavery; it certainly isn't what I would call academic freedom.

In short, Marx aimed at striking off certain fetters on the human spirit. But in communist practice they are heavy and immovable. Where communism speaks of the withering away of the state, Clement Attlee once remarked, the Labor Party speaks of the withering away of property rights. Whether this is wholly desirable or not, it must be recognized that, at any rate, it is something that can really be brought about and to some degree *is* being brought about. Communism says one thing and does another, holds out a goal and moves rapidly away from it. Whose ever the voice, the hands are Esau's; and it is by the work of its hands that communism must at last be judged.

How do you account for the wide acceptance of the ideology in so many parts of the world, if it has the shortcomings that you claim?

Two considerations seem to me quite plausible. First, not only the perspectives in which we view facts, but even what we take to be facts to start with, depend very much on who we are and what is the culture that makes us what we are. I am not for one moment endorsing the communist conception of class science, as though truth is subordinate to class identification. I believe that identifications, loyalties, and aspirations must follow upon a sober appraisal of the facts and not precede them. Yet we must recognize that the human mind is conditioned by the context of its working, and this context is largely cultural, social, and political in substance. So that what seems obvious and beyond question to us might very well not seem so to others, viewing it from the standpoint of their own cultures.

It probably would not seem so even to us, if we were subject to the same influences. I am not talking about anything so melodramatic as what is usually called brain washing. I mean the subtle but all the more significant effect of day by day pressures and persuasions, the unremitting expression of approval and disapproval in society of all we do and say, and thereby of what we think as well. What I am getting at is that it is a mistake, and a dangerous one, to suppose that everyone who sees things differently than we do must be either a fool or rascal. The peoples of other countries who are seriously weighing communism or who have even committed themselves to it, are not necessarily ignorant, stupid, or vicious. I am afraid that many Americans rely too much on the notion that others are victimized by indoctrination, while we ourselves view life steadily and view it whole. I believe that our repudiation of communism has every justification; I reject the superficial relativism of "It's all in how you look at it." But that does not mean that we must lock ourselves into the absolutism of our own perspectives.

The second point I want to make is more specific, and applies especially to the appeal of the communist ideology for the peoples of the underdeveloped countries. Communism speaks to them in terms which are intelligible to them on the basis of their own experience, while we address them in terms which, though familiar enough to us, don't so easily make sense to them. Communism talks about economic facts, and these are homely and concrete; we talk of political ideals, which are abstract and, for them, remote. They know what poverty is, but not liberty, and free land obviously means much more to them than a free press. My wonder is not that communism seems attractive, but that democracy ever does.

We must not forget that the appeal of communism does not rest primarily—or perhaps even at all—on ideological grounds. People like ourselves easily overestimate the effectiveness of words, because we spend so much of our lives in speaking and hearing words, reading and writing them. But the success of the communist ideology, in my opinion, rests on the concrete basis of the Soviet Union's economic progress. Within the span of a single generation or so the peasant economy of Czarist Russia has been trasnformed into one which is seriously competing with the United States—and in some areas apparently outstripping it. The underdeveloped countries of Asia and Africa might well say to us: "We cannot take you as a model for our own growth: you are too rich, you have too many resources, a great population of literate and skilled workers. How can we compare ourselves to you? But forty years ago the Soviet Union was where we are now, and see how far it has come; and China too is making giant strides. Of course your system has achieved a great deal—that goes without saying. It is good, and maybe even the best; but it's too good for us."

Now this may be entirely the wrong view for them to take; but I put it to you, that it is an understandable view. We cannot correct it by persuading ourselves that it makes no sense. Where we see a threat in communism, others see a promise; we look only at the facts of political repression, but they look only at the facts of economic advancement. To pretend that the second is unreal will not make more vivid to them the reality of the first. Democracy will not win adherents abroad on a political basis only, but must seize the initiative on economic questions as well. But now our discussion has taken us beyond ideology to specific issues of foreign policy; and there I must let the matter rest.

How can democracy achieve a sense of mission corresponding to that of communist ideology?

I HAVE GREAT SYMPATHY with this question, and yet I believe that it is misconceived. So many people have been concerned lately with what is described as a loss of national purpose, and there are desperate pleas for its recovery. Our enemies know where they are going, and they are convinced that they know how to get there. But we are groping and unsure; how can we compete with them? We know only that we don't want their mission, but we don't have one of our own; we ask the neutrals not to follow them, but we have nowhere to lead them ourselves. I think this is the feeling that the question expresses. I doubt very much if my reply to it will be altogether satisfying; but it will be sincere.

I believe that in fact our situation *is* a difficult one and that it is a difficulty inherent in democracy. We are inescapably at a serious disadvantage. It is the disadvantage of medicine confronting quackery, and science confronting superstition. For these can claim to cure everything and explain everything—and make the claim with a most reassuring air of confidence. What is offered on the other side must inevitably present itself as partial, piecemeal, and at best only probable. The totalitarian makes no demands on maturity, on thoughtfulness and realism; there is no need for you yourself to participate in the process of policy formation. Why be gnawed by doubt and anxiety when the answers stand ready for you to take? Why assume the responsibilities of democratic citizenship when we stand ready to take them on our own shoulders for you? This is not an easy appeal to offset; but democracy has no alternative than to meet it head on.

It will be said—as it has been said over and over again—that we must make of democracy as unshakeable a faith as communism is for its adherents. We, too, must have our absolutes, or we will be unable to withstand the absolutism of the enemy. I have never been persuaded by this logic. Men can live by their convictions, and die for them too, and still acknowledge a margin for error. On this point I don't know of a more sage observation than Benjamin Franklin's, that nothing's sure but death and taxes; what is usually overlooked is that Franklin made this remark in replying to criticisms of the proposed Federal constitution and demands for guarantees that it would work. There are no guarantees, and that is all that you can count on. A mature man will have the courage to act without them, the courage to put at stake his life, his fortune, and his sacred honor, as the founders of our Republic did. To achieve greatly, we must dare greatly. Democracy has never been able to survive, and will not survive now, without courage.

There is one final point to be considered. You may say: "I am content with less than certainty. I will dare to go forward—but you must tell me to what destination, and in what direction it lies." We have become, it seems, a nation of characters in search of an author who can give meaning to what we do and unfold for us the sequence of events that lie ahead. But democracy means precisely that it is we ourselves who are the authors of our destiny: the characters take over the plot. Democracy means that you don't march behind anybody, and you carry no banner but your own. If you ask me what goals we should pursue, what values to adopt, what purpose to make our own, I will be glad to tell you—on a political platform in town hall. But democracy commits me, not just to giving you the opportunity to tell me *your* goals, values and purposes, but to doing all I can to help you take advantage of that opportunity. For we are not playing a game of one-upmanship, but meeting as equals in the serious business of living the lives of free men.

To those who ask for a mission—in other countries or in our own—I say, you give *me* a mission, and I will offer mine too. Together we can hope to work out something which will be worthy of our dignity as human beings to pursue together. But if you are content to be something less than fully human, if you want only to follow, neither I nor my country stand ready to give you *that* kind of leadership. In that case, you may turn to communism if you choose. It is a crime that carries with it its own punishment.

LECTURE SIX

Indian Philosophy

OUR CULTURE EXHIBITS A STRIKING AMBIVALENCE in its attitude toward philosophy in general and towards Asian philosophies in particular. On the one hand, philosophy is the object of marked deference as the repository of deep ideas and high ideals. Politics looks to the philosopher to define the national purpose, science expects him to serve as referee, art as interpreter, and religion as apologist. And in the society at large, it is awkward for a student of philosophy to identify himself with the corresponding label—as one might be a psychologist or a mathematician—because "philosopher" is so plainly an honorific, which no one can apply to himself. On the other hand, philosophy is viewed as a kind of logic-chopping which overlooks the most obvious matters of fact and common-sense truths, and its ideals are dismissed as part of an idealism that ignores the harsh realities of political life. It was Neitzsche who pointed out almost a hundred years ago that *philosopher* has come to mean *Stoic,* as though no other philosophies have ever existed or are possible; for many people, to be philosophical means to submit apathetically to evils against which men must fight. There is especially a kind of vulgar pragmatism that wants nothing to do with "adversity's sweet milk—philosophy," and exclaims with Romeo, "Yet hang philosophy! unless philosophy can make a Juliet." (I blush to confess that many years ago I expressed some such viewpoint myself.)

Both these attitudes are accentuated, it seems to me, with regard to the philosophies of Asia. We can smile at the folklore of "the wisdom of the East," but if we are quite candid I think we would recognize that very few of us are altogether free of such notions. Psychoanalysts might even suggest that the ascription of intellectual acumen to exotic peoples may result from the same dynamics as are responsible for the familiar attribution of enhanced sexuality to the members of out-groups. Be that as it may, the Indian sage and the clever Chinese are stereotypes whose influence is more widespread than we would ordinarily care to admit. The other side of the ambivalence—for many decades the more intellectually respectable side—is the notion that there is really no such thing as Asian philosophy at all. It is a welter of myth and poetry, religion and superstition, and if systematized at all is more deserving of the attention of the psychiatrist or, at best, of the cultural anthropologist, than of the serious student of ideas as such.

Today, however, more and more people are coming to realize that a new perspective on Asia is called for. In this middle of the twentieth century the time has come for us to examine Asian thought with some care, to try to understand it in its own terms, and then also in terms of its bearings on our outlook and problems. In his *History of Western Philosophy,* Bertrand Russell anticipated that after the close of the war (which was still being fought when he was writing the manuscript), it would become necessary for the Western world to admit Asia to equality not only politically but also culturally. The events of the intervening fifteen years have, I think, completely borne him out. If for no other reason than the political one, the cultures of Asia must be brought sharply into the focus of American attention.

But there is also a distinctively philosophical reason for doing so. I find it ironic that Western philosophy, which throughout the grand tradition presumed to take as its province the whole of man and nature, has been guilty of such shocking parochialism with respect to Asian thought. In fact, to my knowledge Russell's history of philosophy was the first one to acknowledge, even in its title, that it is a history of *Western* philosophy, and not *the* history of the subject. Usually, Asian thought was either casually dismissed in the preface, or relegated to an introductory discussion of the difference between philosophy and religion. Till recent years, in American universities there were not more than a handful of courses on the philosophies of Asia, and philologists had a vastly better acquaintance with the philosophies than did professors of philosophy. All this, I believe, is now rapidly changing.

Part of the reason for the philosophers' dismissal of oriental thought is what I might call the myth of mysticism. It is the notion that all Asian philosophies are of a piece, and that what characterizes them is a certain obscurantism that makes them inaccessible to clear statement and thus invulnerable to criticism. They are first lumped together, then dismissed as impenetrable nonsense—the intellectual's equivalent of "They all look alike, and they're inscrutable." The fact is that the philosophies of Asia are, by and large, as multiple and diverse as are those of the Western world. It is easier to find similarities among various philosophies of Asia and certain European ones than it is to force into separate molds the "Asian mind" and the European one. Kipling and Northrop to the contrary notwithstanding, the polarization of "East" and "West" will not stand up, in the realm of ideas at any rate.

And as far as mystic obscurantism is concerned, Asian philosophers achieved quite early the essentials of Aristotelian logic and of Greek atomism, Humean scepticism, a more or less Kantian "critical philosophy" as well as a post-Kantian idealism, and a good representation of materialist and realist philosophies. The major respect in which the philosophies of Asia differ from those of the Western world, I think—though I must admit at once that I cannot pretend to any scholarship here—is the comparative absence of the influence of science, both institutional and in its patterns of thought. But we need scarcely be reminded that until the modern era science did not have any great importance for Western philosophy either. The failure of science, as we know it in the modern Western world, to develop in either India or China seems to be due to factors also commonly held responsible for the failure of the Greeks to develop science in the modern sense. It is the sharp divorce characteristic of all three cultures between those who devoted themselves to purely intellectual pursuits and those who cultivated the arts and crafts. Science seems to be sired by speculation out of manipulation. In Asia, those who worked with their hands never quite reached the intellectual attainments and status of the artisans of the Italian Renaissance.

If we set aside the stream of scientific influence, it becomes possible to approach the Asian philosophies as not really so exotic after all. To be sure, the language is foreign; but for the Indian philosophies this can scarcely matter, since Sanskrit is, of course, *the* Indo-European language, and its terms are often more easily recognizable to us than are those of the Greek thinkers. In short, the Asian philosophies chiefly differ from the ones with which we are acquainted in respects that depend more on the difference in their cultural settings than in the lines of thought they follow; at worst, it is a question of emphasis rather than of totally different considerations.

There is one more introductory remark that I must make. This is that I shall be speaking about Indian philosophies and not about philosophies in India; because India today is a part of the world community of nations and is very much more European than is often supposed—this especially is true in the realm of ideas. In my opinion, Nehru, for instance, is better understood if we think of him as a product of British higher education than if we try to trace his ideas to their roots in Indian antiquity. A great deal of philosophy in India today is essentially Western. Indeed, this seems to me to be true throughout Asia—and unfortunately so, in my opinion. Many Asians confuse the task of the modernization of their cultures with the very different enterprise of Westernizing them. Students of philosophy in India, Japan, and Free China—to say nothing of Communist China! —are often more conversant with the Western philosophical tradition than with their own cultural heritage. But it is of that heritage that I intend to speak in this and the succeeding lectures, and not of the present state of Westernized Asian thought.

Classical Indian philosophy, then, is contained first of all in the Vedas, the Indian scriptures. These date back to possibly the second millennium before the Christian era, and so are among the oldest writings known. More particularly, Indian philosophy derives from a certain portion of the Vedas known as the "Upanisads." They are long philosophical poems or discourses, remarkable in literary quality as well as in content; there are about a hundred of them, of which about ten are usually recognized as being of special importance. Finally, among the classical sources is one which is perhaps the single most influential text in Indian culture, the Bhagavadgita (usually known just as *the* "Gita"). Sometimes called in translation "The Song of the Blessed Lord," it is a discourse delivered by the best-loved Indian deity, Krishna, who combines in himself something of the personal qualities of King David, Apollo, and Jesus—musician, poet, lover and compassionate helper. The Gita occurs as an interpolation in one of the great Indian epics, the *Mahabharata,* which is comparable in many ways to Homer's *Iliad*. It recounts the story of a great war between rival claimants to the throne, a war in which the gods have also taken sides. Krishna presents himself as charioteer to Arjuna, the hero of the epic, who is reluctant to engage in battle because he knows that opposing him are many of his own kinsmen, noble warriors, and heroes, men for whom he has great love and admiration. The Gita is the discourse delivered by Krishna to Arjuna on the eve of the battle, laying out the path of duty, and setting forth the way to attainment of life's ultimate goal.

These three—the Vedas, Upanishads, and Gita—offer interesting parallels to the Law and the Prophets of the Old Testament, and the Gospels of the New Testament. At any rate, their cultural significance in India is entirely comparable to that of the Bible in the West —the model of all eloquence, repository of all wisdom, and source of all principles for the ordering of human life, both individual and social. Even today it is more or less expected that a candidate for high public office (if not a Muslim) will sometimes have written his own commentary on the Gita or some of the Upanishads, or at least will demonstrate his familiarity with the texts.

Now these materials in themselves are, to be sure, at least as much religious as philosophical, in the sense in which we usually differentiate these two. But on their basis a number of straightforwardly academic schools of thought developed; six are normally distinguished, of which the most important, and the one to which I shall chiefly devote myself, is *Vedanta.* The Indian philosophical development reached its climax in antiquity at roughly the same time as the Greek; was rejuvenated in about the eight or ninth century in response to the challenge of a vigorous Buddhism; and after a period of scholastic decay, enjoyed a renaissance in the late nineteenth century and on into the twentieth. Among the modern figures I want particularly to mention Sri Ramakrishna, the great founder of the mission that bears his name; his St. Paul, as it were, Swami Vivekenanda; Sri Aurobindo, who founded a colony, still flourishing at Pondicherry, to live by his teaching; and Sarvapelli Radhakrishnan, sometime professor of philosophy at Oxford University and now Vice-President of India. (Here, we might admit, is a striking contrast between East and West.)

I want first to make some general remarks about the approach to philosophy characteristic of the Indian thinkers. What I find especially striking in this approach is a remarkable catholicity of outlook. One of the most widely quoted statements in the Upanisads—inscribed in stone on public buildings, and appearing in innumerable epigraphs—is this: "Men call it by many names, but the sages know that it is one." Very early in Indian thought, the viewpoint is expressed that differences among various philosophies and even religions are superficial. So long as the authority of the Vedas is accepted (this defines the "orthodoxy" of the so-called six schools), everything else is quite secondary. And even those whose thought proceeds on a different basis are moving, only more tortuously, to the same end. There is but one mountain, and many paths lead up its sides to the one peak. All mankind is striving for the realization of the same fundamental reality. Thus in the Gita Krishna declares, "Whatever god men worship, they are worshipping me," and, "In whatever form I am worshipped, that worship I accept."

This is in striking contrast to the First Commandment, and more especially to its enforcement throughout the bloody history of Judaism and Christianity. To be sure, Indian philosophers were traditionally (and are today, in my experience) extremely disputatious, and interminably involved in polemic with one another. But I find it remarkable that religious wars and persecutions play such a negligible part in Indian history. Deprivations of life and liberty because of religious belief are as nothing compared to what the Western world has seen. I am not unmindful of the Hindu-Muslim tensions and conflicts in recent times; but this has a national and political rather than a religious significance (just as the position of Israel in the Arabic world today can hardly be compared to that of, say, the Huguenots in sixteenth-century France). Most Americans are unaware that even now, some ten years after the partition with Pakistan, there are over thirty million Muslims in India, occupying a number of Cabinet posts and many other positions of prestige and authority; and the six national universities include not only the Hindu University of Benares but also the Muslim University of Aligarh, probably the most important center of Muslim learning east of Suez, if not in the world. The Indian attitude toward religious differences is this: the turbans may be wound differently, but when you unwind them you see that they are made of the same cloth.

This point of view has occasionally expressed itself (though more often in the Western world than in India) in an aspiration toward a so-called universal religion, or a philosophical "synthesis of East and West." Such movements may find themselves at home in India (as theosophy did), but they are not to be confused with Indian catholicity. Universalism, in my opinion, betrays a radical misunderstanding of both religion and philosophy, of a kind which is involved also in the goal of a universal language. Like language, religion and philosophy have their roots deep in the cultures of which they are parts and products. Just as there cannot be a universal language unless and until there is a universal community (save some medium for purely utilitarian content), so also, as I see it, is the situation with respect to philosophy and religion. In this respect, both are much closer to art than to science or technology. It is absurd to recognize and cherish distinctive styles in art, and demand universality in the style of life—but it is just that style which a culture's religion and philosophy express. Yet to say that they are saturated with their culture is not to say that they are culture-bound—without meaning or value to the members of other cultures—any more than in the case of art. My religion and philosophy are my language in which I try to understand and express my life, just as yours are for you. If we learn each other's language, there is no sense in exchanging our own for some artificial tongue in which we are both illiterate.

Just as remarkable as the catholicity of Indian thought is its tendency to individualize its teaching, as it were. While all truth is one, each individual has his own perspective on it. The differences as well as the sameness must be respected by any philosophy which wants to do justice to the human spirit. To start with, therefore, it is recognized that in each individual career there is a succession of *ashramas,* stages on life's way; a different body of ideas, a different scale of values, a different outlook—in a word, a different philosophy—is appropriate to each of these stages. A man begins his career as a child, a student, with an outlook on life distinctive of his age and condition. When he is no longer a child, he puts off childish things, and becomes a householder, the head of a family, a responsible citizen, with new rights and duties; correspondingly, a new outlook is appropriate for him. As time goes on, if his progress toward philosophical maturity continues, he comes to another ashrama, in which these things in turn are put away from him, and he fulfills new obligations, quite apart from the life of the community. And with a higher level of attainment, he may become an ascetic and hermit, devoting himself entirely to meditation. No one philosophy is right; everything depends on the individual's age and condition in society.

But further, each individual has his own level of attainment even within a given social condition. As we might say, not all new bridegrooms are equally mature; while some obligations are common to all of them, others must surely vary with the individual. Each man has his own *adhikara,* his individual rights and duties, or correspondingly, his individual level of attainment. It is absurd to expect of all men the same conduct, or even the same values, when there are such great differences in the understanding at which they have arrived as they individually progress toward the common goal of all men. In the school of life, the same examination is given to freshmen and to candidates for the doctorate, but different answers are expected of them. Thus in matters of religion, for instance, it is pointless to ask of a Hindu whether he is what we would call a church-goer. Performance of the ritual is a duty at one stage of spiritual progress, but another already lies beyond worship—and even, as we shall see, beyond God. It is paradoxical that we, who put so much emphasis on individualism in economics and politics, have so little room for it in morality and religion, as compared with Indian thought.

Nor is this individuation a matter only of stage and level of progress. There are differences, too, in the path that each man follows, different inclinations and talents. This is called the *sadhana,* the way of worship or fulfillment. "They also serve" is a basic principle. Indian philosophers, I think, would be very much taken with the folktale recounted in Anatole France's *The Juggler of Our Lady:* A juggler joins a monastery especially given to the worship of Mary and is distressed because he is ignorant of the prayers and rituals by which the other monks express their devotion. Having no other skill at his disposal than his acrobatics, he steals down to the chapel in the dead of night and turns handsprings before the holy image. And Mary bows her head and smiles. This was his sadhana, and "in whatever form I am worshipped, that worship

I accept." I have heard a writer's congress in India discuss the pursuit of their craft as their sadhana. One must only be devoted to it, and it can become a form of devotion.

This combination of catholicity and individualization of Indian thought finds expression in an important philosophical doctrine which I find very rich in its implications. It is known as *syadvada,* the "maybe so" doctrine, or the doctrine of "up to a point" or "in a manner of speaking." (It is especially associated with the Jain, one of the non-orthodox Indian schools, and indeed, a distinct religious sect.) No matter how carefully elaborated a philosophy may be, it remains, after all, only a human point of view. It is inseparable from a particular standpoint, and therefore inescapably expresses only a single perspective on a reality which transcends all perspectives. No proposition is wholly and completely true but only up to a point, in a manner of speaking. The proposition must be understood as asserting, "You can look at the matter *this* way"; but this does not mean that there is no other perspective from which it can also be viewed.

Note that it is not just human fallibility that is involved here, as though a proposition is either absolutely true or absolutely false, but we sometimes err in deciding which it is. Nor is it a matter of probabilism, either epistemic or objective. The former is the view that we never know anything for sure; the latter, that *what* we know, apart from the degree of confirmation of our knowledge, is not a flat matter of fact, but always only something that is likely to be the case. All these might be analyzable in terms of syadvada, and perhaps they are implied by it, but they are not to be identified with it. Syadvada is an emphasis on perspectives and an insistence that man can never take up an absolute perspective—at least, short of the point of complete emancipation of the human mind and spirit.

Thus we approach the truth, not by choosing among alternative beliefs and philosophies, but by broadening our perspectives so as to find a place for the several alternatives. The earth *is* flat, within the range of everyday experience; it is crucial that the geometry of a sufficiently small portion of the surface of a sphere is indistinguishably like that of a plane. There is a germ of truth in every false belief, or no one would ever have been tempted to believe it. And there is a germ of falsehood in every true one as well, for knowledge grows, not merely by accretion, but organically, in a way that transforms our earlier ideas as well as merely adding to them. As science progresses, our knowledge of the world is deepened and not merely extended. The Jain parable of the seven blind men and the elephant is, I am sure, familiar to all of us. The trunk of the elephant is indeed like a snake, the leg like a tree, the tail like a rope, and so on; the elephant is like all of these together, and in their togetherness quite unlike any of them. Blind or not, what we know of the elephant or anything else is subject to syadvada.

In this spirit, the Indians regard each philosophy, not as something being offered for exclusive adoption, but rather as a *darshana,* a point of view. The Six Schools ("Sad-darshana") are not strictly "schools" of philosophy in the Western sense, like materialism, idealism, and the rest. They are not thought of as "isms" at all. The truth transcends all of them, and the more of them we can accommodate, the closer to the truth we shall have come. By and large, the Indians reciprocate Emerson's high regard for their own thought and sympathize with his dismissal of consistency as the hobgoblin of little minds. For them, it is more important to be comprehensive than to be consistent. To be sure, a flat contradiction will not help much; what is wanted is a synthesis that combines the element of truth in both the contradictory standpoints. I venture to say that something of this attitude is not irrelevant to India's neutralism in the present world situation. Apart from tactical political considerations, it is congenial to the Indian outlook to hold that the truth does not and cannot lie wholly on one side or the other, nor yet somewhere betwixt and between; what must be found is a larger perspective that incorporates both. The Indians like to think of their own economy as neither capitalist nor socialist; they speak instead of "the public sector" and "the private sector."

This conception of differing philosophies as darshanas must not be interpreted in terms of the Western ideal of "toleration." In the

West, tolerance is either a matter of indifference to the whole issue—this is the basis of much contemporary tolerance of religious differences—or else it is a willingness to let the other fellow go to hell in his own way. The Indian outlook, we might say, is not a matter of tolerance but of integration. It is not that differences are recognized for what they are and accepted as such. The strategy, rather, is acceptance by incorporation. Indian tolerance, fundamentally, is a matter of "Underneath it all, they're just like us." Characteristically, other religions are regarded as types and variants of Hinduism, and the prophets and deities of other world religions venerated as *avatars* or incarnations of one or another of the Hindu gods. When Eisenhower visited India, it was reported that he was widely regarded as an avatar of Vishnu; I seriously believe that if our youthful President Kennedy were to tour India, millions of Hindus would identify him with Krishna.

So much for the general outlook and approach of Indian philosophy. I think we should now settle down to an examination of the specific way in which the Indian philosophers formulate their basic problem and its solution. I have already, I'm afraid, taken twice as long for these introductory considerations as I had planned to, but this is the usual experience with India; it always turns out to be twice as large and twice as complicated as you expect.

The problem of life in Indian philosophy is embodied in the concept of *samsara,* which might be rendered as the endless round of existence. In a literal sense, it is the succession of birth and death and rebirth into another life. I will return to this conception in a moment. But samsara has also a more philosophic significance: it is the Indian word for what we call the rat-race or the squirrel-cage. We go round and round and get nowhere, caught up in a meaningless routine from which we try to find relief in the emptiness of caprice. Our lives are just one damned thing after another, and nothing makes sense. It is all risk and no pay-off, and there is no getting away from it. Each morning we arise to face the day's work, and then have to work at being leisured; we kill ourselves during the day so that we can kill time in the evening and weekends. As Schopenhauer put it, life is an unending alternation of pain and boredom.

I have always felt relieved to find that the sort of problem which we usually diagnose as due to the tempo and complexity of modern civilization was perfectly familiar to the Indian philosophers some thousands of years ago. The problem can't really have so much to do with the pace of modern life but must derive from some constant elements in the human condition, as the existentialists would say. Undoubtedly in every period of history people have felt that the world is going to the dogs, complained that the younger generation has no sense of responsibility and very little sense about anything else, regretted that life was becoming so complicated, and envied their ancestors for living at a time when the world was so simple and life so easy to manage. All this, I think, is nothing other than the form in which our culture has expressed its recognition of what the Indians call samsara, the wheel of life on which we spin round and round.

Now throughout Asia, and especially in India, it is accepted almost universally and without question that when a man dies he is born again. Rebirth is a tacit assumption of every one of the Indian philosophies, so basic that it just doesn't occur to anyone to weigh the relevant arguments and evidence; and this is the state of mind today of the vast majority of even the most educated Indians. But to be born again does not mean to them what that phrase conveys to us. There is no reference here to a spiritual awakening, no concept of the personal immortality of a transcendent soul. Rebirth is meant in a straightforward empirical sense, from which it would follow, for instance, that in principle a man ought to be able to remember his previous existences. In fact, it is widely believed in India that from time to time somebody or other does indeed remember. In much the same way it never occurs to any of us to question the continuity of adult selves with what we were as infants, in spite of virtually complete infantile amnesia. We don't remember any of our experiences as infants, but we recognize—at least in Southern California—that if we lie down in a darkened room with someone sitting behind us encouraging our free associations we may be able to weave together the broken strands of our conscious memories. Rebirth, so far as I have been able to determine, is almost always meant in India in this empirical sense—though I have sometimes doubted the correctness of this interpretation, because I find it hard to understand how an empirical belief can survive with so little evidence in its favor: the trans-empirical ones enjoy the advantage of being independent of the evidence altogether!

It is also important not to interpret rebirth as transmigration. The idea of rebirth does not necessarily involve (and Buddhism even explicitly repudiates) the notion of some substantive entity which persists through successive incarnations. All that is essential to the idea is a continuity from life to life; whether this continuity is provided by a persistent entity or in some other way is a secondary question. I shall return to this question in my lecture on Buddhism.

Now the fundamental point is that rebirth does not in itself provide a release from samsara. It is not an awakening into the True World, the fulfillment of our earthly destiny, and such like. We are born again into this life, and again and again, until the wheel of samsara is broken. The important question is how this can be achieved; rebirth is an incidental to the process and does not play any essential part in the philosophic formulation of either the problem or its solution.

What *is* essential is that the succession of lives—and more to the point, the succession of experiences within any of them—is not random, but proceeds in accord with an inflexible law known in Indian thought as the law of *karma*. It can best be understood, I think, as a principle of moral causation. Western philosophy has relied heavily on a concept of causality as a principle of natural necessity: everything happens just as and when it does because of the workings of causes which are not to be denied their effects. Karma is, as it were, an application of this idea to the sphere of conduct, and especially with regard to the moral quality of the acts performed. Indeed, action is the literal meaning of the word "karma," which originally referred to the ritual acts enjoined in the Vedas, the performance of the sacrificial and other rites called for there. Later philosophical developments generalized it to encompass all action and transferred the element of necessity from the religious injunction to the relation between the acts themselves.

We may say that karma is the collective force of a man's past actions—the pressure of habit and, more basically, of character, which makes a man act as he does. And it is this which determines the content of his life. In the popular view, the externals of the life situation are also determined by a man's karma. In the more sophisticated conception, this is true only in so far as the life situation itself is a reflection of what the man is. (It is in this sense that it is often said in the West that if all the money in the country were to be evenly divided, in a short time it would find its way back into the same hands.) In short, the law of karma has roughly the same content as the Greek aphorism that man's character is his fate. What happens to a man is an inevitable outcome of what he is, and this in turn is a necessary consequence of his past actions. And it is karma that persists from life to life, and not a soul which migrates from one body to another.

But the doctrine that man's character is his fate must not be confused with fatalism. The law of karma is not only not fatalistic but it is even incompatible with fatalism. The fatalist supposes that no matter what he does, the outcome will be the same: if fate does not imply predetermination, it means nothing at all. The bullet either has your name on it or it doesn't, regardless of whether or not you poke your head up over the foxhole to find out if it does—this is fatalism. But for the Indian, you yourself inscribe your name on the bullet by living a rash and heedless life. With every act of this kind you acquire a certain karma, and it will—it must—work itself out. The Indian position is what we have formulated in the West in this way: "Be not deceived; God is not mocked: for whatsoever a man soweth, that shall he also reap."

Yet I must admit that from a psychological rather than a logical point of view, the interpretation of karma as fatalistic is not such a gross misinterpretation after all. For there is a certain apathy which it seems to me to engender, a kind of acceptance, as the workings of karma, of conditions which might be wholly transformed by resolute and energetic action. But the problem is by no means as simple as many Western observers make out: in the West, the Calvinist doctrines of predestination and election seemed to have quite a contrary psychological effect. I find Indian philosophy complicated enough; Indian psychology I must leave entirely to others.

The problem of life, then, for the Indian philosophers, is to work out your karma to its end. For it has an end, a final release from samsara. The Indian outlook is not a pessimistic one, regardless of the initial impression it gives. The law of karma is an opportunity, not a judgment: that a man reaps what he sows is in fact the basis of hope rather than of despair. Samsara is not a trap in which we are caught at birth, and from which there is no release. "Much better never to have been born at all," a wit once remarked, "but not one man in ten thousand has such luck." This is definitely not the Indian point of view. To be born as a human being is already to have progressed very far along the road: the goal is already in sight. It will be achieved sooner or later, in accord with the karma accumulated in the course of our conduct in this life, and in whatever successive lives we condemn ourselves to live through.

This final release the Indians call *moksha,* liberation from this body of death. It is better translated as "emancipation" rather than "salvation." For man is not infected with original sin, innate depravity, or anything of that kind. We do not face a damnation from which we need to be saved. There is no Inferno in Indian thought: we live always in purgatory, till the wheel of life itself is broken. From the Indian point of view, the Divine Comedy plays forever in the second act, until it plays itself out. We achieve moksha, and the comedy comes to an end.

Now before sketching how Indian philosophy proposes to solve the problem I must survey the metaphysical basis in terms of which both problem and solution are stated in Indian thought. This metaphysics is, we would say, literary rather than scientific, a product of what the nineteenth century used to call the "mythopoeic faculty." Such Western philosophers as did rely on myths, like Plato, used them as illustrations rather than for a distinctive content that could not be rendered otherwise. But this interpretation has come to be recognized in our own day as prejudicial. By and large, Western technical philosophy has tended to differentiate itself sharply from the sort of philosophy that is embodied in the works of, say, Dante, Shakespeare, and Goethe. But this differentiation only marks, after all, *our* style of philosophizing; we must beware of projecting it onto the thought patterns of other cultures.

Specifically, the Indian philosopher looks out on the world as a kind of cosmic spectacle and approaches his task more like a critic unfolding the meaning of a work of art than like an engineer explaining how something works. His concept of Creation for instance —one which I find very intriguing—is that the world was created in a spirit of divine playfulness. This cosmic play is called *lilla:* it has been suggested to me that this term may have entered the Western tradition in the name of Lillith, the precursor of Eve who taught Adam to play, and so plunged man into samsara. Be that as it may, the Indian conception of the world is that it is a manifestation of the superabundance of divine energy, poured out with the exuberance of the child at play and the control of the artist at work. The concrete expression of this idea is perhaps the most representative symbol of the classical Indian outlook—the Nataraja or dancing Siva, encircled by the cosmos which is engendered by the dance itself.

In more abstract metaphysical terms, Indian philosophy introduces the category of *prakṛti:* the world process, the ceaseless outpouring of energy by which the world substance is proliferated endlessly into what we experience as the cosmic spectacle. It is what Plato refers to in his *Timaeus* as the receptacle and nurse of all generation, of all coming to be and passing away; or rather, it is this process of becoming itself. I remember among the Fourth of July fireworks of my childhood a little cone which used to be placed on the sidewalk and lit; a seemingly endless and unbroken chain of ash emerged from it—or rather, from the bare cement, apparently; it twisted and turned like a writhing snake in a bewildering variety of convolutions; and around its base there burned a tiny circle of blue flame, giving off a sulfurous smoke. This is my image of prakrti: ash, flame, and all, going on and on out of nothing.

But prakrti follows a path of development: there is a process of cosmic evolution rather than a sequence of random transformations. Indian thought tends toward cycles: there is a corresponding process of involution as well. Each cycle defines a cosmic era or *kalpa*. This is not just a matter of the "ages" or "periods" into which we usually divide human history; the kalpa is metaphysical in scope and constitutes a distinct phase of being of the whole world process. In the West, Nietzsche speaks of "eternal recurrence," and Alfred North Whitehead has speculated about cosmic eras during which the laws of nature remain relatively constant, giving way to other laws in other eras. Today cosmologists are weighing alternative theories, those which conceive of a "steady state" universe, which exhibits essentially the same features in all epochs, and those which postulate a process of cosmic evolution. Contrary to the stereotype of the "timelessness" of what is called the Asian mind, Indian metaphysics would find most congenial those world models that some contemporary cosmologists have formulated in which the universe alternately expands and contracts.

What I find especially interesting is the unimaginable vastness assigned by the ancient Indian thinkers to the kalpas and various other world magnitudes. Indian philosophy has for millenia spoken of larger numbers than almost any encountered anywhere in Western thought until just the last hundred years or so, when the development of astronomy began to require them. Indian philosophy often proceeds by identifying certain elements and then considering the various permutations and combinations that they allow for, which so rapidly increase in number. I venture to say that just as geometry gave a certain cast to Western thought, algebra left its mark on Indian ways of thinking; but this is hardly more than a guess.

Now prakrti is not entirely self-sufficient, for in itself it is only an outpouring of blind forces; something is needed to give it direction. This something the Indians call *purusa,* the silent witness of the cosmic spectacle, all-seeing though in itself powerless. Cosmic evolution is the product of purusa guiding through their cycles the forces of prakrti. The usual metaphor employed to describe the joint working of prakrti and purusa is that of the lame man sitting on the shoulders of the blind as the two of them make their way through the world. This duality is in some respects not unlike the one which Spinoza presents between *natura naturans* and *natura naturata,* nature acting and being acted upon; in other ways like Aristotle's distinction between matter and form; and in still others, like Kant's conception of the phenomenal world and the transcendental ego which provides the manifold in which phenomena are experienced. But it is distinct from all of these, and in its way as rich and suggestive, I think, as the various categories of Western metaphysics. For the Indians, it is, after all, only a darshana, a particular point of view, developed especially in one of the Six Schools, the Samkhya, and given application by the school of Yoga, of which I shall say something later. But reality transcends every darshana, and indeed, in Indian thought it transcends metaphysical categories altogether.

To get at the Indian idea of reality we must approach it through what we might call their theology. The early Vedas exhibit a rather characteristic primitive polytheism. Like the Greek pantheon, a number of deities each presided over his own domain, geographic or in accord with a division of labor, as it were, in the conduct of human and natural events. Such gods could be in conflict with one another as well as with their human subjects; their worship was essentially a matter of propitiating them and retaining their favor. Gradually this polytheism gave way to what has aptly been called "opportunist monotheism," in which a favorite deity, perhaps varying with the circumstances, is regarded as having hegemony over all the others. Eventually a genuine monotheism is reached, with the other deities being conceived of as different names, aspects, or manifestations of the one true God. Such monotheism, I think most of us would say, represents the highest achievement of Western religious thought. But Indian philosophy regards even monotheism as only a halfway house and goes beyond it to a monism in which not only the distinction among the various gods is wiped out, but also the distinction between God and His world, Creator and creation. The ultimate reality transcends all differentiation; this reality the Hindu calls *Brahman.*

Now this word has a number of different meanings which we must be careful not to confuse with one another. In its most literal sense it refers to certain rituals in the Vedas; by extension, it also refers to those parts of the Vedas in which the rituals are specified. Later it becomes the name of one of the deities, the king or ruler of all the gods, who still remains as the chief of the great trinity of Brahma, Vishnu, and Siva. In another usage, it is the name of the priestly caste, in the service of this or any deity. But finally—and this is the sense relevant here—it is a designation for the absolute and ultimate reality of which all else is only a manifestation.

Pantheism is what probably comes to your mind, but this would be a mistake. Brahman is not just manifested throughout nature, but nature is itself a manifestation of Brahman: it is not that God is in all things, but that all things are in God, *are* God. Yet that is not quite true either, for Brahman is not exhausted by nature. It transcends the world process, and all distinctions by which we conceptualize this process. Praktri and purusa themselves are only fragments—or better, appearances—of the one, undifferentiated, ultimate reality. What we experience as nature or *as* anything else is *what* it is only in the perspective of our experience; Brahman is the reality which appears in this perspective or that one.

It follows that nothing can properly be said of Brahman; for every attribution presupposes a distinction between the attribute and its contrary, and every distinction rests on a difference, or it is only words. But Brahman is the undifferentiated reality rather than the difference which appears to us. Whatever question one might ask about Brahman must therefore be answered in the negative: the positive attribution implies that Brahman is one thing rather than another, but there is no "other" to reality. The recurrent phrase in the Upanisads is *neti, neti:* not this, not that. Negative theology of this kind is by no means unknown to the Western religious tradition; but usually it occurs in the context of mysticism, like that of Meister

Eckhart, for instance. In India it serves as the foundation for an elaborate metaphysics. The sage of the Upanisads declares, "I teach you indeed, but you do not understand: Brahman is silence." The paradox is that this teaching generates a voluminous and complex metaphysical literature.

Brahman, then, is the ground of all existence, all being. But since knowledge is the apprehension of what is real, Brahman is by the same token the ground of all knowledge. And for the Indian thinkers, as for Plato and other idealists in the West, it is therefore also the ground of all value. Brahman is, we might say, the core of the true, the good, and the beautiful. Hinduism summarizes this conception in a single term, *saccitananda:* "sat" or being, reality; "citta," knowledge or consciousness; and "ananda" (with which you are familiar as the suffix in the name of every swami), bliss or perfection. The lines in Wordsworth's *Prelude* are not too bad an approximation to this conception of Brahman. Things in nature

> Were all like workings of one mind,
>   the features
> Of the same face, blossoms upon one tree;
> Characters of the great Apocalypse,
> The types and symbols of Eternity,
> The first, and last, and midst, and without end.

And now I can put before you the Indian solution to the great problem of life, and a most remarkable one it is, in my opinion. The path of emancipation leads from the self, through the self, and ends with the Self. Only, it is not the empirical self which is here in question—not the self which we experience introspectively and which enters into interpersonal relations with other selves; this the Indians call the *jiva.* Nor is it the soul in the Judaeo-Christian sense, an individualized purusa, as it were. It is the Self that completely transcends both action and consciousness, body and mind, matter and spirit. This wholly transcendent Self is called the *Atman.* If I am not mistaken, the word "Atman" is closely related in meaning to a number of terms used for somewhat similar ideas in the Western world, like the Hebrew "ruach" and the Greek "pneuma"; it is from a root which eventually gives us our word "atmosphere"—air or breath, and more especially, the breath of life which God breathed into the nostrils of Adam.

Now the cardinal point in the whole teaching of orthodox Indian philosophy is this: that the Atman and Brahman are identical. The ultimate reality of individual human existence and the ultimate reality underlying the whole of being are one and the same. This identity is expressed in the famous formula, *tat tvam asi*. It is easy to make out the English equivalent of these words: "tat" gives us our word "that"; "tvam" gives "thou" (think of the Latin "tuam"); and "asi" is the copula, "is" or "are." We would say: *That thou art!* The ground of being, of knowledge, and of value is nothing other than the Self.

But, of course, it is not the individual self. Nothing could be a more serious misunderstanding of Indian thought than to charge it with the monstrous impiousness of identifying each individual self with God. Any Indian would agree with the Westerner that this would be only a mark of madness if taken literally, and of confused theology if taken in some abstract philosophical sense. The Self which is identified with Brahman is not the self which is individualized, which distinguishes one man from another. It is the Self which we encounter when we transcend individuality, and with it, all differentiation. It is when we do that, and only then, that we come upon Brahman. The Indian thesis is no more megalomaniac than Meister Eckhart's declaration, "The eye with which I look on God is that with which He sees me." I cannot resist the irreverent association of ideas with a story of Köhler's apes: when the psychologist looked through the keyhole to see what his apes were doing, his vision was blocked—one of the apes was looking out of the keyhole at him! An Indian might say: Ape, God, and man are all one, and the door stands open on every side.

Obviously, the basic difficulty with which this conception must deal is the undeniable fact, confirmed in every moment of experience, that this is *not* that. Here I stand, and there is the external world; this hand is a part of me, and this table is not; you are you, and I am I. And outside of and distinct from both of us are stones and trees, earth and heaven and the stars; all these things differ from me and from one another. Every philosophy, if it is to be more than a madman's dream, must somehow accommodate these differences. A Hasidic rabbi once remarked, "If you are you only because I am I, and I am I only because you are you, then you are not you and I am not I." Now we can understand that: self-identity, if it is to be what the existentialist calls "authentic," must have some content beyond sheer differentiation from the other. But to say that I am you; worse, that you are me; and that indeed we are one with the senseless stones—this is surely asking too much, even of a man of faith!

Indian thought must—and does—recognize that there is in fact a world of differentiation which provides the content of ordinary experience and even of scientific cognition. This world is called *maya,* and the concept of maya is of central importance to the whole metaphysics. But it is not an easy concept to grasp. We are tempted to interpret it as illusion, the veil which hides reality from us. But it reveals reality as well as hiding it from us—like a symbol, which both expresses and conceals. The term "appearance" might be a useful translation, for on the one hand we contrast appearance with reality, but on the other hand we recognize that every appearance is *of* a reality.

The point is that appearances are real, if only we take them for what they really are. Even illusions are real, as illusions. I remember my first visit to the Southwestern deserts and my impatience for my first glimpse of a mirage; at last I saw one, only to be told that it was not a real mirage, but only a pond. It is our own self-deception that makes illusions illusory; in themselves, they are just what they are. But the cosmic magician is not fooled by his own spectacle; he sees himself putting the rabbit into the hat and taking it out again, and there is no deception anywhere. *We* are deceived, because we do not see the reality as it is; and becoming aware at last that we have been deceived, we say that it was an illusion. But in fact it always was just what we now see it to be, a reality with no illusion in it. Maya is nothing other than Brahman, for there *is* nothing other than Brahman. The trick is to see through the trick, and recognize maya for what it really is.

In the West, a somewhat similar idea has been formulated in a religious context, in familiar words that are not usually interpreted in this metaphysical way: "When I was a child, I spake as a child, I understood as a child, I thought as a child: but when I became a man, I put away childish things. For now we see through a glass, darkly; but then face to face: now I know in part; but then shall I know even as also I am known." This might very well have been written by an Indian, so far as the content is concerned. For in the Indian perspective, the human problem consists essentially in nothing other than this: that we are deceived by the cosmic spectacle. We see through a glass darkly; we are deceived in ourselves and in the world. We live in the illusion of being an ego, standing apart from all others, and have our being in the world of maya in which we are strangers and afraid. But we are not strangers, either to each other or to the world around us, and there is nothing to be afraid of. Not, "The Lord is with me, I shall not fear"; but, "There is no 'me' outside the Lord, and this, *this* is the kingdom, the power, and the glory, world without end."

In reality, therefore, there is no problem to start with, and so no solution is called for. The secret of the sphinx is that it is we ourselves who pose the riddle. Life is experienced as a problem only because we do not understand it, and just this is the only thing to be understood. Our perplexity is due only to metaphysical ignorance, what the Indians call *avidya.* It is characteristic of the Asian philosophies in general that the human problem is identified as being essentially a problem of knowledge. In this respect it has more kinship to the Greek tradition than to the Judaeo-Christian. The fall of man is not due to his having eaten of the tree of knowledge, but to his having taken only one bite—it is the little knowledge that is a dangerous thing. The Indian might say with the Greek, "Know thyself" or, more accurately, "Know the Self." For when this is known, nothing beside remains to give life surpassing meaning and worth.

All this has a remarkable implication, which the Indian thinker draws with unflinching consistency. It is that the belief in God—and with it, all religious institutions and practices—also belongs to avidya; it is a mark of ignorance, of living in maya. In very truth, theism and atheism, faith and scepticism are equally in error. The religious perspective is error on its way to truth, but it is still short of the goal. For you must not mistake Brahman for God. God is the Creator differentiated from his creation, the sacred set over against the profane. But Brahman is beyond all differentiation, even that which distinguishes God from the world. Some orthodox Indian schools accept the existence of God, but others are quite explicitly atheistic. The word for God in Indian thought is *Isvara*. Now Isvara, like every other existent, is only a manifestation of Brahman. The role of Isvara in those philosophies which find a place for Him is like that of the daemons whom Plato invoked to give the creative principle purchase on reality. He is an intermediary, and not the ultimate. Isvara is a personality; we may say of Him "He," and more important, speak to Him as "thou." But Brahman is only *It,* neither male nor female, neither personal nor impersonal—neti, neti. Isvara also belongs to maya, and must be transcended.

How is a man to go about transcending even the religious outlook? How is he to overcome the metaphysical ignorance which seems to be deeply implanted in the human mind? The answer given by the Indian thinkers is in a general sense contained in the idea of *Yoga.* The word "yoga" comes from a root with which we are acquainted in the word "yoke," as in a yoke of oxen. It means a link or bond, a tying together. By extension, then, it is a way of bringing together what man has thrust asunder—body and mind, matter and spirit, prakrti and purusa; and most fundamentally, Atman and Brahman. Yoga is the method for the overcoming of all the differentiations which in our ignorance we experience as making up reality, but which in fact constitute only the realm of maya.

In the Western world, we usually think of Yoga as consisting of various breathing exercises, unusual postures and gymnastics. This is indeed one aspect of Yoga, the so-called *Hatha-yoga,* as distinguished from the *Raja-yoga* which aims directly at the conquest of avidya, the attainment of insight into the truth of *tat tvam asi.* Hatha-yoga is practiced as physical culture in many parts of the world; whatever merits it may claim or actually have from the standpoint of bodily well-being is of no particular relevance to the understanding of Indian thought. I suppose one of the most famous practitioners of Hatha-yoga in the world is David Ben-Gurion, the Prime Minister of Israel, who reportedly begins each day's work by standing on his head for fifteen minutes; I have heard it said that this is only because he wants to see American policies in the Middle East in proper perspective. I see no harm in supposing that the practice of Yoga in this sense is about as beneficial as, say, Swedish exercises or Turkish baths.

What is of philosophical relevance is that Yoga conceives of the body as the instrument or expression of the mind and soul: it is not a prison for them, not an obstacle to their free working. Yoga aims at achieving a fullness of expression, a mastery of the instrument which is the body. When such mastery has been achieved, quite extraordinary bodily performances become possible. These are in no sense miraculous but belong to the same natural order as the sometimes almost unbelievable skills and powers of accomplished athletes or artists. Yoga, however, also lays claim to phenomena which in our eyes would be supernatural—for instance, levitation and clairvoyance. But it is important to recognize that in the metaphysics of Yoga there is nothing supernatural about them at all; it is rather that they testify to the narrowness of our ordinary conception of nature—there are more things betwixt heaven and earth than are dreamed of in the earth-bound philosophies.

What is frustrating to attempts to make scientific tests of such claims, is that, according to the theory itself, these special powers accrue only at a sufficiently advanced stage of spiritual development; and anyone who has attained that stage is far beyond allowing his powers to be exploited for gain or glory or for the satisfaction of intellectual curiosity. You cannot consistently demand of the prophet a demonstration of signs and wonders: God is not to be tempted. The more usual manifestations of yogic skills, however, are being subjected to extensive physiological and related studies, both here and in India; I am not acquainted, however, with any dramatic discoveries which have been made on this score.

We must not forget that control over the bodily instrument has, after all, only an instrumental value, according to Yoga itself. It is at best only a means for the attainment of a spiritual end; it is not to be pursued for the attainment of other goals, and least of all as an end in itself. There is an instructive anecdote told about Sri Ramakrishna: He was once walking across the countryside with a yogin; they came to a river, and Ramakrishna hailed the ferryboat to take them across. At which the yogin said proudly, "I have practiced sufficient austerities so that I can walk across the river." To this, Ramakrishna replied, "Your austerities are worth two annas"—the fare for the crossing.

The concept of a yoga, then, in its most general sense, is that of a path or pattern of life which leads to realization of the identity of Atman and Brahman. In these terms, Indian thought distinguishes three yogas, which have their counterparts in all major world religions and moral philosophies.

The first of these is *bhakti-yoga,* the path of love, devotion, or faith. This yoga is a particular contribution made by the Gita in its reform of the earlier Brahmanic religion (here "Brahman" refers, of course, to the priestly caste). For the performance of the elaborate Vedic sacrifices could be carried out only by the wealthy, and the study of the Upanisadic philosophy was similarly restricted to those with leisure, as well as natural aptitudes. But bhakti-yoga is accessible to everyone, whatever his talents or station in life. It is the way of worship, or fulfillment, through depth of feeling and sincerity in its expression. Bhakti-yoga is the service of love, both literally and as transformed or sublimated in the arts. Thus Krishna, the central figure of the Gita, is the great lover in Indian folklore and mythology as portrayed, for instance, in the Gita-Govinda, the so-called Indian "Song of Songs." He is also the great musician, usually represented as playing on his flute, and an accomplished dancer. In modern

India, Rabinadrath Tagore might be taken to exemplify this path, as in the Western world we might mention Rembrandt, Bach, or William Blake—not to speak of King David. Among institutionalized religions, bhakti-yoga is emphasized, for instance, by the Hasidim in Judaism, the Sufi in Islam, Zen in Buddhism, and the Pietists in Christianity.

Second is the path of *karma-yoga,* the way of moral action. Here we may think of Ghandi, and in the West of Lincoln and Schweitzer. In Indian perspectives, the things of this world, and worldly values like national autonomy or bodily health, are not lures to sin but pathways to freedom. What is important is that in our involvement with these things we detach ourselves from the outcome of our endeavors, whether they succeed or fail. We are to act *in* the world without being *of* it, do our duty for the sake of duty alone and not for the sake of something external to character which we expect to achieve by our action. For outside the effect on character of what we do, the consequences are in the hands of God; you just fulfill your obligations, and let Him worry about His. This is what we know in the West as the path of works, rather than of faith. But, of course, there is nothing mutually exclusive about the several yogas; devotion to moral action is after all only another full measure of devotion. The Sermon on the Mount expresses bhakti-yoga as clearly as it does karma-yoga.

Most characteristically Indian is the third yoga, *jnana-yoga,* the path of understanding, the intellectualization of wisdom. This is the emphasis in Ecclesiastes and various of the Apocrypha and gnostic writings, and in such philosophers as Plotinus and Philo Judaeus. In India it takes the form of the study of speculative metaphysics, in particular of the system known as the *Vedanta.* The word itself means the end of the Vedas or their culmination; it is the school which attempts to synthesize the various other orthodox darshanas into one comprehensive world view, the understanding of which will bring emancipation.

India, I think, has produced some great philosophical figures, great even on the stage of world thought. I would mention particularly the ninth-century philosopher Sankara-charya, the chief figure in one of the two main wings of Vedanta, the so-called *Advaita* Vedanta. Sankara (the suffix "acharya" is an honorific, meaning Sage or Master) achieved for classical Indian thought what Aquinas did for Christianity, Maimonides for Judaism, and Plato for Greek civilization—a systematic and comprehensive expression of a whole culture. Jnana-yoga, the pursuit of wisdom as distinct from merely empirical understanding, is the central theme of Sankara's teaching, and indeed of the Indian tradition as a whole.

In spite of the sense of other-worldliness in these speculations about Brahman, maya, and the rest, the Indian outlook exhibits a certain realism that contrasts markedly with what is characteristic of Western religious philosophies. (This is just the reverse, isn't it, of the usual stereotypes of East and West.) Specifically, India is quite unequivocal and straightforward in its recognition of death and of sexuality as central facts of human experience. In the Judaeo-Christian perspective, both death and sexuality tend to be glossed over, overlaid with elaborate symbolism and subtleties of interpretation which either make them unrecognizable or assign them a purely peripheral position. Indian art and mythology, religious practice, and even abstract metaphysics accept death and destruction as a part of life, and sex and generation as expressions of divine creativity. Important deities are represented with cobras in their hair and wearing a garland of skulls; others are worshiped at altars which are phallic, not merely to the scholar or psychoanalytic interpreter, but to the worshipers themselves. It would be a serious mistake, in my opinion, to associate such images and rituals with what we have come to call pagan idol worship. For all the gods are but symbols of the one underlying reality; the powerful impulses of love and hate are but human expressions of the forces by which this reality manifests itself in experience. In their personal lives, Indians are more puritanical, I would judge, than most Westerners; but there is no place in their perspectives for the idea that there is something obscene about either sex or death.

With regard to morality in the sense of concern for the welfare of others, Indian philosophy needs no apologies. The goal of moksha, of emancipation, though individual in form (like the Western quest for personal salvation), is thoroughly social in content. In a way, it goes beyond even the prevailing Western conception of moving from egoism to altruism. For the goal is not unselfishness but selflessness, a movement, not from self to other, but from self to Self, in which there is no other. To say "mine" and "thine" is to be a victim of avidya, for we are distinguished from one another only in maya: in truth we are one. Nor does it suffice to lay hold of this truth only in speculation; it must be realized in action, for it is only in action that we can work out our karma. Thus the Ramakrishna mission undertakes an impressive program of social welfare, with hospitals, schools, and the like. And there are many establishments of the type of the Aurobindo ashram, of which I spoke earlier, in which thousands of people live in a comunal life that provides for them daily a concrete expression of spiritual aspiration. Most familiar to the Western world, I suppose, is the reliance on *satyagraha,* moral force, for the achievement even of political ends, as manifested in the life-work of Ghandi, and more recently, in the *Bhoodan* or land-reform movement of Vinoba Bhave.

But there are also certain moral failings which I think are to be laid at the door of the Indian outlook. The philosophy makes much of universality, but its institutional base is in the exclusiveness of caste—and the caste system not only shows no signs of weakening in contemporary India but is apparently even growing stronger. There is a certain moral neutralism to which the Indian is susceptible, because in Brahman even the distinction between good and evil is transcended. The continued emphasis on so-called spiritual progress is not of much help for other sorts of progress and may even be a downright hindrance. Indians have a way of making virtues out of miserable necessity; but it might be less necessary if it weren't regarded as quite so virtuous. And I must also mention the parasitism to which the religious life in India too often degenerates—what I have elsewhere condemned as an expense of spirit in a waste of shame.

Yet for all that, Indian philosophy is as great an expression of the human spirit as is to be found in any culture. It makes of philosophy, not a merely academic pursuit, but a kind of vision of eternal truth —the sort of vision that we find in the West in Plato, Plotinus, Spinoza, and Kant. In the sweep of thought and elevation of expression there is a grandeur in the Upanishads which led someone to describe them as "the Himalayas of the soul," and something of this quality runs unmistakably throughout Indian philosophy. I think no one can fail to respond to it. How we are to view Indian philosophy when we have descended from the peaks is perhaps a different matter. But it is no more than just to remind ourselves of what Plato had to say in his *Timaeus* of the account given in that dialogue of the origin and constitution of the cosmos: "If, then, amid the many opinions about the gods and the generation of the universe, we are not able in every respect to render all our ideas consistent with each other and precisely accurate, no one need be surprised. Enough if we are able to give an account which is no less likely than another; for we must remember that I who speak, and you who judge of what I say, are mortal men, so that on these subjects we should be satisfied with a likely story and demand nothing more." I will myself be quite satisfied if you feel, not about Indian philosophy itself, but about my presentation of it to you, that it is—a likely story.

QUESTIONS

How can the Hindu-Moslem conflicts be reconciled with Indian ideals?

I THINK WE MUST RECOGNIZE first that the perspectives in which this conflict is viewed are very different from the two standpoints. To start with, while *ahimsa* or non-violence is an important Hindu ideal, it does not play any such role in Islam. While Pakistan is by its constitution a Moslem state, India is not in the same way a Hindu one. Successive waves of Islamic conquest of India mutilated and destroyed much Hindu and Buddhist art, because the making of images is contrary to the Moslem faith, while Hinduism, as we have seen, accommodates all forms of worship. In short, there is not here a religious conflict as we have been accustomed to it in the West: whether one religion or the other is the true faith is not at issue—at least, not from the standpoint of the Hindu. The conflict is political, national, and territorial rather than ideological.

Even in this setting, traditional Indian ideals have not been without effect, at least during the lifetime of Gandhi. Shortly after the partition, as you recall, an undeclared war broke out between Pakistan and India, especially in the Kashmir region, and during this period Pakistan asked India for payment of the debt owed her as part of the partition agreements. In the Indian cabinet it was pointed out that if the debt were repayed promptly, the money would be used by Pakistan to prosecute the war, and so payment was refused. When this came to the attention of Gandhi, he insisted on immediate fulfillment of the acknowledged obligation. Only in India, I think, would you find moral principle carried so far; but Nehru has remarked that even in India, only Gandhi would actually do it. It is for just such reasons that Gandhi was and is venerated as *the* embodiment of the Indian spirit. The Gita was Gandhi's favorite text. Although it enjoins the duty of going into battle even against kinsmen if the cause is just, the good fight was always interpreted metaphorically. In India, the Church Militant has never had the literal meaning it sometimes acquired in the West. I have no doubt that Moslems have been persecuted by Hindus just as the other way around; but they have never been the object of a Hindu Crusade.

How does Indian philosophy justify the caste system?

IN PART, CASTE MIGHT BE VIEWED as an institutionalization of that emphasis on different viewpoints and perspectives which we have seen to be so important in Indian thought. There are certain duties which belong to an individual because of his individual circumstances, and others, like ahimsa, which apply universally. Most obligations, however, are intermediate—neither wholly individual nor strictly universal. They depend on the role which the individual is playing in society; others are also performing that role, and other roles are also being played. Caste is, as it were, the expression in social forms of the moral implications of a division of labor.

But the actual institution is, like so many of our own, quite at variance with the ideological principles invoked to explain and defend it. For the classical teaching is that caste is not fixed by birth, but must depend on personal effort and attainment: one is not a Brahman because he is born into the priesthood, but because he lives a priestly life. But in fact, of course, caste has come to mean precisely the impermeable social stratification. The repudiation of caste in this sense was part of the Buddhist reform, and this is not without its historical ironies. Indian public law provides certain privileges for the members of the lowest caste, the untouchables. But shortly before the establishment of the state, some millions of them had become converted to Buddhism, to free themselves from the repressiveness of caste. The outcome was that they forfeited their special legal privileges but found themselves victimized by the same old caste discriminations from which they had suffered before becoming Buddhists.

By and large, Indian sociologists agree that caste lines are being drawn today even more strictly than before. Apologists for the system sound to my ears very like our fellow Americans south of the Mason-Dixon line who are unwavering in their loyalty to democratic principles and institutions, which in their minds, however, are not only not incompatible with segregation, but virtually imply it. "Outsiders," I have been told both in India and in Dixie, "don't really understand our problem." I really don't.

Do the Indians cherish individual rights and freedoms, or are they more sympathetic to a collectivist ideology?

As I POINTED OUT IN MY LECTURE on communism, these are not as clear-cut alternatives as they are usually taken to be. What is important here is that we recognize to what extent our ideas of individualism and of individual freedom are bound up with characteristic elements of the Western cultures. Individualism as we understand it has its roots in Judaeo-Christianity, with its conception of the individual soul standing before its Maker and freely choosing its fate; in the political system of the Greek city-states and the constitutional governments of the seventeenth and eighteenth centuries; in the economic practices of competition in a free market; in social mobility, and equality in interpersonal relations. In most Asian societies, and in India in particular, none of these historical elements is available to give cultural substance to an ideology of individualism.

Most Indians, even today, live in what we might call the enlarged family household: it would not occur to an Indian to complain about having to live with his in-laws. Our conception of family life is basically that of a point of departure for the individual career—the fledgling leaves the nest as soon as he is able and strikes out on his own. A social grouping of any kind is usually thought of by us as a constraint from which the individual must emancipate himself or, at best, a resource of which he can take advantage to achieve emancipation in some other direction. But the Indian does not think of it this way. He sees himself as only a manifestation of the larger social whole, which is the effective psychological reality for him. Group identifications—family, caste, community—are of enormous importance. By and large, to speak to Asians about the denial of individual freedom in the Soviet system is to talk about something they don't understand; and if they did, they wouldn't particularly care.

I don't mean to say that India is a plum ripe for the picking by the communists. Regimentation and strict ideological orthodoxy are also quite foreign to Indian perspectives, as I think the experience in the Indian state of Kerala showed. In my opinion, if India does fall prey to communism, we will see the greatest blood bath that the world has known—millions of people would have to be killed to make communist institutions viable there. But I don't want to pretend to political clairvoyance. The only point I am insisting on is the danger of trying to communicate with other peoples, not in terms that make sense in their own cultures, but in the ones familiar and natural to us. To understand a people, I believe we must understand their philosophy; and other philosophies are not just crude and primitive gropings after the pinnacle of wisdom on which we stand. It may be defensible to view biological evolution as culminating in the emergence of *homo sapiens;* but other species of thought, whether they have survival value or not, are something more than precursors of our own.

What is the relation between ethics and religion in Indian thought?

IN THE WEST, ethics has been regarded, by and large, as resting on a religious foundation. First and most directly, it was thought of as a promulgation of divine law, in a revelation to be interpreted in the context of religious institutions. Afterwards, the idea was that the moral law is dictated to each individual by his own conscience, but with the recognition that the voice of conscience is, after all, the voice of God, speaking to each of us in his own personal accents—ethics still rests on a religious foundation, but with every man his own priest. In another stream of thought, the moral law is embodied in the structure of human reason; but it owes its universality and necessity to the fact that the human mind is, at bottom, a fragment of the infinite mind of God. In short, the major tendency in Western thought is to derive ethics, directly or indirectly, from religion.

In India, on the contrary, morality is a prerequisite of the religious life rather than a deduction from it. The moksha which is the goal of life as Indians view it is by no means identical with moral perfection, but goes far beyond it. True, if one particularly devotes himself to moral achievement, this may become his sadhana; he cultivates karma-yoga, and this is his religious path. But there are other paths as well. In each of them, to be sure, a certain level of morality must be attained; every graduate degree, as it were, requires a certain mastery of English, but not every graduate student specializes in that subject, although some do. Morality is a prerequisite to spirituality, not because morality is itself a spiritual obligation, but because obligations of every kind—whether human, social, personal, or whatever—must be discharged by anyone aspiring to freedom. The ground of moral obligation is to be found in its own nature, and not in the content of spirituality. The Atman is not a moral agent, and God, as we might say, is beyond good and evil.

In the West, spiritual values are thought of as having an essentially moral content: what does the Lord require of you but to do justice, love mercy, and walk humbly with your God? This is the teaching of Jesus as well as of the Hebrew prophets. The Indian outlook is quite different, for morality, like any other system of discriminations, belongs only to maya. It wouldn't be at all correct to say that Indian thought is not particularly concerned with ethics; of course it is! Certain moral principles are common to the various Indian schools, and are shared also with Buddhism, which emerged from India. The point is that conformity to these principles is quite distinct from the goal of the religious life. They are a means to an end, and not justified as ends in themselves. Religion is not, as with us, essentially a system of symbols and sanctions by which a moral code is celebrated and enforced.

Indian philosophy, therefore, has not been particularly concerned, as ours has, to provide a basis for morality. In India, moral values have been taken for granted; in the West they have been problematic at least since the time of the Sophists. Are moral values relative or absolute? Objective or subjective? And if objective, on what does their objectivity rest? A great part of the history of Western thought can be regarded as a series of attempts to answer these questions, whether in straightforwardly religious terms, or in terms which try to also take into account the scientific world view. It is not that the Indian answers these questions differently than we do; he asks different questions. He does not concern himself with the ground of moral obligation, but raises the more fundamental question, Why be moral? When you have done your duty, fulfilled your obligations and pursued the good—what then? What meaning have you found in your life? To what end is it to be lived? Thus ethics gives way to metaphysics, and morality to the religious quest.

Isn't Indian philosophy actually religion rather than philosophy?

If I had been talking about religion—in the conventional sense, at least—the whole discussion would have dealt with quite other subjects. I have scarcely mentioned the major Hindu deities, the cults of Vishnu and of Siva, the characteristic forms of worship, the organization of the church, the specific creeds, and so on. These are the sorts of things that make up, I should suppose, what we usually call a religion. Yet the philosophy undeniably has the sort of preoccupation with first and last things that are characteristic at least of theology, if not of religious institutions as a whole. The trouble is that we project onto the Indian culture a distinction between philosophy and religion which is meaningful and important in the Western world, but which would be felt by the Indians themselves to be confusing and pointless.

There have been times in our own history when the distinction would have been difficult to apply. Would you think of Stoicism, for instance, as a religion? It is discussed in histories of philosophy rather than in surveys of religious sects. Yet it performed for its adherents most of what seem to me to be the essential functions of a religion; their Stoicism was not a merely intellectual belief, but something to live by. There is a sense in which, for my part, I would still defend the conception of philosophy as doing just that—giving us something to live by, a perspective in which a man can find meaning and value in his existence. I believe that, by and large, this has in fact been the substance of the philosophic enterprise in the Western world as well as in Asia. It happens that in the present century philosophy has taken a rather different turn, especially in England and America. When we confront a system of ideas which are really taken seriously, which are expected to affect how a man lives, we have difficulty in recognizing it as what we have so recently come to think of as philosophy.

At the turn of the century, artists in a variety of media tried to pull themselves out of the backwashes into which Victorian art had stagnated. What they produced was so different from the monstrosities to which their contemporaries—including the academicians—had become habituated, that most people had difficulty in recognizing it as art at all. Today we have a clearer perspective, and can see that the so-called revolution of modern art was in fact a restoration of the great tradition, emancipating art from the "prettiness" to which it had degenerated and bringing it once more into intimate relation with the things that really matter. It is my opinion that one of the salutary effects of exposing ourselves to the philosophies of other cultures is that we might be moved to restore to our own the human significance of which it has, I hope only temporarily, lost sight. Call it religion or metaphysics or what you will, if only you make of it something too important to leave in the hands of —the philosophers.

LECTURE SEVEN

Buddhism

GAUTAMA SIDDARTHA SAKYAMUNI, the Buddha, was born in India almost exactly twenty-five hundred years ago. "Gautama" is his given name and "Sakya" the family or clan name; "Sakyamuni" means "the sage of the Sakya," or perhaps more accurately, "the silent one of the Sakya." "Siddartha" means "the all-conquering." He is also known, particularly in Far Eastern Buddhism, as *Tathagata,* which means: "he who has come in this way, in this simple way," or "the ordinary one," or, as we might say in the West, "the son of man." The word "Buddha" is not a proper name but a description. It means "the enlightened one," and so might be compared—and also contrasted—with "Christ," which means, as you know, "the annointed." Gautama Sakyamuni is by no means the only Buddha. He was preceded by six other Buddhas, according to some, while others believe the number was several dozen; and he is to be followed by many other Buddhas, perhaps innumerable ones. Most especially, he will be followed by Maitreya, the Buddha who is yet to come—an important figure in Buddhist art and literature.

The story of the Buddha's life is, in its main outlines, very simple. He was born into the family of a minor ruler of one of India's principalities, and was raised as befitted his station—a prince of the royal house. His life was particularly sheltered until his early twenties, when, according to legend, he left the palace for the first time and experienced a sequence of dramatic encounters: an old man suffering from the ravages of age, an invalid bearing the marks of his disease, a corpse being carried to cremation, and a monk seeking his salvation. The future Buddha was overwhelmed with the realization that old age, sickness, and death were the common lot of mankind; and that while some, like the monk, were trying to come to grips with these great realities, he himself was as one living in a dream.

He had by this time been married and blessed with a son, but he nevertheless determined to leave home and loved ones, to work out his salvation. Thus Gautama set out on the path to Enlightenment by renouncing wealth and position, friendship and love, till he should come to understand what man lives by. This "Great Renunciation," as it is called, is the first step of the Buddhist pilgrimage. Painters and poets have often depicted Gautama's tender but unspoken farewell to his wife and son, as he took leave of them in the middle of the night, slipping away so as not to give them pain or weaken his own resolve. In later years he returned to them, and his son became one of his disciples. These human touches are characteristic and important.

Gautama began by studying philosophy, but found among the academicians no answer to his life problem. He then entered upon a regime of asceticism and self-mortification, in accord with a common practice of the period, and even brought himself near the point of death; but this took him no closer to a solution than his academic pursuits had done. At last, after many wanderings alone and with other seekers, worn in body and spirit but not in his indomitable will, he sat down under a tree—known thereafter as the *bo* tree, the tree of enlightenment—and resolved not to rise up from under it till he had solved the great problem. And so, at the age of thirty-five, he achieved Enlightenment. Rising up, he proceeded to the sacred city of Benares, and there in the park at Sarnath he preached his first sermon, setting in motion, as the Buddhists put it, the great "Wheel of the Law." Thereafter, for a half-century more, he traveled up and down the Indian subcontinent, sharing with his fellow men the great truths to which he had attained.

By about the third century B.C. Buddhism had captured the mind and heart of a good part of India, and in the reign of the great emperor Asoka it became the state religion. It remained a dominant force in Indian life for about a thousand years or so, then went into a decline and rapidly disappeared from India proper altogether, though much of its teaching was absorbed by the parent Hinduism. In this respect as in a number of others, the relation of the two religions parallels that of Christianity and Judaism—in both cases, a new religion emerging from the old to become an international faith, but without any significant hold in the land of its origin.

In the centuries following the death of the Buddha, the movement became crystallized around what Buddhism knows as the "Three Jewels": the Buddha himself; the *Sangha,* the church or community; and the *Dharma,* the teaching or doctrine, which is all that will concern us here. At the time of Asoka, the whole complex of ideas was given a written form, in a codification corresponding to the "Three Jewels," and known as the *Tripitaka,* or the "Three Baskets," which serves as the Buddhist Bible—though without revelation or divine sanction. It consists of the *Sutras,* containing the life and teaching of the Buddha himself; the *Vinaya,* rules of morality and monastic discipline; and the *Abhidharma,* the underlying metaphysics or philosophy. In addition, of course, a great body of other writings grew up, ranging from scholarly commentaries to legend and folklore. Of particular interest, I think, are the *Jataka Tales,* which recount the deeds of the Buddha in a series of previous animal incarnations, in which he already exhibited the character of the Compassionate One.

This sketch of the early development of the movement must suffice; what I want to discuss with you are the perspectives which make up the Buddhist Way.

To start with, it is of the utmost importance to recognize that, unlike the other religions with which we are acquainted, or even other religious philosophies, Buddhism in its pure form is completely naturalistic in outlook. I say "in its pure form" because, like every other religion, it has undergone many changes in the course of its history, and especially in its intitutionalization. Some of its later forms—for instance, in Thibetan Buddhism—have gone so far in the direction of occult metaphysics, if not downright superstition, as scarcely to be recognizable as the teaching of the Buddha. This is a transmogrification not unknown in certain aspects of Judaism and Christianity as well; I shall say no more about it. What interests us is the Buddhist philosophy of life, not its later elaboration into esoteric metaphysical doctrine. Some scholars have even suggested that we use, not the word "Buddhism," but "Shakaism," to convey the focus on the teaching of Sakyamuni. I hope I will make myself understood with the more familiar term.

Buddhism, then, is naturalistic, so much so that it lacks most of what we usually regard as essential to a religion. It has no God, no immortal soul, no creation, no last judgment. The Buddha himself is not a Savior, but a teacher, and more especially, an exemplar of the good life. He was born as a man and died as a man; everything about him is unequivocally within the domain of nature. Every human being, therefore, can aspire to imitate him wholly, and indeed, to become himself a buddha, an enlightened one. The whole drama of salvation, as Buddhism depicts it, takes place on the stage of this life, on this earth. "Within this very body," the Buddha said, "mortal as it is and only six feet in length, I do declare to you are the world and the origin of the world, and the ceasing of the world, and the path that leads to cessation." In this body, in this life, not in some transcendent realm in which we have a being after death. To be sure, statements of this kind can be given an esoteric interpretation: say, that the whole of creation is engendered by the ego. I prefer to take them more simply and straightforwardly, whatever historicity requires. I understand the Buddha to be saying that the world in which the problem of life is posed, and in which it finds its solution, is none other than the familiar everyday world in which this little body, mortal as it is, lives out its span.

With this outlook, Buddhism avoided, by and large, that conflict between religion and science, faith and reason, which played such an important part in the history of Western religious thought. The Buddha himself not only did not appeal to faith, but explicitly repudiated it as a basis for taking up his Way. Do not accept my teaching from reverence, he said, but only from what you find by testing it in your own life, as gold is tested by fire. By their fruits shall ye know them; and not just them, but the truths they live by. He called his teaching the "come and see" doctrine. What he preached was not salvation through his agency, but the path by which each man can reach salvation through his own effort. You are asked to believe nothing, and least of all in him, but only to try it for yourself, and find your own truth. Pascal propounded the argument for the religious life that it was a good wager: the stake in this life is so small compared to the infinite reward or punishment that may face us after death. The Buddha has no place even for this counsel of prudence, where faith is replaced by a calculated risk. No need to wait till after death to discover whether you have been deceived; this life itself will give up the secret. Satisfaction guaranteed or your money back, and you yourself are to be the judge.

In the West, we find a similar naturalism in such deeply moral philosophers as Epicurus and Spinoza. But for us, religion is so closely involved with the supernatural that naturalistic philosophies are automatically presumed to be irreligious, and therefore immoral. In the Talmud and later, "Epicurean" means not only an atheist, but one who repudiates the foundations of any moral or spiritual life; Spinoza was excommunicated, and his writings proscribed by Jew and Christian alike as subversive of both morality and religion. The Buddha was aware of the nihilism to which an undisciplined scepticism can lead. But he refused to ground values in any transcendent dogmatism. The latter was the position of the orthodox schools of Indian philosophy in his day, and the former the position of the materialists and sophists of the period. The Buddha tried to steer a course between them, as Kant did some two thousand years later on another basis. It is this aspect of Buddhism, among others, which is conveyed by the designation given to it by the Buddha of the Middle Way.

Unlike Kant, however, the Buddha was not limiting reason to make room for faith, any more than he set aside faith in order to defend the claims of reason. For him, both have a certain irrelevance, displacing energies that had better be devoted to coping directly with the problem that life sets before us. His orientation is neither idealist nor empiricist, but pragmatic. When you are caught in a burning building, that is no time to discuss the nature of fire, says the Buddha; and if you have been shot by an arrow, no use to inquire into the name of the archer. You must escape from the flames, extract the arrow, heal the wound.

Philosophy for the Buddha is nothing if not practical, as Epictetus also taught. What good does it do to discourse learnedly on the nature of the Good if there is no good in what you do with your own life? And what is a man to make of a theory of truth if there is no truth in him? But the Buddha is not merely a moralist, replacing analysis by exhortation, and understanding by high resolve. Very much the contrary. His point is only that metaphysical speculation is futile if it does not bear on the problems with which experience confronts us. Some of his remarks in this connection have a curiously positivistic ring: "Do not try to measure the immeasurable with words, nor with the plummet of thought to sound the unfathomable: he who asks is deluded, and he who answers is deluded." This strain of Buddhist thought becomes central in Zen, as I shall point out in the last lecture.

Now naturalism is almost always humanistic; this is true, at any rate, of the Buddhist outlook. Buddhism is one of those philosophies that is centered on man, as was the philosophy of Socrates, of the post-Renaissance humanists, or of the contemporary existentialists.

The world presents itself to Buddhist reflection as the scene of human endeavor; the significance that attaches to things derives from the meaning of human life. The problem with which the world confronts the inquiring mind is not a cosmological one but a moral one: not, what is the world made of, but what is man to make of his life in the world—this is the question. Although the Buddhist is interested in knowledge and understanding—indeed, in this above all—what he wants to understand is man, and what he seeks knowledge of is how to live so as to achieve the supreme value that life affords.

Buddhist humanism sets man even above the gods, but without a trace of the impiety of worshiping man as God. To attain Nirvana, the Buddha taught, even the gods must first be incarnated as human beings. The road to heaven leads inescapably through this earth. In Christianity, too, God becomes man, but as a descent into the flesh. In Buddhism, it is the condition of man that not only poses the problem in its sharpest form, but also provides the terms for its solution. Basically, Buddhism is atheistic, not as a matter of positive doctrine, but in the spirit of the French astronomer who, questioned by Napoleon as to the absence of any mention of God in his system of celestial mechanics, replied simply, "I have no need of that hypothesis." Man is the master of his own fate—or can be, if he chooses to be. The Buddha, I think, might very well have endorsed the declaration of Nietzsche twenty-five centuries after him that the gods are dead. We ourselves must achieve what theists imagine to be already provided for us. The gods, if gods there be, cannot lift us to their side; we must make the painful climb ourselves.

But those who have gone before might guide us on our way, spur our efforts, and keep up our courage. When orthodox Jews complete their annual public reading of the Torah, it is the custom to proclaim, "Be strong, and let us strengthen one another!" A Buddhist, I think, would find this congenial to his own outlook. But where the Jew strengthens himself for the arduous task of living by his Torah and so walking with God, in Buddhism religion turns altogether from the worship of God to the service of man. From the standpoint of our

Western tradition, we are tempted to argue that it is all morality and no religion. This is only to say all over again that it is naturalistic and humanistic.

But the service of man is a matter of your own moral achievement; you cannot achieve it for another. In the presence of the great realities we stand alone. Buddhism emphasizes self-reliance and self-responsibility to a degree that has no parallel in the theistic or prophetic religions. "Man is born alone, lives alone and dies alone," the Buddha says, "and it is he alone who can blaze the trail which leads him to Nirvana. . . . The Buddha can only show you the way: it is for you yourself to walk upon it." In particular, rites of purification and penance, atonement and forgiveness have no place in his teaching. "By one's self the evil is done, by one's self one suffers; by one's self evil is left undone, by one's self one is purified. The pure and the impure stand and fall by themselves, no one can purify another." This is a recurrent theme in the Buddha's discourses and sermons; it is contained among the last of the injunctions which the Buddha gave his disciples from his deathbed: "Be lamps unto yourselves; be a refuge to yourselves; hold fast to the truth as to a lamp; hold fast as a refuge to the truth; look not for refuge to anyone beside yourselves." Not even to Gautama the Buddha.

It is time now to ask, what is this problem that each man faces alone, and for which the Buddha points the way to a solution? In particular, how is it to be formulated in naturalistic terms? The orthodox Indian teaching avails itself of the notion of metaphysical ignorance, avidya, by which we are condemned to live in the illusions of maya, in which we are cut off from others and set over against a hostile world, while the reality—self and all—is only Brahman. But all this is completely foreign to the Buddhist outlook. The arrow with which we have been pierced is real enough, and the wound is no illusion. Something is really wrong with the way in which we live, and what must be changed is not in abstract understanding but in concrete action.

The Buddhist teaching is formulated in four theses known traditionally as the Four Noble Truths, and the first of them specifies the problem of life. It is put in terms of the key concept of *dukkha,* translated usually (and misleadingly, as I shall suggest in a moment) as pain, sorrow, or suffering. This, then, is "the Noble Truth concerning dukkha: Birth is attended with dukkha, decay is dukkha, disease is dukkha, death is dukkha. Union with the unpleasant is dukkha, dukkha is separation from the pleasant; and any craving that is unsatisfied is dukkha. In brief, bodily conditions which spring from attachment are dukkha."

Now if "dukkha" is to be understood literally as pain, the First Noble Truth is at best only a half-truth. For there is obviously pleasure in life as well as pain: there is growth as well as decay, health as well as disease, life as well as death; there is union with the pleasant and separation from the unpleasant; and some cravings *are* satisfied. I believe that "dukkha" means something else. It is the element of imperfection, of incompleteness that life always exhibits. Nothing is ever wholly satisfying, nothing in the world ever surrenders unconditionally to the human will. So much of experience is trivial if not downright meaningless; and every fulfillment is tied to conditions and consequences that have no value in themselves. Dukkha is not merely the intermittent frustration of desire, but a quality permeating experience even for the most fortunate of us. The Buddha looks out on the world, and unlike the God of Genesis, does not see that it is good. It is all very well in its way, to be sure; but it was not made for man, and we cannot blot out the sense of our alienation. It is this sense that the existentialists call "anguish," Thoreau calls "quiet desperation" and the Buddha "dukkha."

If any object of desire were complete and perfect, and made wholly ours, it could not remain as it is, and must inevitably remove itself from our possession. For all things are in time, and so subject to change and decay. This is one of the cardinal principles of Buddhism—*anitya,* becoming, impermanence, change. One of the fruitful classifications of philosophies is—to use names important in the Western tradition—into those which follow Parmenides and those which follow Heraclitus: the one localizing reality in something fixed and unchanging, and the other in the ceaseless flow of events, one in substances and the other in processes, one in eternity and the other in time—in a word, one in being and the other in becoming. And if a man takes time seriously—if all that is is other than it was and will be still different again—for such a man the future must inevitably be a ground of anxiety, as the past is a ground of guilt, and there is no peace for him in the living present. And this is dukkha.

Buddhism, like most Western empiricism, does not acknowledge any fixed substances underlying the changing attributes of things. One attribute perishes and another comes to birth, only in its turn to fade into nothingness. The fixities by which we identify a thing as being the particular individual that it is are only relative fixities; they are not permanent but only persistent, lasting just long enough to preserve identity, and continuously giving way to other individuations. It is this confusion between permanence and persistence which vitiates Kant's argument for the existence of substance, that otherwise we could not say that anything changes but only that one thing is replaced by another. Buddhism repudiates not only substance, but also unchanging forms or "universals" as they are known in our tradition, what Whitehead revealingly calls "eternal objects." There are no fixed characters which can be assumed from time to time by the particular things that come and go, like a rack of pigeonholes in a post office into which envelopes are daily placed and removed. In fact, the envelopes are simply stacked into piles, and when the envelopes are removed the piles also disappear to be formed anew with each day's delivery. The characters of things also flow, and all is anitya.

There have been many Heraclitean philosophies which accept anitya, but not the implied dukkha. This is true of the philosophies of evolution or progress and of the various historicisms so characteristic of Western thought in the nineteenth century. In their perspectives, change is welcomed as though it is always a promise of fulfillment coming ever nearer. But for Buddhism, the ceaseless change which is human life carries no guarantees with it. There is no purpose already built into it, no meaning embedded in the unfolding process itself. The fact of change does not provide a solution but sets the conditions of the problem. The dukkha is there to be overcome, and it can be overcome only through human effort.

In the orthodox Indian philosophy, the only effort called for is one of understanding, realizing that beneath the ceaseless shadow-play of maya is the unchanging reality of Brahman, and that this is nothing other than the substance of our own true Self, the Atman. This position is explicitly rejected in Buddhism in its doctrine of *anatma,* no-self—that is, no enduring, substantial self—nothing within the self beyond and beneath those changing appearances which constitute our own experience of the self. The Buddha, twenty-five centuries ago, developed a phenomenalistic psychology which strikingly anticipates the line of thought about the self which we find today in Bertrand Russell, in the last century in William James, or in the century before that, in David Hume, the father of modern empiricism. "For my part,"—this is Hume speaking, but the Buddha might very well have spoken to the same effect—"For my part, when I enter most intimately into what I call *myself,* I always stumble on some particular perception or other, of heat or cold, light or shade, love or hatred, pain or pleasure. I never can catch myself at any time without a perception and never can observe anything but the perception. . . . What we call mind is nothing but a heap or bundle of different perceptions united together by certain relations."

Buddha expresses this view with metaphors characteristic of his own time and place. The notion of a substantial self providing an enduring basis for self-identity is an illusion. The self is like a banyan tree, which grows, not out of a central trunk, but by dropping rootlets from its branches; these take hold in the soil and become themselves the stems from which new branches spread out; the tree may cover hundreds of square yards, but nowhere in the whole thicket is there such a thing as the trunk of the banyan. And the mind of man, Buddha continues, is rather like a monkey swinging in the thicket from branch to branch, endlessly chattering. The self, in short, is subject to anitya as is all else; there is no more permanence within than in the world without.

This has an important consequence for the Buddhist conception of rebirth. For what is it that is born again? There is no self or soul which moves from one life to another, as a man might pack his belongings, leave his native village, and make a new home elsewhere. Man's life is like a flame. We speak of it as though it were an enduring entity, but in fact there is nothing there at all which endures. There is only a continuous process, in which the stuff of the candle ceaselessly becomes the heat and light and smoke of the flame, and only the flame itself persists. When the candle begins to gutter and die down, we light a fresh candle from it. One flame goes out and another begins to burn, and only the flame has passed from candle to candle, which is to say that nothing at all has passed between them, but a process continues. There is no transmigration, no soul moving from place to place, no self which may find itself homeless in the dark with which life is ringed round. There is only a continuous passing along the way, in accord with the workings of each man's karma.

Buddhism takes karma even more seriously, if possible, than do the orthodox Indian thinkers. For it generalizes the law of karma into a principle of universal causality. We may note that such a conception was not very important in Western thought till, say, the end of the eighteenth century; and even then, causality was thought not to apply strictly in the biological sphere, or, at the very least, in the sphere of human behavior. But for the Buddha, the law of causality is the second of the Four Noble Truths: "I will teach you the dharma: that being present, this becomes; from the arising of that, this arises. That being absent, this does not become; from the cessation of that, this ceases." Everything happens as it does in accord with a causal principle. If there is dukkha in human life, something must cause it, and if this cause were removed its effect also would disappear.

The causal relation is not the outer mark of an inner necessity.

There is no mysterious force—as it were, a promulgation by the Creator—impelling nature to obedience. We say a planet moves along its orbit and imagine that the orbit is a path spread across the heavens, while something forces the planet along the path. But the orbit is nothing other than the place where the planet moves. A man lives by the sword, and we imagine that some superhuman agency condemns him to die by the sword; but such a death is nothing other than the last act of a life of violence. The relation between cause and effect is only that of the earlier to the later phases of a single continuous process. The Buddha's conception of causality, like that of the self, is again remarkably like that at which David Hume arrived some millenia after him. In the core of his teaching, the Buddha is an empiricist, though it does not lead him to scepticism: what man is confronted with in experience is to be explained by experience itself.

I think this is the fundamental break between the Buddha and orthodox Hinduism. For the orthodox thinkers, the ultimate reality is substance without causality—Atman or Brahman. There is no causality because there is no change, no process, and indeed, no differentiable parts that can stand in a causal or any other relation. The Buddha's metaphysics is just the reverse: causality without substance. The world process is a network of causal relationships, but there are no things that enter into these relations. The river flows in an unbroken stream, while ripples and eddies form on its surface and vanish once more. Thus Hindu philosophy turns on the grasp of meanings—initially, those of the Vedas, and ultimately, of the symbols of reality which make up the world of maya. Buddhism turns on the grasp of causal relations, initially, in the world process, and ultimately, in the life of man.

For the corollary of the Second Noble Truth, the principle of causality, is that the evil in man's life is man-made and therefore eradicable. There is no such thing as original sin, no innate depravity, no one is foreordained to be damned. If life leaves something to be desired (a misleading expression, as we shall see), if, that is, life is dukkha, there is a cause which has brought about this effect. The solution to the problem of life lies in identifying and removing this cause. Transcendent philosophies in effect either deny the reality of the problem or else content themselves with an unreal solution in metaphysical fantasy. What the Hindus have done with their monistic metaphysics we in the West have done with our monotheistic theology. What they do by identification with Brahman we do with atonement, to be restored to the fellowship of God. But in Buddhism there is no forgiveness, first because there is no one who can forgive, and second because the transgression itself cannot be redeemed. The Buddha, I think, would have endorsed the words which Nietzsche puts into the mouth of Zarathustra, if memory serves: "The consequences of our actions seize us by the forelock indifferent to the fact that we have in the meantime reformed." Every cause has its effects, and they are not to be denied; our recourse is only to address ourselves to the cause, and remove it.

And we *can* remove it: the working of causality does not set limits to human freedom, but on the contrary gives his freedom a purchase on reality. That man is free does not mean that he stands outside the causal network, but that the causes working on him work *through* him, that is, through his knowledge of causes and effects. For the Buddha, as for the Stoics and Spinoza, freedom is essentially the recognition of necessity. No one would be released from a contract on the ground that it was not freely entered upon, if he appealed only to the compulsion of causal necessity: "With my heredity and environment I could do no other." The question is only if he was in possession of his faculties, understood what he was committing himself to, and so on. For in that case the act was free, and, in the plain sense of the words, he could have done otherwise had he chosen to. The question for the Buddha is, How should a man choose to live so as to free himself from dukkha? And this in turn raises the question, Of what cause is dukkha the effect?

The Buddha's answer shares not only the conception of freedom to be found in the Stoics and Spinoza, but also their conception of the source of evil in human life. It is passion, desire, attachment, emotional involvement with things. The Buddhist term is *tanha* or *drsta,* from which we get our word "thirst." If we did not desire, we could not be frustrated; if we felt no attachment, we could not be anxious; if we were not involved with things, their transience or imperfection could not touch us. This, then, is the third of the Four Noble Truths: "Now this is the noble truth concerning the destruction of dukkha: It is the destruction, in which no passion remains, of this very thirst; it is the laying aside of, the being free from, the dwelling no longer upon this thirst."

But the very effort to lay aside thirst may only intensify it as we dwell upon it. Characteristically, we of the West have usually replaced our thirst for the things of this world by an even stronger thirst for the things of another world, freed ourselves from the earthly kingdom only by a subjection to the kingdom of heaven. But he that would find his life must be prepared to lose it. The attachment to Nirvana is still an attachment, and life still remains dukkha. The pursuit of happiness requires that we turn our back on it—happiness, says Nietzsche, is a woman. If happiness does come it is always as a by-product, never the end product; and when we say to ourselves "I'll enjoy it if it kills me!" it usually does. Only those are freed of their thirsts who renounce the thirst for that freedom. So the Buddha counsels, abandon even the good, to say nothing of the evil. "He who has reached the other shore has no use for rafts."

There is a sutra describing a scene at the Buddha's deathbed which I find very moving—not being a Buddhist I can indulge an all-too-human feeling. Among the disciples of the Buddha was an acknowledged favorite, Ananda; if the Buddha could be said to have had attachments, I suppose he was attached to this disciple. As the Buddha lay dying, Ananda stood near him with tears streaming down his face. And the Buddha said, "After all that I have taught you, how can you still feel grief? Is it so hard, then, for a man to get rid of all suffering?" There is another story about an early Christian —Origen, I believe it was—who was discussing his faith with a Stoic, and said to him, "My Lord, when He died, asked forgiveness for those who killed Him; does your faith have anything so noble to show?" To which the Stoic replied, "Mine did what was still nobler; he kept silent." Buddha, like Jesus, is the compassionate one; but like the Stoic, he would root out grief and joy alike, keeping his face steadfast on a world for which no thirst remains.

Nothing could be more unjust, however, than to interpret Buddhism as a counsel of despair. It is tempting to suppose that to end suffering we need only put an end to life itself. The Stoics, as you know, did urge that "the door is always open"; we cannot complain at life's poor show if we are at liberty to leave when we choose. The Stoics' attitude toward suicide is related by many people to the hopelessness of their times; and a similar inference is drawn with regard to Buddhist teaching. But Buddhism repudiates suicide. It is not a question here of the doctrine of rebirth, so that the thought of something after death must give us pause. The point is that suicide does not overcome the thirst but gives way to it. It is not a mark of detachment, but a supreme gesture of involvement with things, as in the case of hara-kiri committed to save face. Or else, it confuses detachment from life with attachment to death, the renunciation of self with self-destruction.

It is this renunciation in which freeing ourselves from thirst, and so from dukkha, essentially consists. More accurately, it is a renunciation, not of the self, but of the illusion of self, for, as we have seen, there *is* no self to which an enlightened one can be attached. Human bondage, as Spinoza put it, is a bondage to ignorance, and through ignorance a subjection to desire and hate. Without the self, there is no soil in which the passions can find root; in the illusion of self, we ask of everything, "What's in it for me?" and no answer can satisfy us. In his so-called "Fire Sermon" the Buddha declares: "The fire of life must be put out. For everything in the world is on fire with the fire of desire, the fire of hate, and the fire of illusion. Care, lamentation, sorrow, and despair are so many flames. . . . Illusion devours you like a flame."

The illusion is that it is what lies outside us that brings us happiness, and we are concerned lest it be taken from us. The truth is that it is just this concern which is the root of the evil, and that lies wholly within. " 'These sons belong to me, and this wealth belongs to me,' with such thoughts a fool is tormented," the Buddha says. "He himself does not belong to himself; how much less his sons and wealth!" Dukkha can be overcome only by self-possession; and as Nietzsche remarked, he who possesses little, by so much the less is he possessed. The Buddha possesses nothing, thirsts for nothing. In the classic iconography his symbol is the lotus, a flower which springs from the filthiest waters; but it floats on the surface and is never wetted by them; it remains untouched, cool and self-contained, complete and perfect, a jewel floating upon the waters.

This, then, is the Buddhist diagnosis of the human condition, and the prescription follows at once. It is a life of detachment, renunciation of the self with its passions, desire and hate, and the words and deeds by which they are expressed. This is the fourth of the Four Noble Truths, the way to the destruction of dukkha by what Buddhists call "the Eightfold Noble Path": right views, right aspirations, right speech, right conduct, a right livelihood, and right efforts, right thoughts, and right contemplation. In the concrete, the Eightfold Noble Path does not differ markedly from the morality enjoined in all the world's major religious philosophies. It is the Middle Way, between sensualism and asceticism, between indulgence of the self and its mortification; for both mark attachment to an illusion, and only the truth can make man free.

The significance of this moral teaching can best be seen against the background of the ritualism to which the Brahmanic religion of the period had decayed. "Reading the Vedas," the Buddha declares, "making offerings to priests or sacrifices to the gods, self-mortification and penances performed for the sake of immortality, these do not cleanse the man who is not free from delusions. Anger, bigotry, deception, self-seeking—these constitute uncleanliness!" How reminiscent this is of Isaiah: "To what purpose is the multitude of your sacrifices unto me? . . . Wash you, make you clean; . . . seek judgment, relieve the oppressed, judge the fatherless, plead for the widow." Like the Hebrew prophets, the Buddha seeks to restore the moral content of the religious life. Like them, too, he finds it in selflessness, and the rooting out of anger and hate. But unlike them, and in agreement with Spinoza, he does not preach the replacement of hate by love, but the replacement of both love and hate by understanding.

Such a path is not an easy one to follow, and the Buddha is under no illusions as to its difficulty. The main thing is to set out and to walk resolutely upon it. The determination to go forward, turning neither to the left nor to the right, is itself the progress along life's way. In spiritual matters, as many mystics have taught, the pure intention is already the deed. "Earnestness is the path of Nirvana, thoughtlessness the path of death. Those who are in earnest do not die, those who are thoughtless are as if dead already." This is the point of the very last words spoken by the Buddha: "Work out your salvation with diligence."

This, then, is the teaching of Buddhism; taken in its entirety, it makes up what is called the Dharma. This word, of central importance in Buddhism, derives from a root meaning to hold or to bear, and so refers most directly to what is held to, the standards or ideals to which we are devoted. It comes to mean the ideal as expressed in words, and so the teaching or doctrine as set forth for those who wish to learn it. Thence it becomes the system of rules, the moral code, which defines the ideal to be realized in human life. As such, it is equated with truth, as this occurs in Judaeo-Christian thought, or with reason, in the role given it by the Greeks. Finally, "dharma" stands for the ideal as realized, for reality itself, therefore, the world process as it presents itself to the enlightened mind.

Buddhism starts with naturalistic and humanistic premises and stays with them to its conclusion. In its original form (as contrasted here with Zen), it is remarkably intellectualistic in its outlook. Unlike so many other religious philosophies, Buddhism does not seek ecstasy but insight. The Buddha is the Enlightened One; the *bo* tree is none other than the Tree of Knowledge. The Buddha is the Tathagata; this word means suchness, being like this, the way things are. The Tathagata is one who sees reality as it is, who sees himself as he is. An Enlightened One is he who lives a life grounded on a thorough understanding of human nature and of the broader nature of which man is an inseparable part. The Buddha was not a pessimist but a realist, and his teaching is the counterpart in Asian thought of the realism to which we have come only in the twentieth century, with Freud.

Like Freud, too, and Spinoza as well, the Buddha proceeds from the axiom that to understand is to transcend. It is not a matter of forgiving what we have understood. For the Buddha, when true understanding has been achieved there is no longer anything to forgive: I have not been touched, and the injury is as much an illusion as is the self. Ignorance and passion, illusion and attachment —these are only the theoretical and practical aspects of one and the same reality. It is easy to see why Buddhism is not enmeshed in the conflict of faith and reason so important in the history of the Western religions. The truth that makes man free is a human truth, a truth about the human condition, and to be attained in the human state.

There is a legend which beautifully illustrates the realism of the Buddha's teaching. A woman had an only son whom she loved, and he died. Overwhelmed with grief, she sought out one holy man after another to restore her son to life, and came at last to the Buddha. "Indeed, I will help you," he said. "Bring to me a handful of mustard seed from a household in which no one has died, neither father nor mother, neither son nor daughter, nor brother nor sister, nor yet servant nor friend." Throughout the countryside the bereaved woman went, from house to house, and though many offered her mustard seed, never was there a house in which no one had died. She came back to the Buddha weeping at her failure to find the seed, and he said to her, "To every house death has come, and is yours alone to be free of it? Be comforted; go now, and bury your son."

Suppose, now, that the Compassionate One had restored her son to life; would it have been in fact an act of compassion? Would she not have had to bear her grief yet once more, or leave her son an orphan with his grief? There is no escaping anitya and karma; all is transient and governed by causes. But we *can* escape from dukkha, from the illusion of self and its possessions, from thirst and attachment. The way to live is the way that leads to the conquest of self and its desires; all else perpetuates illusion. Freud is perhaps more tolerant of self-deception than is the Buddha, for he acknowledges that a touch of fantasy may be necessary to make life bearable. The Buddha sits unmoved looking out on life as it is.

The Enlightened One does not deceive himself for he is freed of self. Buddhism, therefore, does not enjoin altruism but selflessness; and certainly not sentimentality, but action rooted in understanding. One whose conduct is so determined is known in Buddhism as an *arhat,* the closest equivalent, I suppose, to what we call a saint. The word means literally a worthy one, one who has slain the enemy—the enemy, that is, of peace and freedom: desire, attachment, illusion. Now selflessness by no means implies indifference to the sufferings of others; the arhat is detached but not callous. He has emptied himself of passion and replaced it with compassion, not only for other men, but for all sentient beings. Nothing touches him, not because his self has contracted to a dimensionless point, but because it extends through all that lives and suffers.

In his specific moral teaching, the Buddha comes very close to Jesus: "By the practice of lovingkindness I have attained liberation of heart," and again, "Whoever would nurse me, let him nurse the sick." This is surely not so very different from Jesus' words, "Inasmuch as you have done it unto one of the least of these my brothers you have done it unto me." And the Christian injunction, "Love those that hate you" is paralleled by: "Hatred does not cease by hatred at any time; hatred ceases by love," or better, "Let a man overcome anger by love, let him overcome evil by good; let him overcome the greedy by liberality, the liar by truth." The Sermon at Benares is some five centuries and five thousand miles from the Sermon on the Mount, yet not so very far away after all.

The historical setting in which Buddhism appeared gives particular relevance to its moral teaching with regard to caste. "Go into all lands and preach this gospel," the Buddha declares. "Tell them that the poor and the lowly, the rich and the high, are all one, and that all castes unite in this religion as do the rivers in the sea." Beneath the differences that divide one man from another is a common humanity, with which alone the deepest questions in life are concerned. Yet it would not be quite right to interpret Buddhism as having initiated a movement of social reform along the lines which run in the West from the ancient Hebrew prophets to contemporary Christian socialism. The Buddha made no attempt to transform the social structure of Indian society. What he was rebelling against was the Brahmanic monopoly of religious rites, their insistence on their own indispensability. The consolations of religion, the Buddha urged, are offered equally to all men; for each the door is open to his own salvation.

I think, however, that Buddhism does face the serious problem of how to cultivate detachment without weakening the impulse to improve man's lot, whether in society or against the forces of nature. It is all very well to preach equality in matters of the spirit; but for my part, I would not wish to minimize in the slightest the moral obligation to institute equalities of a more mundane kind. Similarly, I find myself very much drawn to the standpoint of the Buddha, the Stoics, and Spinoza that nothing outside me can touch me, and only I can wrong myself; but I do not want to forget for one moment man's inhumanity to other men. I cannot deprive another man of his life, his liberty, or his pursuit of happiness, then seek to silence him by counseling him to give up his attachment to these things. Buddhism tells me that in doing so I damn myself; but the fact remains that I am also wronging another. I do not say that this is a fatal objection to the Buddhist philosophy, but it is at least what is usually called "a serious difficulty."

And now, to what does the Buddhist pilgrimage lead? What is the outcome of the understanding of the Noble Truths of dukkha and karma, of detachment and the Eightfold Path, of the earnest endeavor and diligence in the Middle Way? It is the achievement of *Nirvana*. The literal meaning of the word is "blown out," as might be said of a candle. It is the extinction of the fires of desire and hate, of the flame in which there flickers the illusion of self.

Negatively, therefore, Nirvana is the destruction of attachment and ignorance, the freeing oneself from dukkha. In positive terms, it is the attainment of detachment and enlightenment, in a life filled with compassion; it is, we might say, the peace that passes understanding.

The important thing is that Nirvana is in no sense a heaven with which the faithful are rewarded by a divine judge, nor something reserved for a life after death. It is a state of being to which a man can attain in this life, on this earth. "Those whose mind is well grounded in knowledge," the Buddha says, "who, without clinging to anything, rejoice in freedom from attachment, whose appetites have been conquered, and who are full of light, they are free even in this world." As for the immortality which in the Western religions is so closely tied up with our ideas of salvation and the like, in Buddhism it lies only in the achievement of character and the perpetuation of its moral influence. As the Buddha lay dying, he said to his disciples, "Do not weep, saying 'Our teacher has passed away and we have no one to follow.' What I have taught will be your teacher after my departure. If you adhere to it and practice it uninterruptedly, is it not the same as if my body remained here forever?" One who is fully enlightened, who has entered into Nirvana, has not achieved personal immortality, but lives forever in a selfless present. The Buddha has no longer a name, no identity; he has become a nobody, just a man—Tathagatha.

Before concluding, I want to say something about the development of the Buddha's thought in the institutionalized religion. The early doctrine, as I have pointed out, was independent of any theistic assumptions, if it was not, indeed, explicitly atheistic. But some time after the death of the Buddha, his teaching was absorbed into the background of the older religious perspectives, and he himself was in effect deified. Today when we think of Buddhism, there probably comes to mind a recollection of an image of the Buddha and worship being accorded it. But for some centuries, although there was a considerable development of Buddhist art, the image of the Buddha himself never figured in it. He was represented only by what iconologists call his "traces"—footprints, an empty chair, a place where he was or might be expected to be, but never the Buddha himself. And although the emperor Asoka caused to be carved in stone the Buddha's teaching, he did not mention the name of the Buddha. As time went on, however, the Buddha became a deity, and even his name entered into various sacred and quasi-magical formulas.

In the course of many centuries, the religion developed institutions not unlike those familiar to us in other faiths. Two branches of the religion are to be distinguished from one another. The older, flourishing in Ceylon, Thailand, Burma and elsewhere in Southeast Asia is known as *Theravada* Buddhism—literally, the doctrine of the elders. In the Far East, the prevailing form of Buddhism is known as *Mahayana*—literally, the greater vehicle, the Theravada being referred to as *Hinayana* or the lesser vehicle. The word "vehicle" has the sense of a course or way, and specifically, a way of life—as contrasted, for instance, with a mere darshana, as the Indians term it, an outlook or perspective rather than a principle of action.

Characteristic of Mahayana Buddhism is an emphasis on a certain ideal which, in all fairness, also plays some part in Theravada. It is that of the *Bodhisattva:* one who has virtually attained complete enlightenment, but who refuses to enter into Nirvana so long as other sentient beings are still suffering. He has, as it were, completed all the requirements for the degree, but instead of graduating prefers to remain to help his fellow students. When the Buddha was sitting under the *bo* tree, Mara, the Prince of Darkness, visited him with many temptations, sending his seductive daughters, for instance, to lead the Buddha away from detachment. And the last and greatest of the temptations was this, that having attained Nirvana, he leave this life altogether. But the Buddha rose up from under the *bo* tree and devoted many years to helping others find the way and walk upon it to attain their own salvation.

In spite of this social element in Mahayana thought, however, it is the Theravada which is particularly concerned with what we would regard as moral action in society—care for the sick, the widow and orphan, and so on—while Mahayana philosophy turns rather in the direction of metaphysical speculation. Faith and a certain mysticism become more and more important as contrasted with the role of understanding and reason in the older teaching. Ideas are developed reminiscent in many ways of such Western streams of thought as neo-Platonism. Like the *logos* of the neo-Platonists, the Word which is bodied forth in things, *dharma* is taken in Mahayana thought to be itself the ultimate reality, the Buddha-nature lying at the heart of all existence.

The whole development reaches its culmination in the fascinating and somewhat bewildering concept of *Sunyata,* usually translated as Nothingness or the Void. It is an idea to be found in mystic speculation the world over—not sheer emptiness, but that indescribable Void which the mystic experiences as fullness of being. Zen Buddhism, to which I turn shortly, is a sect of Mahayana, and were Zen to indulge in speculation, Sunyata would be central to it. I know of no better expression of this idea of Nothingness than in a haikku composed in the spirit of this metaphysics:

> My hut in the spring:
> True, there is nothing in it . . .
> There is everything!

QUESTIONS

Does Buddhism allow for freedom of the will?

BUDDHISM BELIEVES THAT MAN IS (OR CAN BE) FREE; but it does not believe in freedom of the will. For the latter phrase implies the existence of something which stands outside the causal sequence that makes up the world process; the former has nothing to do with whether there are causes of action, but rather with the content or meaning of action. Let me explain this a bit further.

The metaphysical problem of free will, which has drawn so much attention in Western philosophy, would have been dismissed by

Buddha, I think, as irrelevant to his practical concern. No dialectical proof or refutation of the idea of free will can have any bearing on the actual conduct of life. Suppose a man were convinced that he had no free will, convinced, that is, that he must necessarily do whatever it is that he is going to do; he still faces the task of coming to a decision. For until he has made the decision, his determinist philosophy won't tell him what action it is that is necessary. Countrariwise, a man who is convinced that he does have free will must still consider carefully all the forces working on him to shape his decision. For without such consideration he would not in fact be using his supposed free will, but defaulting to necessity.

The point is that in either case we must distinguish between deliberate choice and mere whim or caprice; between an informed decision and one springing from ignorance and error; between action following reflection on available alternatives and their conditions and consequences, and action into which we are plunged by overpowering emotion or thoughtless routine. All these distinctions remain in force whether there is such a thing as free will or not. A man who acts in the first way is a free man, and otherwise not. Whether he is at liberty to act as he freely decides to act is of course another question. He may be in chains and still free, or quite at liberty and yet in bondage to his own slavishness. This line of thought has been developed at some length by Epictetus, Spinoza, and Dewey among Western philosophers. It is, in my opinion, the standpoint also taken up by the Buddha. The important thing, of course, is not to satisfy ourselves that, being human, we are indeed free; the thing is to become free men, and that transpires only as we use what freedom we have to achieve an ever greater emancipation from our human bondage.

How can a Buddhist love others yet renounce desire?

Buddhism seems to be asking us to do two very different things at the same time. On the one hand, we are to abandon our emotional investments, to detach ourselves, to renounce self. On the other hand, we are to be compassionate and devote ourselves to the service of others. The Eightfold Noble Path distinguishes at every point between what is right and what is not right, and the Buddhist must certainly care whether he chooses the one or the other. Yet how can he care, while recognizing that caring itself is one of those flames which is to be distinguished? This is the general form of the problem; and let me say at once that I think it does pose difficulties. But a solution is not impossible.

Consider the difference between a doctor's concern for the health of his patient, and the concern of someone emotionally involved with the patient. The mother loves the child as being just the person he is, related to her in just that way; for the doctor, the child is one patient among numberless others, distinguished essentially only by his medical condition. But just because the mother is so deeply attached, it is likely that her conduct will serve to gratify her own intense feeling rather than to further the well-being of her loved one. (Doctors, in fact, habitually do not treat the members of their own family.) The work of the healer is surely compassionate, and just for that reason requires detachment.

In short, Buddhism does not wish to blur the distinction between love and hate, or between right and wrong, but wants only to objectify it. What it repudiates is that concern for others—indeed, for the self as well—which is wholly a matter of subjective feeling rather than of objective understanding. In its most obvious form, this is what we know as sentimentality. "O, it breaks my heart—I must do something about it!" But what does it matter that *your* heart is breaking? What room is there for love in this illusion of self? It is not compassion for others that is acting in you, but your own passion, directed inevitably to your own gratification and plunging you inevitably into dukkha. Suffering, whether your own or another's, can be overcome only through selflessness. The Buddhist ideal of the wise man, the sage, is of one who is never overwhelmed by his feelings, yet never acts unfeelingly. This is what Buddhism calls the Middle Way—between heartlessness and the bleeding heart. There is something godlike in this detached compassion; whether it answers fully to the god in man, I cannot say.

How can Buddhist detachment result in action to achieve social justice?

THIS QUESTION IS REALLY A SPECIAL CASE of the preceding one; I think it is sufficiently important to be separately stated, but I'm afraid I cannot give it a separate answer.

The difference between Hinayana and Mahayana Buddhism is of particular relevance here. Mahayana tends toward a kind of monasticism, which has the effect of a withdrawal from political and social problems. I am aware that Mahayanists themselves would argue this point; nevertheless, such is my impression. In Hinayana Buddhism, on the other hand, there is much more worldliness, in the sense, that is, of adaptation to the conditions of life in society rather than in the monastery. The monastery itself is recognized as a social institution, having its own functions to perform for the society—for instance, as a center of Buddhist learning. Compassion must express itself in action, and under the conditions of modern life, at any rate, action cannot be effective save as it works through and is directed toward various social agencies, like the family and the state.

The question is whether such action is compatible with detachment. But isn't this attitude what we ourselves ask of our political leaders? We want them to rise above partisanship and to serve selflessly; this is what we call statesmanship. The statesman is above the struggle, not as being indifferent to the conflicting values and interests, but as viewing them all with objectivity and understanding. To be detached, to renounce the self and its desires as Buddhism urges, means to live our lives without partisanship. The Bodhisattva is, as it were, a statesman of the spirit; and to enter Nirvana means to be done with politics forever.

Did Buddhism in its time do for the individual what we do today by psychoanalysis?

THE ANSWER IS "No," but it needs a footnote.

The institutions of every culture, including our own, simultaneously perform a variety of functions. An institution identified as religious may nevertheless also be performing some of the functions of educational institutions, economic ones, social, military, and medical too. I have no doubt that the Buddha and those associated with him, like many clergymen today, have at various times so related to others, in their compassion for human suffering, as to contribute toward the alleviation at least, if not the cure, of mental illness. But I think it of cardinal importance not to confuse these various functions. A church which is providing a meeting place for young people is not necessarily thereby serving a spiritual end, however important that service may be from a moral or social point of view. The consolation of faith may have its own value, but it is not lightly to be identified with the value of therapy for psychopathic grief.

The point is that the problem of the philosopher, and especially of the religious philosopher, is an existential one, while that of the therapist is a purely historical one. That is to say, the former is a problem in which a human being is involved by the sheer fact of his humanity, quite apart from the particularities of his individual circumstances. It has nothing to do with how he was toilet-trained, whether he was bottle-fed, how his parents treated him, his early sexual experiences, or anything of that kind. The existential perplexity will express itself in these and other areas of his life, for he does not cease to be human in becoming a particular personality. But it is not dependent on these particularities.

The problem for therapy is essentially different. Therapy is concerned with illness, and I cannot make sense of the concept of illness unless I can contrast it with some notion of health. And this is to say precisely that the therapeutic problem is not universal, an inescapable consequence of the human condition. The therapist can always say of his patient, "If only he had been born to other parents; if they had raised him differently; if he had escaped certain traumatic experiences; if at certain critical junctures he had made other decisions; and so on, and so on; then, he would not now be mentally ill, or at any rate his illness would take quite a different form, and call for quite other therapeutic measures." But there are no such ifs that can stand as qualifications to the Buddhist analysis of dukkha or to comparable ideas in other religious philosophies.

Of course, you are quite free to object that the problem of the religious philosophies is altogether a spurious one, that preoccupation with it is itself a symptom of mental illness, and that the whole problem would disappear if the therapeutic task were solved. I do not myself take this view, though I agree that a strong case can be made for it. But unless you come to this conclusion, you are committed to the recognition that it is one thing to diagnose and treat mental illness and quite another to diagnose and treat, as it were, the perplexity posed by the human condition. There is unquestionably such a thing as psychopathic grief or manic joy, and the therapist can deal with it. But the question whether all grief and joy are to be renounced by the enlightened one, as Buddha seems to say, is one which cannot be answered solely in terms of psychotherapy without being begged.

It cannot be denied that these two kinds of problems invite comparison with one another and encourage an analogical way of thinking. Whichever one we are discussing, we apparently find it useful to borrow terms from the other universe of discourse—therapists apparently can't help talking about values, nor religionists about peace of mind. The word "salvation" itself comes from a root which means health, still preserved in the word "salutary," for instance. But I believe that these usages are less a result of strict analogy than of metaphoric extensions of meaning; and still less are they the outcome of generalization and abstraction of features common to the psychological and the existential problem. Buddhism may contribute, in its way, to mental health, but that is not its purpose, as I see it. Its problem begins where that of the therapist leaves off.

Undoubtedly, very much more needs to be said to clarify and support this viewpoint; but footnotes must not be indefinitely prolonged.

I am impelled, however, to add a closing remark. I cannot call your attention to the confusion of religious and psychotherapeutic functions without an awareness that some such confusion might also arise with regard to my own educational purpose here. I have heard that Sinclair Lewis was once invited to lecture at a university on the craft of the writer. He began by asking for a show of hands of all those students seriously interested in becoming writers, and almost every hand in his audience went up. At which he said, "Then why aren't you home writing, instead of wasting your time at lectures!" I hope that I have raised no expectations that I will terminate this discussion by declaring to you solemnly, "Go now, and work out your salvations with diligence!" It is no part of my purpose to persuade you that all is dukkha, and enjoin you to walk on the path of enlightenment. On the contrary, I hope that, far from renouncing your desires, you have acquired a greater thirst—for the understanding of Buddhist thought.

LECTURE EIGHT

Chinese Philosophy

For most Americans, I am afraid, Chinese philosophy consists of either proverbs or jokes, with the proverbs not very philosophical and the jokes not very Chinese. That a culture so rich and venerable should be so crudely caricatured is perhaps shocking. But even more shocking, in my opinion, is the pervasive contempt for the Chinese people and its civilization which has marked so much of the Western outlook and which is manifested to this day, especially in our country, in restrictions on immigration, housing, citizenship, and in various other ways. In the last decades, of course, the situation has changed markedly: China is no longer an object of ridicule but of serious concern. Our attitude has moved quickly from contempt to fear, but without ever having been anything in between. Surely it is time, and long past time, for a serious and responsible endeavor to understand China, and on the part of the American public, not only the missionaries, scholars, and diplomats.

This means an understanding of Chinese thought—its outlook on man, society, and nature. Quemoy and Matsu, after all, are not the centers of Chinese civilization, but on its periphery, and I am talking about more than geography. To be sure, Communist China has established itself on a Western footing: Karl Marx is more important than Confucius, and Lenin than Laotzu. But I venture to say that even Communist China is still Chinese. To what extent traditional perspectives have had an impact on the new society I am not in a position to judge. I think it safe to say that an understanding of the tradition is by no means irrelevant to our concern with Chinese communism. It is true that the communists are rewriting the history of Chinese philosophy as a history of class struggle reflected in conflicts between materialism and idealism. We should at least be aware of what history it is that is being rewritten. And, of course, in Free China the tradition remains a living reality. In this lecture I shall deal only with the tradition; how it has been transformed by the communists is, to be sure, of enormous importance. But this is a subject which for me remains hidden behind the Bamboo Curtain.

Philosophy has probably played a greater role in the history of Chinese culture than in any other, making itself felt in every phase of life—in religion, in art, and most notably in government. For a period of some two thousand years, continuing through the nineteenth century, examinations for the civil service tested the candidate largely on his knowledge of the Chinese classics. I rather suspect that worse principles of selection have been used by various governments East and West; but I can hardly pretend to an unbiased judgment. Be that as it may, a knowledge of Chinese literature, and even of the specifically philosophical literature, has been regarded by the Chinese themselves—especially by the educated classes and the bureaucratic elite—as being of the very first importance. This assessment cannot fail to be taken into account in our own approach to the subject.

Now a close approach is not easy to make. Apart from the differences between their culture and ours—this is a difficulty, after all, with regard to any of the Asian philosophies—the Chinese language presents special problems to the student of Chinese thought. It is my understanding that this language is not logically articulated, as the Indo-European languages are, but builds up complex ideas by suggestion and imagery. Over and above whatever difficulties there are in interpreting philosophical prose, and especially that of another culture, there are difficulties posed by the language itself. Scholars who know the language may disagree very sharply with one another as to just what is being said in a particular passage, say of Laotzu, quite apart from questions of philosophical interpretation. I have been told that even the grammar of the sentences is by no means always unequivocally clear.

Yet this trait of the language is not altogether without its compensations for us. Because of the nature of its linguistic resources, as well as for other reasons, Chinese thought tends to express itself in an extraordinarily concrete way. Western philosophy, by and large, has aspired to abstraction, as F. S. C. Northrop has emphasized, and in the modern period has often abandoned prose altogether for the symbolism of a mathematical logic. Nothing could be more foreign to the Chinese philosopher. The problem of government, for instance, has been one of the central themes of his thought; but nowhere in the whole corpus of Chinese philosophy do we find the question raised of the nature of Justice, in the way in which Plato, for example, poses it. And the idea of formulating axioms of, say, utility or social welfare, to which Platonism has brought us in modern times, is unthinkable in the Chinese perspectives. We may not know with precision what a Chinese philosopher is saying, for he himself is not precise; but it is correspondingly easier to see what he is getting at and what difference it makes in the conduct of affairs. The grasp of his thought calls for imagination and sympathy; for my part, I think that a philosophy which makes no demands on the sensitivity of its reader has somehow impoverished itself.

The concreteness of Chinese thought is only one of a configuration of traits which can be described in ecological terms, as it were: it is a rural philosophy. Western thought, on the whole, is urban; it embodies an outlook that we might expect to have been developed in the Greek city-states, and subsequently in the urban centers of later Western civilization. It is cerebral, sophisticated, cosmopolitan, and sceptical, withdrawn from nature save as providing materials and instruments for human technology. Meyer Schapiro once called my attention to the curious fact that the illustrations chosen for discussion in modern Western philosophy are characteristically small, manipulable artifacts: pennies, pencils, watches, and chairs. The Chinese philosopher turns rather to mountains and clouds, animals and plants. It is a farmer who is speaking, or at any rate someone to whom the country is more meaningful and precious than the city. We have had in the West our Lucretius, Thomas Jefferson, Thoreau, and such like; but their outlook is not nearly as characteristic as the corresponding perspectives are in China.

Specifically, the Chinese look out on the world as something dynamic and relational. It consists, not of fixed substances with attributes which can be abstracted and ordered into some logical system, but of concrete affairs and interactions exhibiting constant changes. This is not the abstract philosophy of process in the Buddhist doctrine of anitya, or in the Western metaphysics of the type of Heraclitus, Hegel, and Whitehead. For "process" and "event" may enter into as fixed a world order as "substance" and "attribute." As we are likely to put it today, the question is only whether time enters as a real variable into the formulation of natural laws. For the Chinese, natural law does not "govern" change but only reflects it in a schematized form. But the schematization is a reality several times removed from the concreta of nature itself. The Chinese thinker would probably have had less sympathy with Newton's *Principia* than with Walt Whitman's "When I heard the learned astronomer. . . ."

The changes that make up the affairs of man and nature are viewed as being cyclic in character. All that happens will happen once more in due course, in its proper season. The season is everything, as was also emphasized by that rural philosopher of our own tradition, the author of Ecclesiastes. Nothing is forever done, but makes its way back to a new beginning. The Chinese call this the "Returning"—an idea richly exploited by Toynbee among others.

Whatever goes up must come down, but not with finality, as we are likely to think: it must go up once more, and again and again. "Reversal is the movement of the Tao," Laotzu says, in a spirit reminiscent of Heraclitus: "The way up and the way down are the same." It is easy to see why a farmer looking out on the world notes particularly those aspects of it which mark the interaction between his own efforts and the workings of natural forces. The outcomes of such interactions manifest themselves in recurrent patterns of events, as day gives way to night and day once more, as the year follows the familiar round of the seasons, and rain gives way to drought; the plant goes from seed through seedling to maturity, it flowers, and then it drops its seeds to begin again. This is the paradigm of Chinese cosmology.

Very early in Chinese thought speculation turned to the notion of two fundamental powers, forces, or constituents of this cyclic process, derived, like the idea of the cycle itself, from homely experience. They are called the *yin* and the *yang*—the male principle and the female, action and passion, matter and form. These renderings are characteristically Western, I am afraid, being abstract and metaphysical. In Chinese thought, yin and yang are concrete; they are not transcendent essences, but characters intertwined in all natural processes. They are complementary as well as contrastive and in their togetherness make up every whole. They are not the two moments of a dialectical opposition, which generates a higher synthesis, but rather two modes of unitary being—as sexuality is a twofold manifestation of the life-force which is actualized in the union of the two.

Yin and yang are not merely cosmological principles, but make up the content of human life as well. Nature, you may say, is personified in being conceived through these categories. But man in turn is, as it were, naturalized—he manifests within his own being the structure and workings of the cosmic process. The Chinese do not draw a sharp line, as Western thinkers are inclined to do, between cosmology and ethics—or more concretely, between man and nature. Man is a part of nature; he is in nature and nature is in him.

Prometheus and Faust have no analogues in Chinese culture: the aim is not to conquer nature but to live in harmony with it. Yin and yang work through man and nature alike: the forces that actuate human conduct move the stars through the heavens. Like Plato's *eros,* the creative principle does not set man apart from the cosmos, but unites him to it. There is something here of Faust after all: the eternal feminine draws us onward.

These perspectives, then, must serve as a background against which we can survey the two major movements of Chinese thought: Confucianism and Taoism. I shall consider them in order.

Kung-fu-tzu or "Master Kung" is the Chinese name for the man we know as Confucius; "tzu" is an honorific, like the Indian "charya" or the Western "doctor" or "saint." Confucius lived some time in the sixth century before the Christian era, roughly a contemporary of Ezekiel and the Buddha. By profession he was what might be described as a migratory intellectual worker—moving about from place to place and offering his services as schoolteacher, tutor of princes, civil servant, and adviser on the conduct of affairs in personal life, in business, and above all in government. In the two or three centuries following his death, his teachings were crystallized into a definite Confucian philosophy, as represented in the so-called idealistic wing of *Mencius,* in about the fourth century B.C., and the realistic wing of *Hsuntzu* a short time later.

In these early centuries Confucianism was in no sense a religion, but rather what we would call today an intellectual or social movement. By the time of the Han Dynasty—roughly contemporaneous with the ascendancy of Rome—it was codified into an orthodoxy, serving as both the official ideology and the state religion. In the next several centuries it became more and more firmly established on an authoritarian basis, till at last the rival religions and philosophies—Buddhism and Taoism—were officially abolished. Chinese culture, however, was too complex and heterogeneous to be served indefinitely by any single outlook. Confucianism continued to interact with other movements of thought, both indigenous and imported from India. In the twelfth century it was revised and modernized into the form of what is now usually called neo-Confucianism. Of particular importance here was the great synthesis carried out by *Chu Hsi,* whose philosophy was the most influential in China till Western ideas began to have an impact in modern times. The role of Chu Hsi is to be compared with that of Plato, Aquinas, Maimonides, and Sankara in providing a synoptic expression of a whole culture.

The Confucian philosophy is, above all, a humanistic one. Morality, which is the major preoccupation of Confucian thought, is based squarely on the conception of a common human nature. The Chinese character that we interpret as "ethics" is derived from the character for "man," while our own word "ethics" comes from the Greek for custom or usage. The Chinese character for "morality" derives from the symbol for the human heart. Confucius speaks over and over again of "the cultivation of the person, the root of everything besides." The business of philosophy is to teach man how to be worthy of a man's estate; and the teaching is grounded in a down-to-earth conception of human nature.

The basic virtue which a man is to cultivate the Chinese call *jen* or human-heartedness. (It is pronounced, so far as my ears can judge, as though it were spelled with an initial "r," for reasons that I have never had satisfactorily explained to me. No doubt for similar reasons, "hs" in Chinese—as in the names Hsuntzu and Chu Hsi—is pronounced as though it were "sh." Let us file these conventions of spelling and pronunciation under the heading of "the mysterious East" and proceed.) Now jen or human-heartedness plays the part in Confucian thought of righteousness in Judaism, charity in Christianity, detachment in Buddhism, and so on. It is the fundamental quality of character on which all else depends. "What is virtue?" Confucius was once asked. "To love your fellow man." "And what is knowledge?" "To know your fellow man." Man is everything; jen is just being wholly a man. We speak in a comparable way of being "humane"; but this has rather too much of mercy in it, not enough of love, and no connotation of justice. Jen is all three. It is the quality of humanity in its fullest sense.

But it is not quite accurate to think of jen as an attribute of the isolated individual. It is not what we would call a personality trait, but something manifested in interpersonal relations, a quality of the role being played or action being performed rather than of the abstraction called a personality. Ethics, in Chinese thought, is always social ethics; the qualifier is for them a redundancy. The central problem for Chinese moral philosophers is what we in the West mark off as the special province of the political philosopher, or even the political scientist. It is the problem of government. The good man is to be found in the concrete only in the good society; it is in social patterns and practices that his goodness manifests itself.

The tendency in the West has been one of increasing depersonalization of human relations. In the familiar formula, we have moved from a society of status to a society of contract, freely entered into by the contracting parties. But the outcome has been that we tend to define the human being by the functions which he has contracted to perform. He is important to others, not as an individual, but as a functional element in a depersonalized social structure. The strangers whom we encounter identify themselves to us by the roles which they are playing in the situations which the encounter calls forth as points of reference. In China, traditionally, it is the other way around. The role is defined by the person who is playing it. What is primary is not the office but the concrete human being who is discharging the duties of the office. We pride ourselves on having a government of laws, not of men. For the Chinese, such an arrangement would have little to recommend it, even if it were realistically workable. No doubt their perspective leads to what we would condemn as favoritism and other abuses of administration. But in their view, ours is altogether dehumanized; there is no room for jen in it all. Jen has its seat in the human heart, but it is there as a potentiality. It can be actualized only in the interactions of a man with his fellows—interactions to which the participants bring their full humanity.

Now usually, when a philosophy is concerned with what is to be found in the heart of man, we expect it to be otherworldly, or at any rate, not worldly-wise. For in our own culture, moral and spiritual values are thought of as rooted in the soil of transcendence: they spring from heaven not earth, and are nourished by faith rather than reason. But of all the great law-givers and culture-heroes, Confucius, I think, is far and away the most earthy and realistic. There is very little mystic sensibility in his character or teaching—comparatively speaking, at least. He sees himself as giving practical advice, and his hearers take it as such; he is perfectly willing for his philosophy to stand or fall with its practicality.

Like the Buddha, Confucius refuses to discuss miracles or the supernatural, not because there is nothing here to discuss, but because there would be no point to the discussion. "While you cannot serve men, how can you serve the gods?" Confucius asks. "While you do not understand life, what can you understand of death?" First things first is the principle. Of course, a transcendentalist would not take issue with this principle, but he would apply it differently. For he would give priority to a concern with God, the soul, and immortality, and on that basis would then address himself to mundane questions. Confucius does not hesitate to invoke the name of "Heaven" in expounding and justifying his views. But what we translate as "Heaven" does not have quite the sense in his teaching that it conveys to our ears. It represents the realm of values, of ideals—spirit naturalized, at home in the everyday affairs of this life. "The way of Heaven is evident. Let me not say that it is high aloft above me. It ascends and descends about our doings."

Such an attitude must not for a moment be confused with the vulgar pragmatism which dismisses altogether things of the spirit. The Chinese is practical, but he makes a point of extending his practicality throughout the domain of value. As he puts it, he wants to keep his feet in two boats, though even in the crowded Chinese rivers this is not always easy. This world and the other both have their claims. But there is no dualism here, no bifurcation of experience and corresponding partitioning of duty. Heaven "ascends and descends about our doings" on earth. The angels first mounted Jacob's ladder before they climbed down: they were here to start with.

The Confucian approach to morality is thus realistic but without cynicism—at once practical and principled. Practicality requires that principles be accommodated to the actualities with which we are confronted and not merely reserved for the goal of aspiration. "The moral life of man may be likened to traveling to a distant place: one must start from the nearest stage. It may also be likened to ascending a height: one must begin from the lowest step." It is the starting point which was his peculiar concern: the question to be tackled is always, "What do I do now?" Simple as this consideration is, it is remarkable how often it is overlooked, whether by the contemporaries of Confucius or by our own. A large part of political debate as well as of inner conflict seems to occupy itself with what should have been done then, instead of what is to be done next. Confucius never wavers on this point.

What impedes the moral life is less often a lack of principle than too much of it—that is to say, principles so high that they have no purchase on what lies before us at any given moment. "The path of duty lies in what is near," Confucius explains, "and men seek for it in what is remote. The work of duty lies in what is easy, and men seek for it in what is difficult." We find morality, as we conceive it, unattainable, and blame the frailty of our human nature; but the fault lies rather in the weakness of our conception. How easy it is to exercise ourselves about the admission of Red China to the United Nations, or the unilateral suspension of nuclear testing; how much more difficult to be concerned with problems that have their locus in the family circle, the school, the neighborhood community. We do not see the moral issues here, close at hand; or we imagine that they are of vastly less importance, without asking, "Important to whom?" The result is that moral action is seen as an obligation on others, and that moral values are felt to be correspondingly inaccessible to ourselves. Because we are not the movers and shakers, we read ourselves out of the moral community altogether, then grieve at our alienation. But Confucius asks, "Is virtue indeed so far off? I crave for virtue, and lo! it is at hand."

The thing is to live by ideals that are adjusted to the real possibilities in both character and circumstance. Confucius said, "I know now why the moral life is not practiced. The wise mistake moral law for something higher than what it really is; and the foolish do not know enough what moral law really is. I know now why the moral law is not understood. The noble natures want to live too high, high above their moral ordinary self; and ignoble natures do not live high enough, that is, not up to their moral ordinary true self. There is no one who does not eat and drink, but few there are who really know flavor." The ordinary self is quite moral enough, indeed the only locus of morality. Here Confucius parts company with Buddhism and the Western moral philosophies. In these, morality depends upon conquest of the self. The attitude of Confucius toward human nature is like that toward the encompassing nature of which man is a part: the aim is not conquest, but a life in harmony with it. Such harmony does not constitute surrender to brute fact, but only a repudiation of moral fiction.

The realism of these perspectives leads to a recognition of certain basic needs whose satisfaction is a precondition of moral conduct. Thus Mencius, idealist though he was, remained close enough to the outlook of Confucius himself to draw attention to the importance for morality of economic security. "If beans and rice were as plentiful as fire and water, such a thing as a bad man would not exist," he remarks. Much the same point was made by his contemporary Aristotle: before a man can live well, he must be able to live. Aristotle, in fact, has much in common with the realistic idealism of the Confucians, especially with their emphasis on the capacities of human nature, and the importance of circumstance in allowing the potentialities of the good to be actualized. At any rate, the Confucian morality is not an exhortation to pursue the higher values and to disregard so-called material wants. Confucius, I think, would have had little sympathy with either Plato or St. Paul. Morality is to be achieved in the human state, and there is no escaping the body and its needs.

But of course, a man may succeed in filling these needs and still fail in moral achievement. He may have his rice but submerge his human nature in its animal base. Plato had a point after all: better a

Socrates dissatisfied than a pig satisfied. What is needed is moral aspiration; in its absence, the most favorable circumstances are no more than wasted opportunity. On one occasion, the duke of the principality in which Confucius was teaching was seen out riding with a beautiful companion, who was, however, of dubious repute; and Confucius remarked to his disciples, "I have never yet seen a man whose love of virtue equaled his love of woman." No sense in offering moral instruction to those who have no wish to learn. But given the wish, if outer conditions are also met, there is no limit to what can be achieved.

The failing of the ignoble man who is lacking in moral aspiration is matched by the moralist who loses sight of the realistic conditions of fulfilling aspiration. Moral reform characteristically addresses itself to the largest issues in the broadest arena—a new world is in the making! But time and again it meets with defeat, and at last gives way to cynicism and despair: "The world, it is the old world yet, I am I, my things are wet, and nothing now remains to do but begin the game anew." The whole enterprise, for Confucius, is misdirected. Moral reform can begin only with the self; when we have succeeded with ourselves, we can put our families in order; and from the family the principality; thence to the state, and so at last to the community of man. How absurd for a Rousseau to write treatises on the education of the young, while his own children are abandoned with neglect; how ridiculous is the posture of a noble who presumes to rule a kingdom, while he is not even the master of his own household; how futile and dangerous the endeavor of a state to reform its neighbors when its own affairs are in disorder. The art of government must be mastered in the small, in the kingdom of the self; and its domain is to be extended step by step.

This is Plato's logic: the state is the individual writ large. Only Plato was so lacking in realism as to suppose himself capable at one stroke of instituting the ideal republic. He never troubled to ask himself, as Confucius surely would have asked, where will I find the philosophers to govern it? He assumed that he had a system of education which would infallibly produce them. Aristotle may have learned better by his own experience as tutor to Alexander the Great. Confucius, too, was enough of a teacher to know how little one man can learn from another.

This realism of his has one more implication for ethics. It is that the requirements of morality will necessarily vary with the changing context of moral action. Circumstances inevitably alter cases for any morality that aspires to the reshaping of circumstance. "With me," Confucius once said, "there is no inflexible 'thou shalt' or 'thou shalt not.'" For how can such inflexibility be reconciled with a realistic assessment of the potentialities of moral achievement afforded by nature in a concrete case—the nature in both man and his environment? Morality must be, as the pragmatist would say today, contextual; principles do not degenerate to expediences merely because they have been adapted to what is really possible in that context. Otherwise they may remain pure—but also sterile. "In our land," someone once boasted to Confucius, "a man will report even his own father for theft." This is the absolutist morality of the Communist countries today, but Confucius would have none of it. Virtue is for the son to cherish his father, and the father his son.

This is not simply one absolutism replacing another. It is the refusal wholly to abstract principles from the concreta in which alone they can be made to work for the attainment of virtue. Confucius was once asked what he thought of the principle of repaying evil with good. "In that case," he replied, "with what would you repay good?" In the abstract, the principle presents itself as the highest morality; but in the concrete, it fails to discriminate the moral quality of the actions to which we are responding. What then becomes of justice, for instance? And how is the good to be encouraged and evil restrained if we deal with both alike? There are unquestionably moral principles to be learned, and Confucius devoted himself to teaching them. But really to have learned them means indeed to be able to choose those which the situation requires, and to make them effective in the situation.

Morality thus becomes, as with John Dewey, a matter of reflective deliberation. We cannot rely solely on habit or routine, and certainly not on spontaneous impulse. The ideal is to be able to make moral choices spontaneously and habitually; but only the most cultivated character approximates this ideal. But even with regard to the need for reflection and deliberation Confucius is realistic and moderate. On being told that so-and-so acts only after thinking it over three times, Confucius remarked dryly, "Twice would be enough."

What, now, is the content of the morality that Confucius enjoins? First of all, Confucius is a thoroughgoing conservative, in the strict sense of the term: he wants to preserve the best that has been developed in society, and to order the life of man in a way which maximizes the achievement of the good already discovered in human history. Confucius is an empiricist in ethical theory, always justifying his moral prescriptions by appealing to the lessons of experience. But it is a retrospective empiricism, not an experimental one, like that of the pragmatists, for instance. There is no spirit of adventure in social arrangements: "Let's try this and see what comes of it, then we can make up our minds about it." The reference is always only to what has already been tried, what has already been found wanting or shown itself to be successful. The only social science that really matters is history.

It is easy to see why, in these perspectives, the scholar and man of letters has such an important role in society. The past is the only guide for the present, and continuation of tradition the only path to the future. And it is the scholar who is the bearer and guardian of tradition. Civil-service examinations testing the knowledge of the classics are not merely a device to recruit into government only the members of a privileged class, in the way in which a knowledge of Latin and Greek might have served at one time in Britain. The classics are in fact the substance of sound public policy, taking the place of the treatises on economics and such like that we might expect an administrator to have mastered.

The problem in Confucian thought is always only that of getting the right system of morality, law, government, and then enforcing the system. For all his realism and contextualism, Confucius does not take seriously the passage of time and the changes that time inevitably brings—an indifference to time is just the essence of conservatism. The past is forever present, at least in potentiality; our business is only to actualize this potentiality. The right system has already been found, and in the Golden Age men lived by it. Our task today is to reinstate the pattern of excellence of the days that have gone before. A philosophy such as this is understandable in a society which for so many centuries remained fixed and unchanging.

Throughout most of its history China exhibits a feudal, hierarchical social structure. Each individual is characterized by a distinctive status in society, and may be viewed as a point of intersection of countless lines of deference and authority, extending in one direction to those above him in the hierarchy and in the other to those below. We may think here of the patriarchical family in which everyone stands in fixed personal relations to others, on the basis of which obedience and respect are called for, in the proper directions and modes of expression. The Chinese tend to view every social complex —a business enterprise, a state, or whatever—in this image. It is thought of as having an individual founder, who is to be venerated by every participant in the complex as the source of its being and the supreme authority for its working. There can be no thought of bringing the system up to date, as we would say. As embodied in the person of the patriarch himself, it is age and not modernity which is the hallmark of merit.

It is to be expected that the ideals generated in such a society are the ideals of a leisure class. The achievement of the system must be measured by the attainments at the top of the hierarchy. It is here that the value, the very reality of the complex, is localized—somewhat in the way in which the Platonic Idea serves for the concrete particulars that crudely embody it. Social arrangements are devices for the preservation of a cultural heritage: the end they serve is to make possible—for the right people—a life of cultivated leisure. "I do not expect to find a saint today," Confucius said, "but if I find a gentleman I shall be quite satisfied." Saintliness is unwordly and unrealistic; but aspiration, learning, and character may very well succeed in producing a gentleman.

In my opinion, the values embodied in this ideal must not be dismissed too lightly. I hope I need not yield to anyone in my personal dedication to democratic and equalitarian principles. But the contributions to human happiness made by the gentleman seem to me quite considerable. I, for one, would feel much easier in my mind if there were many more cultured gentlemen in positions of power and responsibility in the world today. It may be true that the devil finds work for leisured hands to do; but history is also full of boors who made themselves busy doing the devil's work. The social philosophy of Confucius is undeniably vulnerable to very severe criticism, along lines which I am happy to think few contemporary Americans need spelled out. But I think it must also be acknowledged that in Confucius the values of conservatism are put in the best possible light.

The Confucian ideal of a cultivated gentleman centers around the notion of *li* or propriety. It is made up of standards of protocol, etiquette, and the performance of ritual. The tradition speaks of three hundred rules of ceremony, and three thousand distinct rules of deportment. In their entirety, they define what we might call "good form." Form in this sense is not decadent artificiality, but naturalness and simplicity. What is important about li is that it develops character in the direction of dignity, poise, and a certain seriousness. One cannot be frivolous or foolish and at the same time observe the proprieties. A true gentleman exhibits always what Confucius describes as ease without pride; he is satisfied and composed no matter what befalls.

To attain this dignity and composure, the Confucian cultivates the polite arts, such as music and poetry. The experience of beauty is an ingredient of the good life, not so much for what it is in itself, but because of the effect it produces. The conventions of art reflect, in their measured harmonies, all that is best in conformity to tradition. Elegance, grace, and polish are virtues in both art and life. The revolutionary artist, however, the creative genius who breaks through the academic mold to reveal new possibilities in his materials—or in the life of man—such an artist has no place in these perspectives. Like Plato, Confucius prizes art only when it is in service of ideals already established for it, either by the state or by tradition. There is no doubt that art can serve very effectively to this end, but I doubt very much whether this is the most significant contribution to life that art can make.

Ceremony and ritual come to be important for Confucius in much the same way. They give concrete expression to the requirements of li. They provide an intrinsic satisfaction in the dignity and grace of their performance. But beyond that, they reach deep into the organization of the personality, molding its impulses and providing channels for their expression in ways that develop the character to which a good man aspires.

The realist Hsuntzu particularly addressed himself to the basic problem raised by the Confucian emphasis on ritual: how can a thinking man, a man of integrity, perform rituals that seem to presuppose beliefs which he cannot in all honesty accept? Ceremonies honoring departed ancestors, for instance, make it seem that those who perform them believe that their ancestors have not really departed; must we accept such notions or repudiate the ritual? The answer which Hsuntzu gives is a remarkable anticipation of Coleridge's theory of poetry as involving a "willing suspension of disbelief"—he speaks of "deceiving ourselves without being deceived." Ritual must not be taken literally. There is a kind of make-believe in its performance, but no falsehood or hypocrisy. It is a fiction which serves, not to deny the facts in their nakedness, but to cloak them in the garments of a civilized people.

Now li provides the form of the moral life, but not its content. This is embodied in the concept of *yi:* righteousness, performance of duty. In the West, from the prophet Amos down through Kant and beyond, we have tended to conceive of ethics in terms of moral obligation, fulfillment of the moral law. Right and wrong are the primary moral ideas, and good and bad only secondary. Moral obligation is usually contrasted with natural inclination, what we ought to do with what we want to do. Confucius aims at overcoming any disparities between these two. But what we ought to do is not determined by the object of desire. We are to do it simply because we must, not because we are aiming at a certain outcome. The Confucian speaks in this connection of "doing for nothing," a notion quite similar to the karma-yoga of the Bhagavadgita. We are to detach ourselves from the fruits of our action, and perform it simply because it is our duty. The outcome does not matter; especially, it does not matter whether the outcome is gratifying or not, whether or not it satisfies our desires. There is only one outcome of action that is of moral relevance: the effect on the character of the man who does his duty or evades it. This is the principle of yi.

In a passage which I think has a peculiarly modern relevance, Confucius explains to his disciples why he is so concerned with politics in spite of the low likelihood of realizing moral values in the political arena. "The reason why the superior man tries to go into politics is because he holds this to be right, even though he is well aware that his principles cannot prevail." One can be a realist and still pursue an objective which, under the circumstances, simply cannot be attained. Even though the action is foredoomed to failure it may still be done, if it is the part of a human being to act in such a way. For in that case, the action will succeed after all, in the thing that matters most. I think this is the spirit in which the Jews of the Warsaw ghetto rose up against the Nazis. They surely did not expect to be able to sweep the Wehrmacht out of Europe; but they were resolved, if they could not live in dignity, to die as befits the human estate. A Confucian gentleman of the Han dynasty might very well have viewed the matter in just this way.

As we might expect of Confucian humanism, the basic duty is not defined in terms of man's relationship to God; and naturalism implies that it will also not be defined in terms of some transcendent essence—a soul or Atman—embodied in man. Confucius grounds it in the homeliest of human obligations, those derived from the family structure. "Filial piety is the root of all virtue, and the stem out of which grows all moral teaching. It commences with the service of parents; it proceeds to the service of the ruler; it is completed by the establishment of character." To be a good man one must first be a good son; then a good citizen, a good father, a good employer, a good ruler. A man who does not recognize his first and most immediate obligations cannot be expected to discharge the subsequent and more remote responsibilities. The duties arising out of the family pattern call for just that human-heartedness which is the core of all other virtues.

In Mencius, the family pattern is projected onto the political structure. The state is conceived as an enlarged family, a moral institution having as its objective the development of the moral character of the citizenry, the members of that family. It must be ruled, therefore, by a philosopher-king concerned, as a father would be, with the moral well-being of his subjects. They, in turn, should feel towards him a filial gratitude and devotion. If he acts otherwise, however, he forfeits the right to the loyalty of his subjects. On the contrary, they themselves have, not only the right, but the positive obligation, to carry out a revolution against him. For his disregard of moral principle betrays the fact that he is not their lawful ruler but only a usurper, "a mere fellow," as Mencius says. We thus arrive at the Confucian ideal of "sageliness within, kingliness without"—moral character given political expression.

The demands of yi come to a climax in what Confucius calls "the principle of reciprocity," which is familiar to us as the Golden Rule. Confucius gives it both the negative and the positive formulation: not doing what we would not have done to us, and doing as we would be done by. The superior man exhibits the virtue of *chung-shu,* conscientious altruism, that concern for others which is expressed in the habit of putting ourselves in their place as we deliberate our own choices. And in making his choices, whether or not others are involved in his action, he is guided also by the principle of the Golden Mean, by temperateness and moderation. Like the Greeks, the Chinese approached moral issues by way of essentially aesthetic categories, harmony and proportion, or what they call *chung-ho*—a quality manifested equally in character, in events, and in the cosmic order. The whole moral structure is then capped by jen, the human-heartedness or benevolence which infuses yi. The ideal of the sage is to attain that condition in which he is able to follow his heart's desire, to act solely on natural impulse, without violating in the least the claims of either propriety or duty, li or yi.

This raises the question whether man's original nature—as it is in itself and apart from the workings on it of the natural and human environment—is basically good or evil. This is the issue which divides the realist from the idealist wing of Confucianism, Hsuntzu from Mencius. It is the position of Mencius that is most characteristic, I believe, of the Chinese outlook. "There is no man who is not good," Mencius says, "as there is no water which does not flow downwards. But you can strike the water and it splashes up. And you can make human nature turn to evil in the same way." Nurture has its importance, to be sure, but its function is not so much to shape the human being in the mold of morality as it is to free him for his innate moral growth. "What else is education," Mencius asks, "but the recovery of good feelings that have strayed away?"

And they stray easily, so easily! The substance of the whole Confucian philosophy amounts, I think, to this: that life should be so ordered, in society and in the individual personality, as to allow the fullest development of what makes us most truly human—moral feeling experienced with esthetic sensibility. The restraints of tradition, like those of classical art, are no more than the channels of free expression. Outside them all is inchoate, disproportioned, and ugly. One who really knows how to submit to them thereby becomes their master and makes of life itself a masterpiece. But we must serve our apprenticeship, and practice unceasingly the principles of the great art.

All this is movingly summarized by Confucius himself: "The way in which a man loses his proper goodness of mind is like the way in which the trees are denuded by axes. Hewn down day after day, can it—the mind—retain its beauty? But there is a development of its life day and night, and in the calm air of the morning, just between night and day, the mind feels in a degree those desires and aversions which are proper to humanity, but the feeling is not strong, and it is fettered and destroyed by what takes place during the day. . . . If it receive its proper nourishment, there is nothing which will not grow. If it lose its proper nourishment, there is nothing which will not decay. Hold it fast, and it remains with you. Let it go, and you lose it."

But there is another major stream of Chinese thought which teaches just the contrary: Don't hold fast; let it go! Taoism is second only to the Confucian philosophy in importance for Chinese culture; and in certain areas, like poetry and painting, it is possibly even of the first importance. It is mystic, spiritual, unworldly, withdrawn—everything that Confucianism is not. But I suppose I should warn you that in this very brief sketch it is impossible for me not to exaggerate differences, so as to bring both perspectives into sharper focus.

Taoism (the initial letter is pronounced roughly as if it were a "D") is associated with the teachings of *Laotzu,* a personage of somewhat doubtful historicity—his name means only "the old Master." He seems to have been a contemporary of Confucius; there are legends that the two philosophers met, though they could not have had very much to say to one another. The most important figure of Taoist thought is a philosopher of the fourth century B.C. named *Chuang-tzu;* there are in fact some scholars who regard him, rather than Laotzu, as being the actual founder of the philosophy. The most influential work of Taosit thought is usually ascribed to Laotzu; it is called the *Tao Te Ching,* translated as "The Way and Its Power," and ranks with the *Analects* of Confucius as a Chinese philosophical classic.

There is a body of crude ideas known as "Taoist" which must be more or less sharply distinguished from the philosophy, though it may have constituted the matrix out of which the more refined conceptions later developed. This early, or at any rate, vulgarized Taoism was chiefly concerned with achieving longevity, preserving the sexual powers, and such like. As might be expected, it was associated with a variety of quasi-magical prescriptions and practices, and has continued down to modern times in the form of popular superstitions, folklore, and so on, which Western ignorance so commonly mistakes for the substance of Chinese thought. I find it interesting that in many cultures philosophies expressing what may be a very sophisticated mystic impulse become intertwined with occultism, magic, and a more or less erotic preoccupation with the body—Pythagoras, gnosticism, cabbalah, and Yoga all exhibit many parallels to Taoism in this respect. But I will not venture here on an explanation.

As a philosophy, Taoism presents us with that emphasis on the cultivation of the inner resources of the personality which is so central a theme of Indian and Buddhist thought as well, and which is so important in our stereotype of the so-called oriental mind. Confucianism is at least as characteristic of the Chinese mentality and is very much alive to what lies outside the self. But its worldliness does not fit our Western prejudices; we are likely to feel that Taoism is somehow more truly Asian. It is always a pleasure to encounter something that matches our preconceptions—Santayana even regards this as essential to the experience of beauty. If so, Taoism is undoubtedly among the most beautiful of the Asian philosophies!

The central idea is that of the *Tao*—a rational, moral principle to be found in nature itself. The Tao is, as it were, the whole system of li conceived as making up the natural order of the cosmos. It is close to what the Buddhists call dharma, and what we know in the Western religious tradition as the logos, or in secular philosophies from the Stoics to Hegel as a world Reason. The Tao is a principle embodied in things; a sage is one who is able to incorporate this principle in himself, who identifies with it, who manifests it in his life. The Tao thus defines the way in which a man is to live; the word "Tao" is usually translated, in fact, as "the Way."

For the filial piety of the Confucians, therefore, the Taoist substitutes a kind of natural piety. An identification with nature, rather than with man, is the root of all virtue, and the stem out of which grows all moral teaching. Not, however, the nature that presents itself to earth-bound perception, for this is but an intimation of the Tao and not its substance. The hard actualities of what we see dissolve before the inner vision, and the less there is to look at the more there is really to be seen. The Tao itself is Nothingness, like the Sunyata of Mahayana Buddhism. It is this Void which appears in much Chinese landscape painting. The Taoist withdraws from men to the lonely mountains and climbs above the peaks into the clouds. "He who needs others is forever shackled," says Chuang-tzu, "and he who is needed by others is forever sad. Drop these shackles, put away your sadness, and wander alone with Tao in the kingdom of the Great Void."

Revising my manuscript, I sit here now looking out into a northern California fog. Earth and sky are gray, blank, and bottomless; the bough of a blue oak twists across my window, darker gray and black, with patches of yellow moss and wet green leaves; and there is no sound at all. This, I suppose, is the very edge of that kingdom. But we have all been trained to respect boundaries; and who among us would venture abroad without our passports and visas, inoculations and credit cards? The shackles and sadness of which Chuang-tzu speaks are familiar enough; if we do not wander alone with Tao, I do not know whether it is because we are lacking in sense or in sensibility—and perhaps, after all, it is because we have both. "The woods are lovely, dark and deep, but I have promises to keep, and miles to go before I sleep, and miles to go before I sleep." The Taoist is one who makes no promises and has nowhere to go at all.

Even in China, to wander alone with Tao is not a life to which most men are suited, though there are few, even among Confucians, who are not in some measure drawn to it. Taoism makes the descent from Nothingness to existence, accommodating itself to the man who is not prepared to forego entirely human relations and a place in the world of affairs. It does this with the concept of *te,* which in our abstract metaphysics we might translate as essence, intrinsic quality, power, or virtue. It is the Tao that is responsible for the existence of anything, and indeed of everything, as we might say of God. But the te is what makes each existent the particular thing that it is rather than something else. The te marks off its kind, its distinctive nature. The te, therefore, is revealed in the natural, spontaneous actions of the thing, by which it shows forth its own true character rather than the traits imposed upon it from without. For man, the te is nothing other than his inborn powers or capacities. It is what the man himself really is when these powers have not been tampered with by his own self-conciousness, or circumscribed by society with its laws and morals. What Oscar Wilde said in jest the Taoist takes seriously: ignorance is an exotic bloom that withers at the touch—education is deadening, and especially if it consists of moral instruction.

In making each thing what it is, the te is the locus of the specific virtue or excellence of the thing. If Tao is a Platonic notion, rather like the Idea of the Good, te is Aristotelian, the nature or essence of each concrete particular, which at once differentiates it and determines wherein *its* good lies. The word "virtue" itself still has for us the sense of distinctive power or capacity, as when we say that something produces a certain effect "by virtue of" some aspect or other of its nature. The Taoist, like Aristotle, states this equivalence in the reverse direction: fulfillment or realization of innate potentiality is virtue. Thus, as the Taoist has it, "Everything is what it is, is good for something, is all one—the Tao."

As applied to man, the te corresponds to what we might call the integrity of character, perhaps what the existentialist means by genuineness. If only we lived in accord with the te all would be well for we are all just what we are, and the specific goodness of each thing lies just in its own true nature. But man perverts things, perverts himself, forces on himself and on nature something extrinsic, and so unnatural. Evil is perversion, a turning aside, a denial of the te and so a moving away from the Tao.

It is only man who separates himself in this way from nature and from his own nature. We put it in our religious tradition, "God hath made man upright; but they have sought out many inventions." Ecclesiastes has much to say to the Chinese and especially to the Taoists among them. All that civilization prides itself on is man's work, and it cannot compare with God's. Of the landscape paintings inspired by the Taoist perspective we might very well say that every prospect pleases and only man is vile. But he is vile only in abandoning his humanity, in "improving" upon it, as he supposes. He reaches out for more and thereby lessens himself, scales the heavens to his own damnation. Be content, the Taoist enjoins. Be true to your own nature; live by the te. This is the basic Taoist principle. Beneath all the multifarious forms of nature is only the one Tao, and all else is trivial. "Hold to the core, hold to the core!"

This means to strip away the artificialities of civilization, to do away with the so-called refinements of polite society. The ideal which the Taoist follows is something he calls *p'u:* it means literally unpainted wood, and therefore refers to what is simple, plain, unadorned—or, in moral terms, innocent, ingenuous. Through Zen, which was much influenced by Taoism, this ideal finds realization in Japanese architecture, for instance, in which materials are used in their natural condition. Lacquer and gilt are for the Confucians; the Taoist is content with things as they are. The Chinese tell a story of an artist who painted a picture of a snake, realistic in every detail; and not yet satisfied, the artist then proceeded to paint four feet on the snake. "Painting feet on the snake" is the Taoist expression for overdoing it, abandoning p'u, perverting nature into civilization. We start out well enough, in the innocence and simplicity of childhood; what we must do is to become as little children once more.

It is easy to imagine how the Taoist is repelled by Confucian ceremonialism. It is all painting feet on the snake. When Chuang-tzu was questioned concerning the traditionally eleaborate preparations for his funeral, he replied: "With heaven and earth for my coffin; with the sun, moon and stars as my shroud; and with all creation to escort me to my grave—is not everything for my funeral all prepared?" What else, indeed, is needed? Such a dismissal of the forms of civilized living and dying was no doubt shocking to the Confucians; but it also must have appealed strongly to another side of the Chinese character. There are surely times for all of us when the constraints of good form, however much they contribute to gracious living, are felt to be burdensome and, at bottom, pointless. For the Taoist this is a permanent state of mind.

The ideal of p'u may be given a moral content as well as an

esthetic one. It means plain living, and without high thinking either. We adorn ourselves with possessions, and they become our shackles. Chuang-tzu says: "The fox and the panther—it is the value of their fur that brings them to disaster. Strip away your fine fur!" This means holding to the core. The acquisition of property is painting feet on the snake, or we would say, gilding the lily. The man himself is good; but how is he to find himself amidst all his possessions?

Advertisers and such like have argued for some time that our "way," the American Tao, depends upon continued stimulation of desire so as to consume the products of an ever expanding economy. The Taoist wants rather to limit desires, to simplify his life, and not only to make do but to do without. "This earth we walk on is of vast extent," Chuang-tzu said, "yet in order to walk a man uses no more of it than the soles of his two feet will cover." This is echoed in a Russian tale, I think by Tolstoi, called "How Much Land Does A Man Need?," in which a man is given as much land as he can ride around in one day; of course, he pushes himself to the utmost, falling dead of exhaustion at the end of his efforts, and is buried in all the land he needs. The moral of the story is by no means unfamiliar to us, and we are weekly enjoined to lay up treasure only in heaven. But one who lives by that philosophy is little better than a tramp—as must have been true of many Taoists, for that matter. He who wanders alone with the Tao down Main Street will not find himself alone for long. And with good reason, I think, for in a complex society the satisfaction of even simple desires is no simple matter. I can imagine Confucius arguing that even rice requires cultivation and polish; and can man exhibit his virtue without them?

The Taoist, however, is content to remain just as he is. He has no ambition, for what he wants to attain is Nothing. A central theme in Laotzu is the idea that what is important is non-being rather than being: it is the emptiness that is useful in a room, not the walls, the emptiness and not the clay that gives the bowl its value. A man makes something of himself just when he abandons ambition and spurns achievement, when he is humble and yielding. In Taoism this is known as "the spirit of the valley," an important element in the teaching of Jesus as well. What is low shall be lifted up on high, and the meek shall inherit the earth. The Taoist does not aspire to skill but is content with his awkwardness; he is incapable of being clever; his strength lies only in his ceaseless yielding. Such a man may strike us as a fool, but he belongs to the tradition of what we call "the fool of God." He is so naïve and simple-minded, so innocent and inept as to be even laughable; but as Laotzu says, "If it were not laughed at, it would not be the Tao."

It is in this spirit of the valley that Laotzu enjoins "Never too much, never be first." If you are first, you are trying too hard; and it would be better if you didn't even try at all. Laotzu is not saying that it is the last who shall be first, that success crowns the efforts of one who is content with failure. The idea is rather that success and failure are all one, if only we hold to the core. The opposite sides are the same if they are seen from the center of the moving circle, from what Eliot calls "the still point of the turning world." The Taoist asks us to look at all things in the light of heaven, of the Tao, *sub specie aeternitatis,* Spinoza would say. In the light of heaven, what is there to be seen that is not already ours? What differences make a difference to one who walks with Tao? Every effort, whatever its object, betrays the fact that we are determined to go our own way and not on the Way. The outstanding trait of Satan was—ambition.

This brings us to the most characteristic of the Taoist conceptions, the doctrine of *wu-wei,* non-action, doing by not doing, letting things happen of their own accord. It is, we might say, civil obedience to the governance of the Tao. Force, contention and struggle are quite futile. Water is harder than the hardest granite, because it is perfectly yielding; it cannot be cut through. That which offers no resistance cannot be overcome. And were we ourselves able to overcome it, no end would be served. It is best just as it is. "Consider the lilies of the field . . . they toil not, neither do they spin . . . even Solomon in all his glory was not arrayed like one of these." Don't toil, don't spin, the Taoist says; not because your Heavenly Father will provide, but because you will provide for yourself in letting yourself be. Above all, don't toil after moral achievement; don't set about cultivating yourself, in the manner of the Confucians, trying to make something of yourself. For you will succeed only in producing something made—artificial, unnatural, indeed monstrous. Li and yi, propriety and duty, ceremony and gentility, these are all shackles and sadness. The Tao is free and open before you; there is nothing for you to do.

The last thing you should do, Laotzu insists, is to tamper with men's hearts, to try to make something of others. "The heart of man is like a spring; if you press it down, it only springs up higher." In the Freudian idiom, the repressed always returns, and civilization is nothing other than systematized repression. Chuang-tzu tells the story of the city-dweller who was visiting a country cousin and wished to help him in his labors; so he stole out to the field where the tender young shoots were growing, and painstakingly pulled each plant a few inches out of the soil—to help it grow. The doctrine of wu-wei amounts to just this: don't help plants grow. Let them reach out for sun and rain of their own accord; it is the natural growth, the only possible growth. The efforts of the educator and moralist are at best futile, and at worst destructive of every human good.

The same must hold true, then, of the institutions of state and church; and Taoism does not shrink from this implication. It is laws that make criminals, religion that makes sinners. Where there are no locks, how can there be thieves? Where there are no pious rituals, who can be guilty of omitting to perform them? The Taoist is a thoroughgoing anarchist but not, like the Western anarchists, because he believes that the state is a device by which the rich and powerful few exploit the many. On the contrary, he is an anarchist because he sees government as a futile and dangerous altruism. "To love the people," Chuang-tzu says, "is to harm them; to side with those who are in the right in order to end war is the way to start fresh wars." I rather think that if Laotzu and Chuang-tzu were alive today, they would have every right to say "I told you so"; but being Taoists, they would certainly refrain from saying it.

There are other schools of Chinese thought, deserving at least our bare acquaintance. But the Confucian and Taoist outlooks, between them, are quite comprehensive. The one explores the possibilities for the good life in a stable and rational social order; the other directs attention to the boundless inner resources of the individual. Realist and idealist, naturalist and mystic, Aristotelian and Platonist —these are the sorts of polarities with which we usually mark out the range of philosophical possibilities. The Chinese take something from both; it was Lin Yutang, I think, who observed that every Chinese is a Confucian when he succeeds and a Taoist when he fails. I suppose that when he is uncertain about the outcome and beset with anxiety, he turns to Western philosophies. All in all, one might do worse than to follow his example.

The Chinese outlook as a whole can best be summarized by tracing the path of moral degradation as the Chinese see it, or in the reverse direction, the path of moral ascent. The supreme achievement, the condition of the sage, is to be at one with the Tao, in harmony with the will of earth and heaven. When the Tao has been lost, there remains the te, native goodness, and the moral man is at one with himself, at peace with his own intrinsic nature. When that has been lost, there remains jen or human-heartedness; morality finds a basis in sympathy. If there is no jen, morality can still rest on the foundation of yi: man does his duty even if it runs counter to his own inclinations. When yi has been lost, there remains at any rate the li, the outer forms of moral action; there is at least a formal recognition of moral principle. But when li is also abandoned, there is no longer anything distinctively human.

Taken in reverse order, these are also the stages of moral progress. One begins by learning the rites and ceremonies, the proper forms of action. Morality initially is only a matter of what "just isn't done" or what of course "we" all do; this is the morality of custom and conformity. Custom is enforced by social sanctions and these become internalized: li gives way to yi, and the forms of morality acquire a content of moral obligation. In this way impulse is subject to controls which begin to form character: moral obligation is reinforced in the personality by the workings of moral sentiment, feelings of benevolence and sympathy—yi gives way to jen as the basis of action. As jen takes hold more and more, the roots of character are deepened and integration is achieved: there are no longer conflicts between thought and feeling, inclination and obligation. One acts as a whole man, true to his own intrinsic nature, the te. Such a man at last breaks through the boundaries of the self, to identify with the principle of harmony in the cosmos itself, the Tao.

And now words fail us. "The Tao that can be spoken," says Lao-tzu, "is not the true Tao." But we need not feel frustrated: when we have come to the Tao, there is just nothing more to be said.

QUESTIONS

How do the Chinese reconcile the Confucian, Taoist, and Buddhist elements in their outlook?

It is quite characteristic of the Chinese to adopt simultaneously a number of different viewpoints—this is true of traditional China, that is; today, I take it, there is only one viewpoint, that of the Communist leadership. In the tradition, a variety of religious observances might be practiced, not just by the members of the same family circle, but even by the same individual, according to the circumstances. A man might be married in the Buddhist rite, face illness as a Taoist, and be buried as a Confucian. The Chinese attitude is not quite like that of the Indians toward the darshanas, that each is only a limited perspective on a truth that transcends any of them. It is not an attempt to go beyond a partial truth to the whole truth by adding more parts. It is rather that each religion or philosophy is felt to be appropriate to different life situations—as we might say that a man should be a realist in business and an idealist in personal relations. Only, for the Chinese this does not fragment the personality or compartmentalize the culture. No lines are drawn to serve as rigid barriers; there is instead a kind of pragmatic fluidity, an accommodation without anxiety to differences from others and within the self.

We, on the other hand, are likely to react to differences, I think, in one of two ways. The first is, in effect, to deny the difference—"We're saying the same thing in different words"; "Our ends are the same, we differ only as to the means"; "After all, they're just like us, at bottom"; and so on. I call this acceptance by incorporation. The second is an acceptance by repudiation: the difference is recognized, but the issue is dismissed as unimportant or irrelevant. It is a matter of hair-splitting or logic-chopping, much ado about nothing; and the repudiation ranges from "Who cares?" to "A plague on both your houses!" Neither of these seems to me characteristic of the Asians, to say nothing of the fundamental Western orientation that one view (mine) is right and all the others wrong. In China especially there seems to me a genuine capacity for appreciation of a variety of points of view. What is remarkable is that this capacity does not express itself in an unthinking eclecticism but in a coherent and distinctive outlook. How this has come about I cannot pretend to explain.

What sanctions, if not religious ones, can Confucians rely on to enforce moral principles?

I MENTIONED EARLIER that the Chinese character for "morality" is derived from the one which represents the human heart, while our word "ethics" is from the Greek for custom or usage, and the word "morality" from its Latin translation. They are close to the Confucian conception in referring to social patterns, folkways, conventions in the broadest sense—in short, the way things are done in the society. Now in every society, the fact that things are done in a certain way becomes itself the ground of value in doing it that way. The patterns of action characteristic of the society draw to themselves social sanctions by which they are enforced and preserved. The normal becomes normative, and a description of the pattern has in itself an imperative force—the phrase "It just isn't done" conveys "Thou shalt not do it!"

The Confucian philosophy, more, I think, than any other, faces squarely this feature of human society. The ethical theory doesn't merely come to terms with it but takes it over for its own purposes. It is as though for once in a way the moral philosopher confronting social patterns which pose the problem for his ideals says to himself, "If you can't lick 'em, join 'em." The core of his position becomes the maintenance of a system of conventions conceived as only giving an explicit form to the patterns already established by tradition. In this way the familiar agencies of social control are put to work on behalf of morality—the family, church, school, and state. These are in fact the agencies of greatest importance for formulating and enforcing moral principles in our own society, as in every other. For Confucius, this fact is not a necessary evil, but the basis for the achievement of the greatest good.

Does the Confucian emphasis on the patriarchal family and state make it susceptible to dictatorship?

THE MORE I BECOME ACQUAINTED with various philosophies, the more I marvel at the power of the human mind to make of them whatever suits its particular motivations. My feeling is that no matter what the dominant philosophy of China had been, the manipulators of public opinion would have been able to engineer consent to their ideology. I think it is not too hard to present Confucian ideas as paving the way for the teachings of Marx and Engels and Mao Tse Tung. In fact, I am told that something of this kind is being done, though I have no direct acquaintance with the literature. On the other hand, I think it is also possible to present Confucianism as the direct antithesis of the communist ideology, failing only because it did not have a sufficiently powerful institutional base. I have heard a number of scholars of Free China talk of Confucianism in these terms. On the one hand, there is the emphasis, in Mencius for instance, on the moral content of governmental action, and the moral basis of its authority. On the other hand, certain ideas in the realistic wing of Confucianism, and in general the emphasis on conformity, obligation, recognition of authority, and so on, are comparatively easy to assimilate into the communist ideology, if they do not themselves reinforce its appeal.

The question is a perplexing one; for my part, I do not know what goes on in men's minds during a period of rapid and radical social change. Ask yourselves what part was played by Christian thought in Russia in the decades immediately preceding the Bolshevik revolution. There are in Europe Christian Socialist parties which regard communist ideals as identical with those of Christianity, or which argue, at any rate, that a truly Christian life can be lived only in a socialist society. And we are all familiar with the contrary view that communism is directly antithetical to everything that the Chirstian religion teaches. Who is right on this point? Plainly, everything depends on how both Christianity and communism are interpreted.

Now I don't know how anyone can prove that one interpretation of a philosophy is right and another is wrong, because the interpretation itself *is* the philosophy. We can argue only about the semantic question: which shall we *call* "Christianity," "communism," "Confucianism," or whatever? It is interesting that Confucius himself presented his own program of social reform as resting on a kind of semantic principle. All he aimed at, he said, was "a rectification of names." The trouble is that these days a "father" is not really a father, a "son" is not really a son, nor the "ruler" a ruler and the "citizen" a citizen. What Confucius was concerned with, as he put it, was that each man become really the thing that he is called. Something of this kind might also be said, I suppose, with regard to philosophies. But I am not so rash and presumptuous as to venture here on a rectification of philosophical names.

To what extent can China's lack of progress for so many centuries be attributed to its philosophies?

THAT QUESTION puts me in the awkward position of having to remind you that its philosophy is not the only influence working on a society, and probably far from the most powerful influence. I believe that philosophy is important to an understanding of culture; at any rate, some people (and I among them) find it the most fascinating element in culture. But the more attention we devote to it, the easier it is for us to lose our own perspective and come to see the philosophy as the only significant cultural reality. This is the typical intellectualist error, and I would be sorry to think that I am more than normally guilty of it. I have tried to present the bearings which any philosophy has on the problems of the men who have that philosophy; but I would not have you suppose that an understanding of the philosophy alone allows us to explain how and why the problems arose and are dealt with in particular ways. I think it likely that Indian philosophy, for instance, can be assigned some measure of responsibility for the great social problems that India now faces, but some measure only. With regard to China, I must simply plead ignorance; I just don't have enough acquaintance with Chinese institutions to venture an opinion on how they have been shaped by the thought of Confucius, Laotzu, and the rest. I would like to say something, however, about the concepts of progress and stagnation that are involved in the question.

It seems to me an unwarranted assumption that social problems are essentially the same everywhere, so that if another culture has not solved them as effectively as we have, the ideas which we have brought to bear on them must be superior to theirs. The West has made progress, while Asia has stagnated until it adopted the Western outlook. Ergo, Asian philosophies are intrinsically inferior from a social point of view. I believe that this common line of argument (seldom stated so baldly, of course) is mistaken for two reasons.

In the first place, problems are differently defined in different cultures, in ways that are directly relevant to differences in the corresponding philosophies. A poor solution to *our* problem may be an admirable one for theirs; we cannot insist on the superiority of our own formulation without begging the question at issue. The farmer who irrigates his fields with a bucket may be well aware of a more "efficient" arrangement, and yet feel that if he begins to rely on machines he will himself become no more than a machine. Something is achieved by the work of his own hands that no technology can achieve for him. You may say that his is a "reactionary" point of view, which stands in the way of progress; no doubt most Chinese today would say so. But I must confess that his position, while I do not share it, strikes me as being not altogether without justification.

In the second place, even if the problems which the Asian cultures face are to be formulated as we have formulated ours, we must not forget the enormous differences in the natural and human resources available for their solution. In particular, the state of technological development is so very different that the effect, if any, of differences in philosophical outlook must be entirely masked—except in so far as they might account, in turn, for the respective technologies.

I have several times hazarded the opinion that classical Indian philosophy makes for a certain apathy and withdrawal; but I would be hard put to it to defend this opinion. Every traveler feels, I am sure, that the natives just don't do things sensibly, and that if *he* were running the country, things would be very different. I freely admit that when I first went to India I shared this universal reaction. But as time passed and I became aware of the enormity of India's problems and how little is available for their solution, my attitude changed markedly, till at last I felt that if I were in the Indian government, what I would do is—go to Switzerland! I have boundless admiration for the heroic efforts which India is making toward its own social reconstruction, but I doubt very much whether the replacement of classical Indian thought by modern British philosophy—or by American philosophy, for that matter—would contribute markedly to the success of those efforts.

How is it that man is so central in Buddhist and Chinese philosophy, while human life is so cheap in Asian practice?

For my part, I repudiate the assumption on which this question rests. The notion that human life is of little account in Asia is, in my opinion, nothing but a prejudice. It is one thing to recognize the fact that poverty, disease, and illiteracy are widespread among vast populations; it is quite another to jump to the absurd conclusion that this shows that the Asians just don't care.

What is more, it is not hard to imagine representatives of the various Asian philosophies that we have just surveyed challenging the corresponding assumption that our own institutions and practices reveal such a great regard for the sanctity of human life. This is not the place, nor is it my intention, to spell out a wholesale indictment of Western civilization, and what man has made of man. But if we ask the Asian, "What good is your humanistic philosophy, when human beings are so miserable in your society?" it seems to me only fair that we consider also the counter question. It is easy enough to point to the vastly higher standard of living of the Western countries; but can this so easily be identified as expressing a higher regard for the sanctity of human life? May it not reflect, instead, a concern with the human being only insofar as he represents manpower for the technology and purchasing power for its products? I can imagine the Asian continuing with the charge that our technology has dehumanized man rather than emancipating him, and has brought us all to the point where it is no longer a question of the sanctity of human life but of the survival of life at all on this planet.

Let me make it quite clear that I am not myself endorsing this attack; I rather think, on the contrary, that it also expresses certain prejudices and relies more on stereotypes than on realistic images. But there is enough substance in it, I hope you will agree, to make it embarrassing—so much so, that we might be well advised to withdraw our own question. The wisdom of the East may not have done very much for the Easterner; but surely it is the beginning of wisdom in West or East to hold fast to the vision of what is yet to be done in our own lives.

LECTURE NINE

Zen

In one of his essays Montaigne remarks that no one is exempt from talking nonsense: the misfortune is only to do it solemnly. I want to assure you that I am going to make a special effort, not to avoid nonsense—that is impossible in talking Zen—but to avoid solemnity. I would like to invite you to do likewise, or at least to relax your efforts to grasp Zen: the more you relax, the more you will be able to grasp. The dominant style of Western philosophy—style of thought, I mean, not just of writing—has been ponderous and even grim. It is suggestive that we speak of a man as being in "dead" earnest, while "lively" connotes playfulness. Is it, as Santayana has suggested, only the approach of death that makes us philosophers? Can we so lightly assume (paradox indeed!) that gravity of demeanor is essential to the philosopher? Philosophy, after all, is the love of wisdom; and what is to be said of a lover who behaves always as though he were in church?

To begin, then, our adventure in nonsense. I must first enter a disclaimer. I shall be speaking of Zen largely (but not exclusively) as expounded in the writings of Daisetz Suzuki, who, as a member of the Rinzai sect of Zen, tends to make it rather more bizarre and paradoxical than is true of the other major sect, the Soto. In either case, the Zen that concerns us is a branch of Far Eastern Buddhism, not of West Coast dilettantism: it has incomparably more to do with Japanese tea than with Italian coffee. Whoever lays claim to being Zen, in the sense in which I shall speak of it, is first of all identifying himself as a Buddhist, and by implication is associating himself with Japanese culture. For almost everything which we in the West identify as characteristically Japanese is either a product of Zen or bears unmistakable marks of Zen influence: the Noh drama, haikku, flower arrangement, the tea ceremony, gardens, swordplay, and even the Kamikazi.

This, in my opinion, is what it means to be a living philosophy: that it plays an intimate part in the life of some particular people, that it infuses and informs a particular culture. I cannot find much significance in a philosophy that affects the speech habits of academicians but has nothing to do with behavior patterns in science, art, religion, politics, or interpersonal relations. In this sense Zen is one of the most vitally significant philosophies known to me: millions of people have really lived by it and view their lives through its perspectives. A full appreciation of Zen is therefore impossible without an appreciation of the culture of which it has been a significant part. Unfortunately, the limitations of both my time and my knowledge impose corresponding limitations on my treatment of Zen. I shall try to deal with it as though it can be abstracted from its cultural matrix, in the hope that thereby its possible relevance to our own culture will be made more apparent.

But in performing this abstraction, we must beware of interpreting Zen in terms of what belongs only to our own culture. In particular, we must recognize at the outset that Zen is not a religion in the usual Western sense. It has no sacred books or symbols, adheres to no special dogmas, performs no characteristic ceremonies or rituals. It is, to be sure, a branch of Buddhism; but what is distinctively Zen, as contrasted with other Buddhist denominations, does not depend on any of those features which we in the West usually regard as essential to a religious identification. For instance, Zen has nothing to do with theology; its aim, Suzuki has said, is "to see into the work of creation and not interview the creator." It has nothing to do with a Heaven, nothing with an immortal soul. When a Zen Master was asked how we could be sure of a life after death, he replied, "Leave that to Buddha, it is no business of ours." This is reminiscent of the remark attributed to Heine on his deathbed: "Of course God will forgive me —that's his business!" But the conventional religionist is not usually content to leave it to Heaven.

There are comparable dangers also in interpreting Zen as a philosophy in the Western sense. It does not offer a new logic, a special ethics, or a distinctive metaphysics of man and nature. In particular, Zen must not be interpreted as a kind of pantheism, monism, nature mysticism, or indeed any kind of transcendentalism. To be sure, it bears some resemblance to such philosophies; but, as I hope to make clear, the similarities are quite superficial. For these various schools are involved in just what Zen wishes to avoid—the pointless endeavor to trap life in a metaphysical net instead of simply living it. Zen, I think, shares the attitude to such an endeavor of e. e. cummings:

> O sweet spontaneous
> earth how often have
> the
> doting
>
> fingers of
> prurient philosophers pinched
> and
> poked
>
> thee

Zen renounces this embarrassing enterprise in favor of a forthright embrace.

The reason that Zen sets itself against philosophizing—though Zen hasn't much to do with reasons either!—is that philosophy is inescapably a matter of words. If it isn't entirely occupied with what words mean and how they should be used (as is true of much Anglo-American philosophy today), at any rate it is concerned with finding the right words by which to convey its teaching. But as far as Zen is concerned, there just aren't any right words; what Zen has to say simply isn't sayable—or at least, it isn't sayable simply. Now there have been philosophies which have held that language moves among shadows and stands in the way of grasping the substance. Bergson even defined metaphysics as the science which dispenses with symbols, and Wittgenstein concluded his logical analysis of language with the pronouncement "Whereof one cannot speak, thereof one must be silent." There is, indeed, a long tradition of so-called negative theology in Judaeo-Christianity as well as in Hinduism, according to which we can affirm nothing of God or the ultimate reality, but say of It only that It is not this, not that. But the position of Zen is not the conclusion of a philosophical analysis either of language or of reality. Its silence is an expression, not of an abstract mysticism, but of a preference for living life rather than talking about it—a conviction, indeed, that it is the talk that most interferes with the living.

You may complain that if Zen doesn't talk it can't teach; and Zen will counter, Who ever said that it *is* a teaching? It is *we* who come to Zen in the expectation of being taught; but what we have to learn is precisely to get rid of such expectations. A monk once approached a Zen Master and asked to be enlightened about Zen. The Master said to him, "Come again when there's nobody around, and I'll tell you what it is." The monk waited impatiently for an opportune moment, and some time afterward came again to the master and implored, "Now there is no one about—tell me the secret." The master said, "Come up closer," and when the monk did so the Master whispered to him, "Zen is something that cannot be conveyed by word of mouth." First he heightens the expectation: apparently there *is* a teaching, too important indeed to be broadcast indiscriminately; and just when the monk believes that the secret is about to be revealed to him, he is told: How could you have imagined that *any* words could be that important!

Nevertheless, human culture is made up of words—our very humanity depends on our capacity to use symbols. How can we avoid them? Even to say that Zen cannot be conveyed in words is to use words to convey something of Zen. Nor do we escape the dilemma just by being silent. As Suzuki reminds us, "A stone lying there is silent, a flower in bloom under the window is silent, but neither of them understands Zen. There must be a certain way in which silence and eloquence become identical." We cannot escape the dilemma, but must learn to live with it; and just that is what it means to know Zen. When the monk who has some acquaintance with Zen tries to get round the difficulty by asking the Master to show him the Way without using words, he gets the reply, "Ask me without using words!" There *is* no way around. The classical formulation in Zen is that of a man who is hanging on to the branch of a tree with his teeth, suspended over an abyss; and now someone comes along and asks him to expound the basic teaching of Buddhism. If he opens his mouth he is lost; but how shall he dismiss the questioner? This is the dilemma, not just of teaching Zen, but of learning life.

The upshot is that in Zen language is used, not for what it says, but for what it does. Its significance lies in its pragmatics rather than its semantics. The point to an utterance in Zen lies in the part played by the act of speech in the particular interpersonal situation in which the act occurs. If we abstract the content of the words from the concrete situation of which the words are only an incidental part, what we get is either hopelessly irrelevant or altogether nonsensical. What appears to be a dark saying is just something that is not meant to be looked through; and when we realize this, we see through it at once. This is what we must try to do with Zen: not understand it, but see through it. The propositions of Zen are to be treated as Wittgenstein counsels the reader to treat the propositions of his *Tractatus Logico-Philosophicus:* we are to "climb out through them, on them, over them"—and then throw away the ladder.

Zen expresses itself, therefore, not in a discursive exposition of doctrine, but in a recounting—or even better, a re-creating—of interpersonal situations between Master and monk in which words may or may not play a part. It may be a situation in which monk or Master asks a question and receives a reply, or one in which the Master reports an encounter between another Master and monk, perhaps adding his own comment. Such encounters are called in Japanese *mondo,* which means literally a question-answer; we might say a dialogue, anecdote, or vignette. The mondo, told in particular circumstances, has a part to play in those circumstances, not because it transmits a meaning encased in its words, but because the words serve to awaken the hearer to a realization of what he already somehow knew. The teaching is not in the mondo but in the act of its being spoken and heard.

It is for this reason that we find so much paradox, contradiction, and irrelevancy in the mondo. What is being said doesn't matter so much—or rather, the words in themselves are not a very good index to what is being communicated (lovers, too, may say a great deal to one another with sweet nothings). Often the Master will reply to a question just by repeating it, as though to say, Do you know what you are asking? for if you do, your question just won't arise. He may reply with an exclamation, a grunt, a cough, or—most characteristically—a ferocious roar. He may make use of gesture and action; especially famous is the Master's staff, employed, not to point to words on a blackboard but literally to beat the nonsense out of the student, with the help of Newton's physics rather than Aristotle's logic. Even more violent methods may be employed: one of the great Master's servered a disciple's finger, and another hacked a kitten in two before the assembled monks. Zen apologists speak of such actions as a kind of shock therapy, expressing the tender concern of the Master for the monks' enlightenment. Be that as it may, what is said in Zen can be understood only as we understand action, not discourse: we must ask, what is the speaker up to, what is he getting at. It is not his words but the fact that he utters them, then and there and in just that way, that has the latent meaning.

If Zen is nonsense, then, it is a special kind of nonsense. But we have a right to ask what this nonsense is about. What is the problem to which Zen addresses itself? What is it the monk wants to find out that the Master already knows? And it's no good to tell *us* to come again when there's nobody near. Yet what Zen has to say is not of much more help: There was an old woman who was born at the same time as the Buddha, and they lived in the same place throughout their lives. The old woman did not want to see the Buddha; whenever he came near, she did all she could to avoid him, running here and there to hide herself. But one day, finding it impossible to run away, she covered her face with her hands—and lo! the Buddha appeared between each of her ten fingers. This sutra quoted by Suzuki is about all we are told concerning the problem of Zen: it is that problem which is inescapable. You will recall in connection with existentialism the comment that there is nowhere for man to go out of this world, no tavern in which he can overcome anxiety, no jail in which he can expiate guilt. I think it is this that Zen is getting at in telling us that we cannot escape the confrontation of the Buddha. We cannot help trying to find meaning in life, and life is just the same sort of nonsense that Zen is. We cannot hide from ourselves; but what are we to do if we come out of hiding and find nobody? If there *is* someone there, there is no problem, no need to study Zen; the Master will dismiss you, for you are yourself the Master, and indeed, as Zen makes perfectly explicit, you are the Buddha.

So instead of telling us what the problem is, Zen insists that the whole trouble is just our failure to realize that there is no problem. And of course this means that there is no solution either. This is the position taken by Zen from the very beginning. According to tradition, Zen was founded early in the sixth century by a monk named Bodhi-Dharma, who brought Buddhism from India, the land of its origin, into China, whence, after some centuries of interaction with indigenous Chinese philosophy and religion, it moved into Japan. Suzuki relates that Bodhi-Dharma was once invited by the Emperor for an audience. The Emperor told him how many monasteries he had built, how many sacred writings he had caused to be copied, how many nuns and priests he had invested, and asked, "How great is the merit due to me?" "No merit at all," was the answer. Startled, the Emperor asked, "What is the Noble Truth in its highest sense?" Since the Buddhist doctrine is canonically presented in the so-called Four Noble Truths, the question is often asked, What is *the* Truth, or the One True Word, or simply, the Word—in short, what is the essential teaching of Buddhism? So when the Emperor asked, "What is the Noble Truth in its highest sense?" Bodhi-Dharma replied, "It is empty, no nobility in it whatsoever." In astonishment, the Emperor demanded, "Who is it then that is standing here before me?" "I do not know, sire." The Emperor could not understand him and Bodhi-Dharma went his way; the audience was at an end. You see what kind of an impression Zen left from the very beginning!

For all its apparent formlessness, Zen is really very stylized. Many of the mondo are as strictly patterned as the classical ballet or a chess gambit: we must learn the openings before entering on our own combinations. One of the standard opening gambits is to ask, "Why did Bodhi-Dharma come out of the West?" That is, what was his mission, what is the message that Zen brings? The Master replies, "Come forward, and I'll let you know." And when the monk steps up, the Master boxes his ears with the words, "There! The secret is out." With this blow Zen demonstrates in a striking fashion how radically different its standpoint is from those of the Western philosophies. It may agree with existentialism that there is no escaping life; but for Zen there is no wrestling with the angel in the dark night of the soul. There is nothing to be grappled with, no secret to be wrenched out of the very heart of things. Western philosophy has remained in the circle that runs from Pythagoras to Kant and back again: its aim is to penetrate the mysteries of existence, for knowledge is power; but power in turn wraps itself in mystery. Zen, on the contrary, absorbed from Chinese Taoism the repudiation of conquest—even the conquest of self. The monk pleads, "O Master, pacify my soul!" "Bring me your soul and I will pacify it." "But Master, I have searched and struggled, and have been unable to find my soul." And the reply is, "It is already pacified."

In short, the Zen solution to the great problem of life, as Suzuki has pointed out, is not solving it at all: "the not-solving is really the solving." Philosophy is itself the disease for which it pretends to be the cure: the wise man does not pursue wisdom but lives his life, and therein precisely does his wisdom lie. What does the Preacher say, "Go your way, eat your bread with joy, and drink your wine with a merry heart; for God has already accepted your works. . . . But be admonished: of the making of many books there is no end, and much study is a weariness of the flesh." This is the wisdom that Faust comes to in the end; Zen starts with it. I think it rather remarkable that the classic of contemporary scientific philosophy, Wittgenstein's *Tractatus,* comes also to the same result: "We feel that even if all possible scientific questions be answered, the problems of life have still not been touched at all. Of course there is then no question left, and just this is the answer. The solution of the problem of life is seen in the vanishing of this problem." This, I think, is what Zen means to say; but it cannot actually say it without betraying its own principles.

And now you've caught me: if Zen acknowledges no problem and offers no solution, how can it have "principles"? The dilemma remains—my teeth are holding tight to the branch, and how shall I speak? This is what the man of Zen might say, and the more he is pressed, the more he will insist that there is no Zen in him at all, and in any case there is nothing to it. Of course we are not convinced, at any rate not at the outset; and I must say it is my intention to try to persuade you that he is not deceiving you in the least! But still, there must be something there that we are trying to lay hold of. If not a philosophical or religious doctrine, it is at any rate a point of view, or maybe better, a point of action, as it were. How shall we characterize it?

To start with, Zen stands firmly opposed to any tendency to dilute the rich concreteness of life with watery abstractions. So too the psychoanalyst must combat a certain sort of patient's defense mechanism which consists in glossing over his behavior with the standard terms of the psychoanalytic vocabulary. The monk asks, "What is my self?" and the Master replies, "What would you do with a self if you had one?" No good purpose is served by the abstraction when it becomes a device for this kind of intellectualization. Accordingly, the Master does not answer the question, but answers the need which impelled it, or rather, answers in such a way as might help bring the questioner to an awareness of the concrete substance of his life.

This is a frequent and important tactic in Zen. A Master was one day sweeping the ground in the monastery when one of the monks said to him, "You are such a wise and holy Master, how is it that dust ever accumulates in your yard?" The Master replied at once, "It comes from the outside." The dust, of course, is symbolic, a classic metaphor in Buddhism for whatever tarnishes the clear mirror of the mind. The Master was saying that all was clear until the question arose. The point is more explicit in another mondo: "Why should a holy place like this attract dust?" "There! another particle of dust!" It is as though one breaks the silence by asking why it's quiet—how much noise we make with our questions! Yet something of Zen is lost if we interpret these mondo only in this symbolic way. For if this is what the Master meant to say, why didn't he say it? A contemporary English or American philosopher might address himself to formulating a semantic theory of admissable questions, and his teaching would consist in expounding the theory. But it is just such formulations and expositions that Zen takes to be pointless. Note that the Master was in literal truth sweeping the yard, a simple and concrete action that flowed naturally out of his life in the monastery, no part of being a "philosopher." Dust *does* come in from the outside; and when he said "There! another particle of dust!" no doubt there really was one, and the sweeper was understandably annoyed at seeing it. What the Master was doing was as much a part of his instruction as what he said; and even more important, what was said didn't in the least interfere with his going on about his business.

Sometimes, however, Zen does make the point verbally and explicitly. There is a mondo which Suzuki tells as follows. A group of monks were engaged in philosophical dispute concerning a fluttering penant which was on a pole in the monastery courtyard. One monk urged that, since the pennant is an inanimate object, it is the wind that makes it flap, to which another objected that the wind is also inanimate, so the flapping is an impossibility. A third protested that the flapping is due to a certain combination of causes and conditions, while a fourth proposed the theory that after all there is no flapping pennant, but the wind moving by itself. The discussion grew quite animated when the Master came among them and broke in with the remark, "It is neither wind nor pennant that is flapping, but your own minds." And that put a stop to the argument. This mondo concerns one of the greatest of the Zen Masters, yet I make bold to say that there is not very much Zen in it. It is too much of a witticism, almost a joke. It was a debater's point that the Master made and won; he might better have hauled down the pennant, or saluted it, or done whatever it was that the time and place called for. And the monks themselves were only half serious; it was obviously no more than an undergraduate bull session. The real problem is how to keep from remaining undergraduates all our lives.

What Zen is getting at is that the really serious questions, as we imagine, the ones we suppose to bear on the deepest human concerns, the profound religious and metaphysical questions—such questions should never have been asked at all. The mere asking involves us in a network of abstraction in which we become hopelessly enmeshed. It is not that we cannot manage the abstractions themselves: it isn't so hard, after all, for a student to master the idiom of a Kant or Whitehead or the rules governing the transformations of the symbols of mathematical logic. What we can't manage with these abstractions is our lives. We imprison ourselves in our own conceptualizations and think we will escape if we can only make the system more subtle and complex.

We have become so accustomed to wearing a mask of rationality, Zen mght say, that we cannot recognize even our own faces. It is an almost universal assumption of Western philosophy (and most Asian philosophy as well) that the solution to the great problems of human existence can be arrived at if we carry our rationality far enough, if we try hard enough to make sense of existence, uncover its intrinsic reasonableness. The standpoint of Zen is that exactly the contrary is true. If we were just to turn our backs to the whole enterprise, suddenly nothing would remain for us to strive for. The monk says to the Master, "Yesterday you declared that the whole universe is one transpicuous crystal; how am I to understand that?" To which the Master replies, "The whole universe is one transpicuous crystal, and what is the sense of understanding it?"

Here, I am afraid, Zen is treading on dangerous ground. The repudiation of the pernicious *use* of reason is too easily transformed into an acceptance of faulty reasoning. In the West we have become familiar with this possibility in a certain strain of romanticism.

—To think that two and two are four
  And neither five nor three
The heart of man has long been sore
  And long 'tis like to be.

Quite so; and yet an impressive documentation can be provided for the thesis that poor arithmetic is also very bad for the human heart. In its strictures against the mask of rationality Zen does not always distinguish as sharply as I think it must between the view that reason has improper uses and the view that the use of reason is improper. We can—and I believe we should—accept the first and at the same time unequivocally reject the second. All that Zen needs to maintain is that the use of reason in the attempt to cope with the basic religious and metaphysical concerns is ill-advised. And on this point I think that Zen is quite right.

What we must see clearly is that Zen is not rejecting one metaphysics or theology in favor of another. It is the whole metaphysico-theological enterprise that is being repudiated. So far as concerns the actual living of our lives, there is little to choose among the various constructions. They are all metaphors, as it were, and while a change of metaphor may satisfy the critics it will never lift us from literature into life. We become so accustomed to particular conventions of symbolization that we forget altogether that we are dealing with symbols and mistake convention for nature itself. Suzuki tells the story of a famous painter of bamboo who executed a commission with his customary skill, painting an entire bamboo grove in red. "The patron upon its receipt marveled at the extraordinary skill with which the painting had been executed, and, repairing to the artist's residence, he said, 'Master, I have come to thank you for the picture; but, excuse me, you have painted the bamboo red.' 'Well,' cried the Master, 'in what color would you desire it?' 'In black, of course,' replied the patron. 'And who,' answered the artist, 'ever saw a black-leaved bamboo?'"

We do not get rid of the mask of rationality if we merely cover one mask with another. There have been many philosophies of unreason—intuition and the like—but from the Zen viewpoint they are still philosophies. As I see it, Zen does not counsel us to think with our blood, but only warns us against what F. H. Bradley called the bloodless ghosts of metaphysics: to converse with shadows the metaphysician himself becomes a shade. It is possible to make a rationale even of unreason. A monk asked the Master, "Who is the Buddha?" and the Master struck him. Now the monk had learned a lesson or two—or so he thought—so he hit the Master back. At once the Master said to him, "Ah, there was a reason for your striking me, but no such reason for my striking you." This left the monk entirely at a loss; whereupon the Master struck him and drove him from the room. There is no sense in planning to be spontaneous, or in calculating how not to be a schemer.

Now Bradley and his fellow absolute idealists of the late nineteenth century also held that logic is inadequate to life, inadequate even for a coherent account of reality. Our conceptions of space and time, things and the self, they argued, are shot through with contradiction. But to their mind this called for a new logic by which we are to penetrate Appearance to Reality. For the Hegelians there was a dialectic by which contradictions are continuously resolved into a higher synthesis. Zen has nothing to do with all this; it has no use for deeper logics and higher syntheses. As Suzuki brilliantly put it, Zen contents itself with just calling a spade a not-spade. The traditional practice in the Zen monastery was for the student to demonstrate the degree of his attainment by composing a poem testifying to his insight into Zen. One of the earliest and most famous is this:

> Empty-handed I go, and behold the spade is in my hands;
> I walk on foot, and yet on the back of an ox I am riding;
> When I pass over the bridge,
> Lo, the water is still, but the bridge flows.

Suzuki himself, if I may presume to say so, is in my opinion a Master and not merely a scholar of Zen. Nothing in the classical literature that he cites seems to me to excel his own formulation: "The stone maiden dances, the wooden horse neighs; in a handful of water scooped up in my palm the mermaids are seen dancing to their heart's content." What a contrast with our own pathetic Mr. Prufrock:

> I have heard the mermaids singing, each to each.
> I do not think they will sing to me.

There is no sense of tragedy, and certainly no pathos, in Zen's unblinking acceptance of the dilemma that is life. Zen has no time for such reflections. You simply stand, walk, or sit; hold your spade in empty hands; and bridges flow, stone maidens dance. Zen does not aim at proving that these things are so; just scoop up the water in your own palm and see the mermaids.

If we do not see them, Zen would say, it is because we look through a veil of words. Zen is direct and immediate, but words are mediators; we relate to life as though it were a government we have not officially recognized and with whom we communicate, therefore, only through the good offices of a third party. We want to "understand" life, but that only means that we want to put it into words—we are groping for the intermediary. The bridge that does not flow does not connect the two banks but only holds them apart. Or, to use Suzuki's metaphor, Zen must be seized with bare hands, with no gloves on, and the same is true of everything in life. Religion and philosophy try to fit us with gloves with which we can safely take hold. Zen does not offer us pious assurances that there is no danger, exhorting us to have faith. It simply declares that you cannot take hold in fear and trembling, and gloves will not help you one bit.

The Master once held up his staff before his disciples and declared: "Call this a staff and you make an assertion; call it not a staff and you make a negation. Now don't assert and don't negate; what is it? Quick, quick!" This is a classic figure of the Zen ballet. The Master asks a question and demands an answer immediately, without a pause for what we call reflection—that is, without letting us move further and further away from the reality of which we are trying to take hold. Do we not find ourselves at a loss in such a case? Yet the more we reflect, the more we are unsettled and perplexed. In the mondo, one of the monks—obviously a very superior fellow—instantly stepped forward, pulled the staff out of the Master's hands, broke it in two, and holding up the two ends said, "Now what is this?" The meaning of life manifests itself in the living of it or not at all, and certainly not in any collection of words, however "profound." We stand in a vast hall with doors on every hand, and as we turn irresolutely from side to side, one by one the doors are closing.

Of course reflection has a part to play, and words, as instruments of reflective action, are by no means expendible. What Zen is getting at is that so often we treat the words not as the instruments of life but as its very substance. We confuse the words with the realities they stand for. "A basket is welcome to carry our fish home," Suzuki says, "but when the fish are safely on the table why should we eternally bother ourselves with the basket?" It is especially in the area where philosophy and religion border on one another that words get out of hand. We worship an image, work magic with symbols, and conquer in a sign. And all these mark out for us—so we suppose—a special realm, the realm of the spirit, the holy. But nothing is more inimical to the life of the spirit than to encapsulate it from life in this way. This is why a certain Master instructed his monks to wash out their mouths with soap when they uttered the word "Buddha." Note, please, that this is not a matter of the Buddha's name, like that of the God of the Hebrews, being too awesome to utter; on the contrary, taking the Name is most likely to be in vain precisely when we most regard it as sacred. The Master once slapped a monk when he was bowing before an image of the Buddha. The monk defended himself: "Is it not a laudable thing to pay respect to Buddha?" "Yes," answered the Master, "but it is better to go without even a laudable thing." The instruments for the attainment of spiritual value so easily usurp intrinsic value themselves: that the letter can kill is a commonplace of all religious experience. The point is that religious symbols can draw sustenance only from a religious life; and such a life cannot consist only in the use of the symbols, or it does no more than close an empty circle.

The fatality in words is that they offer themselves as material with which to construct another world than God's, a fantasy world, a world empty, as Zen might say, of the universal Buddha-nature. Zen is distrustful of words and thoughts because it is determined not to be seduced by illusion. We in the West say, "The mind is its own place, and in itself can make a heaven of hell, a hell of heaven"; but we forget that these words were spoken by Satan, the Great Illusionist, and himself the greatest victim of illusion. Zen wants no commerce with anything but realities; the business of the mind is to know its place, and its place is not its own. A Master was once asked, "We have to dress and eat every day; how can we escape from all that?" What a world of trivialities we live in—so the monk feels; all this fuss over bodily needs and social conventions; all the endless restrictions imposed by the laws of nature and of man. If only we could do away with them, once for all, and enter into the Heavenly Kingdom where we can live a life of pure spirituality! "We have to dress and eat every day; how can we escape from all that?" The Master replied, "We dress, we eat." And when the monk complained, "I do not understand you," the Master said to him, "If you don't understand, put on your robe and eat your food." Just accept the facts for what they are; and there's no occasion either to wax philosophical with the reflection, "That's life!"

Essentially the same question was asked of another Master: "Summer comes, winter comes; how shall we escape from it?" We are caught in the rat race, an endless round of meaningless effort, deadening routine; surely it was not for this that God shaped man in His image, and breathed His spirit into man's flesh! Life must have some meaning, and where shall I find it? How well the Master understood the questioner, for he asked in turn, "Why not go to the place where there is neither summer nor winter?" (Now you're talking! This is just what I had in mind.) "Where can such a place be found?" And the Master replied, "When winter comes you shiver, when summer comes you sweat." This is the only place after all. "Here at least we shall be free," Satan promises; the poor monk was on the point of forgetting that *that* place is Hell. The Master's solution to the problem of life was just to shiver in winter and sweat in summer. And if we're not solemn about it, I think myself that he was right.

We must not do Zen the injustice of charging it with standing opposed to any attempt to master the environment: the monks, after all, do not live on a diet of wild berries and roots, but cultivate their gardens. What is being called for is not a passive submission to things as they are, but an active—even joyous—acceptance of what we in the West call the existential constraints on the human condition, the facts of life, so to say, as distinct from the particular circumstances in which we might happen to find ourselves. However advanced his technology and medicine, man must still live by the sweat of his brow, still come to terms with the prospect of death. The Garden of Eden is behind us forever, and those who dwell on the memory live with the curse still ringing in their ears. For Zen, the round of summer and winter becomes a blessing the moment we give up the fantasy of eternal spring. As I approach Zen—inescapably, through the background of our own Judaeo-Christian tradition—this is what it means to me to shiver and sweat, to put on our robes and eat our food.

Once out of Eden, we must see God everywhere or we will not see Him at all. Zen is to be found in the ordinary affairs of everyday life or nowhere. Correspondingly, there is as much "spiritual" truth in the simplest matter-of-fact observation as in the most profound metaphysical propositions—indeed, more! The Master is asked, "What is the most wonderful word?" This is the same gambit as the Emperor's question to Bodhi-Dharma, what is the noblest truth, the one true word. Here the Master replies, "What do you say?" or perhaps better, "What say you?" This has a duality of meaning characteristic of Zen. The Master probably didn't hear the question and is asking to have it repeated; or maybe he heard the question and answered it—the most wonderful word is just what you yourself are saying. But put this way it has almost become a metaphysical doctrine; if we intellectualize it, the whole point is lost. The dual meaning serves this purpose, that the perfectly ordinary one ("I didn't hear you") provides an anchorage against floating off into the abstractions of the esoteric meaning ("Every word embodies the ultimate truth of Buddhism"). If we become caught up in the second interpretation, the Master sharply pulls us back to the first. When he was asked about the "first word" (another variant), the Master coughed, at which the monk remarked, "Is this not it?" But the Master at once rejoined, "Why, an old man is not even allowed to cough!" And yet the monk was right, if only he hadn't stopped to think about it and say so. But staying with the mundane sense won't do either. "What is the one word?" "What do you say?" The monk then repeats his question, but now the Master replies, "You make it two."

The way of Zen is nothing at all special, and this, of course, is what makes it seem so extraordinary. Asked what is Zen, the Master once replied, "Your everyday thought." Perhaps better might have been, "Your everyday action," or maybe even simply, "Everyday."

Life becomes a riddle only when we spend it anxiously searching for the answer: confronted by the Sphinx the way of Zen is, if Japanese, to take a picture of it, and, if American, to carve initials on it. Life is not a metaphysical exercise, but people live it like those amateur musicians who are always "practicing" the piano but never play it. The monk who complained that in his three years in the monastery he had never been given any spiritual teaching was brought up sharply by the Master: "When you bring me tea, do I not take it? When you bow to me, do I not acknowledge your greeting? When was I ever at fault in instructing you in matters spiritual?" What more was it that the monk wanted to learn? Apparently, he wanted to transcend life but not to live it, to paint masterpieces but not bother with either brush or canvas. The Master once treated a visitor to some cake; the visitor asked, "They speak of our not knowing it while using it all the time—what is this 'it'?" The Master innocently picked up a piece of cake and offered it to his guest, who finished it and repeated the question, at which the Master said, "There you are! It is used every day, but they don't know it!" Zen is in the tea and cake, and not as symbols of a sacrament either, but just as the ordinary things they are, as ordinary and as miraculous as everything else in the world.

This is the point, is it not, if I may venture to make it so explicit—that there are miracles all around us, and we miss them only because we are straining to hear the sound of the ram's horn by which we imagine so special an event must be announced. How simple, genuine, and moving is Suzuki's account of the matter: "There is nothing extraordinary or mysterious about Zen. I raise my hand; I take a book from the other side of this desk; I hear the boys playing ball outside my window; I see the clouds blown away beyond the neighboring woods: in all these I am practicing Zen, I am living Zen. No wordy discussion is necessary, nor any explanation. I do not know why, and there is no need of explaining, but when the sun rises the whole world dances with joy and everybody's heart is filled with bliss. . . ."

Now this is the classic teaching of Zen, so far as I am acquainted with it. Unfortunately, the devotees of Zen are human beings like the rest of us, and in their practice depart from the true spirit in about the same degree as we find in any other of the world's great religions. The insight of the prophet is codified in law, inspiration becomes institutionalized, and the outcome is often scarcely recognizable as embodying the original teaching. I was myself once almost bodily thrown out of the meditation hall of a Zen monastery because, although I had of course removed my shoes, I had neglected to take off my socks as well. Custom, I suppose, is king everywhere, and trifles are taken as seriously in the actual practice of Zen as in any doctrinal religion.

Thus the teaching of Zen is that discipline and meditation, although they have an important part to play, as we shall see, must not be allowed to interfere with a simple and natural life. This point is made in Senzaki's story of the two monks who came to a ford in a river where a young girl was helplessly waiting to cross. The man of Zen picked her up, waded across, and set her down on the other bank. His companion, an orthodox Buddhist, was obviously distressed, and as they walked on their way he at last broke out in reproach: "You know perfectly well that we monks are not even permitted to touch a woman, and here you have held one in your arms!" To which the other replied, "I set her down by the river; are you still carrying her?" Looking at Zen as an actual institution, with its set of characteristic patterns and practices, I am afraid it must be said that many of its followers are indeed still carrying her. I do not mean to be making an invidious comparison with our own religious institutions—it would be foolish to invite attention to the beam in our own eyes. Perhaps it is flatly impossible, from a psychological and sociological standpoint, to preserve a spiritual insight in an institutional form. The law, after all, is intended for ordinary men, not prophets. But I think it important to be reminded that the Zen with which we have been made acquainted in the West is likely to be the careful distillation of a precious essence and not the crude mixture that makes up the historical reality. A Japanese student of Judaism and Christianity would in the same way be well advised to remember that the Synagogue, Church, and State are not too clearly represented in the Book of Job, Isaiah, or the Sermon on the Mount.

To return, then, to the teaching of Zen. Sooner or later the question must be faced, how Zen is to be attained, if it is so simple and ordinary. How can we live our lives so straightforwardly, so free of intellectualized complications, that the meaning of life no longer puzzles us? The answer that Zen gives is probably disappointing in a characteristic way, but I think that it is also characteristically homely and honest. It is just to go after Zen with complete earnestness and sincerity. To my mind this is the same as the counsel of Ecclesiastes: "Whatsoever thy hand findeth to do, do it with thy might." And I think that William Blake was getting at the same thing when he said that if the fool persisted in his folly he would be wise. The great thing is to keep at it, and to put all you've got into it. A monk asked the Master to play him a tune on a stringless harp (I shall say something about this kind of absurdity shortly). The Master was silent a few moments, and then said, "There! do you hear it?" And when the monk replied, "Alas, no, Master!" the Master reproached him with, "Why didn't you ask me louder?" Like the author of Deuteronomy and the Hasidim of eighteenth-century Judaism, Zen puts its reliance on whole-heartedness and intensity of effort; nothing else will do, and that alone is enough.

If we have learned not to look for the secret, we have yet to learn, Zen might say, that it is we ourselves who must do the not-looking. The last and greatest obstacle is to free ourselves from a dependency on a source of what we still imagine to be spiritual instruction: the Master, the prophet, priest, philosopher, or psychoanalyst. We think to move him with compassion for our plight, so he will take us by the hand and lead us to our goal, play us a tune on a stringless harp. But Zen insists, in agreement with other Buddhist sects, that salvation cannot be sought outside the self, and to attain Nirvana we must give up our attachment even to Nirvana. The last words of the Buddha exhorted his disciples to be lamps unto themselves, and to work out their salvation with diligence. For Zen, we cannot even take the Buddha as a model, and, in the current Western idiom, rely on transference, identification, and introjection to heal us.

There is, indeed, a strong temptation in Zen to imitate the Master. Even we probably feel about these mondo that it's not too hard to get the hang of it; we might well be able to do it ourselves. And I cannot resist asking once more, What is this "it" that we can so easily learn to do? Surely nothing of any particular significance in our lives. The Zen Masters were quite well aware of this temptation for the monk just to imitate and addressed themselves to the task of making him realize that the outcome would be only an *ersatz* life. A Master asked one of the monks, "What do you understand by this: 'Let the difference be even a tenth of an inch and it will grow as wide as heaven and earth'?" There are some obvious intellectualizations we might go into: it means that you must discipline yourself with firmness, you must not waver for one moment, and so on and so forth. But the monk had learned something, so he replied instead, "Let the difference be even a tenth of an inch and it will grow as wide as heaven and earth." The Master rejoined, "Not at all, that just won't do!" Now the perplexed monk said, "I cannot do otherwise; how do you understand it?" To which the Master replied, "Let the difference be even a tenth of an inch and it will grow as wide as heaven and earth." It was clear at once to the Master that the monk was imitating him, and he himself imitated to make it clear to the monk. When the little girl puts on mommy's high heels she neither walks nor runs in them, but only stands and admires herself in the mirror—and therein lies her childishness.

The Master may indeed be important to you, but with the importance that attaches to whoever is before you at that moment. You can take hold of Zen only by direct and simple action, in interpersonal relations as in all else. One of the most famous of all the mondo concerns a military man who confronted a Master with a problem: "A man once kept a goose in a bottle, feeding it till it grew too large to get through the bottleneck. Now, how to get the goose without killing the goose or breaking the bottle?" The Master said to him, "O officer!" to which he replied, "Yes, Master," and the

Master exclaimed, "There! The goose is out of the bottle!" It was only a puzzle after all, and we see through it in the immediacy of the interpersonal relation in which it is posed. God said, "Abraham, Abraham!" and he answered, "Here am I." There is here no metaphysics of I and Thou, no self-mortification, no torturing of either flesh or spirit. Life need not be transfigured by so-called spiritual exercises: it is enough if I call and you answer me.

The problem of the goose in the bottle is not posed by life but is of our own making. We conceive of the human mind as being locked up in its own experiences and formulate elaborate epistemologies to explain how we build up an external world out of our perceptions. We struggle to establish the conviction that the whole choir of earth and furniture of heaven are not figments of our own imaginations. What is worse, each man lives in his own dream, and how can the dreamer reach out to establish contact with any other? In this dream world I alone am real and every other human being a fabled monster. With Alice we say, "I'll believe in you if you'll believe in me." But on these terms faith is not easy to come by, and there is no one to enforce the contract. This is the problem with which we come to the Master, and he says: Here am I, another person; I speak to you, you hear me, understand me, and answer me; and together we sit and drink our cup of tea. Now tell me again, what is it that is worrying you? The goose has come out of the bottle easily enough; indeed, it never was in the bottle.

Of course, Zen does not content itself with waiting for such a release. Like every other religion it imposes a discipline which is meant to enhance our capacity for answering when we are called —in Zen, our capacity for living life without bothering ourselves with the artificialities by which we complicate it. The method with which we are best acquainted in the West (though it is characteristic chiefly of the Rinzai school of Zen) is that of the *koan*. The word means literally a public theme or document, rather like the "thesis" which a candidate for a degree must defend before the assembled faculties. It is in Zen a mark of the student's qualification for progressing to another stage on the road to enlightenment.

There are some seventeen hundred classic koans; the student works on one, and when he has mastered it proceeds to another and another. Enlightenment by no means depends on solving all the koans; but then it is in any case not a matter of completing any fixed set of requirements!

The koan is an unanswerable question, an impossible task, a paradox to be resolved: how to hear the sound of a stringless harp or the clap made by only one hand, or how to get the goose out of the bottle. It is a dilemma from which we cannot escape by intellectualization. The student struggles with his problem until he realizes as fully and vividly as may be that his thinking will get him nowhere with it, and then the problem vanishes. It is not solved but dissolved; he simply takes the dilemma by the horns and throws it behind him. And then another may confront him and still another. The goal is to arrive at a condition in which such dilemmas no longer arise before him, in which life is no longer a problem to be solved but is just to be lived.

The Zen method for dealing with the koan is to engage in a characteristic activity which we might call "meditation" were it not for the intellectualist connotation of that word. Historically it derives from the pattern of meditation in Yoga, called *dhyana* in Sanskrit, *ch'an-na* in Chinese, thence *zenna* in Japanese; its practice is called *zazen,* and the room of the monastery in which it is practiced is therefore known as the *zendo*. The word *zen* is thus an abbreviated reference to this basic method of seeking enlightenment. The monk or serious student spends many hours daily sitting cross-legged and immobile, often in conjunction with various Yogic breathing exercises, and working on his koan. He must struggle with it till he is driven to such an extremacy that suddenly he breaks his way through. No magical efficacy attaches (in theory, at least) to the bodily posture and disposition; it is just the one in which we can be most comfortable and free from the distraction of bodily sensations. At any rate, that seems to be true for the members of the Asian cultures; if Zen were genuinely to take hold in the United States, I think it should avail itself of the psychoanalytic couch.

Now the practice of zazen is not an end in itself but is instrumental to the mastery of the koan. For us the posture may be exotic, but there is nothing esoteric about the process. There is something very like it in Walt Whitman's "I loaf and invite my soul"; indeed, there is a good deal of Zen in Whitman. The practice in the zendo differs only in this, that there you must stop loafing and really work at it. But we are not to forget that the koan itself is also only an instrument, and all our struggles with it may be less effective than some sudden and intense experience—the smashing of the water jug with which the old woman earns her livelihood, or the sight of a morning-glory in full bloom entwined about the well in the courtyard. Or perhaps enlightenment may come through the friendly offices of a vigorous Master. Such a one raised his staff once before the assembled monks and declared, "This staff of mine is meant for people of the second and third grades." A monk asked, "What would you do if one of the first grade should turn up?" You can guess what happened to the questioner, but it is harder to know whether that promoted him to the top grade.

And now, what has been achieved when this highest grade is attained? We in the West speak of salvation, as the Hindu does of moksha or the Buddhist of Nirvana; in Zen it is called *satori.* Translations are dangerous, and especially here, for we are accustomed to think of the goal of the religious life as having its locus beyond the world of the senses. But satori, we are told over and over again, is in no way in conflict with the world of sense. When we have made a little progress in Zen, we think the river is no river and the mountain no mountain; but after satori, the river is a river and the mountain is a mountain. We do not enter another world but view the one real world from another perspective—or if it is another, it is only in the sense in which, as Wittgenstein remarked, the world of the happy is quite another than the world of the unhappy. Satori brings about, as it were, a Copernican transformation: we no longer experience ourselves as the fixed center about which all revolves. "It all depends on the adjustment of the hinge," Suzuki has said, "whether the door opens in or out." Satori is only that small adjustment; it is not the experience of a transcendental object but a transcendence of the perpetual bifurcation of experience into subject and object. We must not think of a Heaven in which we are rocked in the bosom of Abraham; it is on this earth that we stand face to face with the living God. The antitheses of the earthly and the divine, the sacred and the profane, time and eternity—all these belong to just that apparatus of pernicious intellectualization that Zen wants to dispense with once and for all.

Yet I hope I have said enough about Zen for you to anticipate that it does not make much of a fuss about satori: there's not much to it, after all. Achieving satori is at bottom not an achievement—the marksman rejoices when he examines the target, but it is neither the examination nor the shot that gives cause for rejoicing: his arrow stood in the bull's-eye from the very beginning. Man is not in bondage, struggling for freedom; he is already free. If there is a bondage here, it is the Spinozistic human bondage which consists only in ignorance. Our Western religions begin with man's eating of the fruit of the tree of knowledge; for Buddhism, the story begins rather with ignorance. The enlightenment to which Zen aspires consists in the realization that there is nothing to aspire to, that we already have everything for which we are struggling. "How can I get away from the triple world?" the monk asks. The "triple world" in the classical Buddhist metaphysics is the world of phenomena, the world of sense, of brute fact, of triviality and meaninglessness. The Master replies, "Where are you now?" Why try to get away when you have already arrived? What is all this talk of returning home when not for one moment have you been away? The rider on the donkey, Suzuki says, searches for the donkey.

Satori is not an attainment, in short, but a realization of what we have had all along. In that case, of course there is no secret, no esoteric teaching in the custody of the Master, no special path on which only the devotee can learn to walk. A Confucian poet came to a Master and wanted to be initiated into Zen. The Master quoted him a passage in the *Analects* in which Confucius said to his disciples, "Do you think I am hiding something from you? Indeed, I have nothing to hide!" Now they were walking in the mountains, and the wild laurel was in full bloom. As they went on in silence, the Master said, "Do you smell it?" When the poet said "Yes" the Master continued, "There, you see? I have nothing to hide from you." The same point is beautifully made in a seventeenth century haikku by one of the Japanese emperors:

> Smiling eyebrows are opened.
> Is it cherry or peach blossom?
> Who does not know?—Yet nobody knows.

There is no more of a secret in Zen—and no less of one!—than the difference between cherry blossom and peach blossom, blooming every spring, and sending out their fragrance to all men, like the gentle rain falling on the just and unjust alike.

In Buddhist iconography, enlightenment is represented by the opening of a third eye, in much the sense in which we speak of listening with the third ear. The third eye does not open on a hidden world, somewhere beyond; it only represents really seeing what is in this one. This is why it is wrong to think of Zen as mysticism, at least of the usual kind. Zen does not find tongues in trees, books in the running brooks, sermons in stones, and good in everything. There is water in the brook, a tree is a tree, and a stone is a stone; and that indeed is good, but it is also bad. It is just what it is. To make a symbol of every reality deprives the symbol of anything to symbolize, and deprives reality of any significance. To put the meaning of life somewhere outside it is to make life itself empty. But it is just this sense of the emptiness of life that we are trying to overcome when we turn to religion or philosophy. To think that rivers and mountains are, "underneath it all," something entirely different is no kind of enlightenment, and certainly not Zen. Just the way things are is quite enough to evoke awe and wonder. With Aristotle, the Western world finds the beginning of philosophy in this awe and wonder; Zen ends with them.

I conclude with a legend recounted by Suzuki which I think captures the spirit not just of the Zen teaching but also of its cultural setting, to which I have been able to do no justice at all. A great painter was commissioned by the Emperor to do a landscape on one of the walls of the palace. When the Emperor saw the finished work he was filled with admiration at the marvelous scene—forests, mountains, clouds, a great sky. "Look!" the painter said. "In the cave at the foot of this mountain lives a spirit." He clapped his hands, and the door at the mouth of the cave opened. "The interior is beautiful beyond words," he continued; "permit me to show you the way." So saying, he passed within. The door closed after him, and before the astonished Emperor could say a word, everything faded to white wall before his eyes. The painter was never seen again. I would like to be able to tell you of the beautiful interior, but like yourselves, I see only the blank wall . . . and maybe a faint trace of brush strokes.

QUESTIONS

What need is there for a Master at all?

ZEN RECOGNIZES very well the logic of this question. We might say that the Master is needed in order to lead his disciples to an awareness that he is expendible. This paradox is perhaps familiar to us in the relationship of a psychoanalyst to his patients. But while the first phase of psychoanalysis encourages the establishment of what is called "transference" to the analyst which is later to be itself analyzed and broken, in Zen the dependency is attacked from the very outset. Traditionally, the Master does not accept any disciples, on the grounds that he is not a Master, he has nothing to teach, and there is nothing in Zen anyway. I hope it is clear that this is not just a conventional idiom, a polite lie. The Master takes it seriously enough; it is only the enquirer who is incapable of appreciating its truth. There is a Hasidic story which is very much to the point. A Hasidic saint appeared in a certain community, and in a short time a good part of the congregation withdrew from the synagogue and spent their time in his company. Summoned by the rabbi for this challenge to established religious authority, the saint assured him he would soon put a stop to it. Accordingly, on the Sabbath he arose and announced that he was as much a sinner as everyone else, had no particular sacred learning, and exhorted his hearers not to follow him. Of course they flocked to him more than ever. Once more the rabbi summoned him. "This time," he said, "you must tell them that you are a great saint, a master of scriptures and commentaries, and prepared to give instruction in the path to the True World." At this the saint shook his head. "Not even if my rabbi commands me could I bring myself to tell a lie."

Zen institutionalizes this point of view as follows. Whoever applies for admission to membership in the monastery is just flatly refused, perhaps even rudely. If he is in earnest, he might decide nevertheless to remain waiting at the monastery gate. Perhaps toward the evening someone might emerge and hand him a bowl of rice. This might continue for several days. At night he might be told of a corner somewhere where he can find a place to sleep. And after some time has passed in this way, the Master may say to him, "Well, as long as you are hanging around, eating our rice and sleeping under our shelter, you might as well do some work!" He is assigned some menial chore, and proceeds to learn Zen as best he can—which is just what the rest of the monks are doing. Of course, this is by no means a perfectly standard procedure or it would lose its point; but something of the attitude expressed is quite characteristic. It demands the utmost sincerity and determination on the part of the aspirant. And it conveys at the outset that no one can teach him how to live; he must learn for himself, and just that is the most important thing that the Master can teach.

Does Zen have any room for a sense of guilt or moral responsibility?

THERE IS of course in Zen no theology of original sin or innate depravity. Our word "salvation" is from a root which means health or healing; but Zen has no use for the implied conception of a spiritual pathology to which belong the sense of guilt and anxious concern with the state of the soul. Just go on about your business, Zen says, and don't bother yourself with what you call your spiritual welfare.

But this is not to say that your actions are to be heedless and self-centered. Just the contrary! It is precisely the egoist and sensualist who is most calculating, most anxious to get all he can. And neither is the Zen ideal a life of *dolce far niente*. A man must work, and Zen would warmly endorse the Western view that to work is to pray. Suzuki quotes with approval Meister Eckhart's declaration that what a man takes in by contemplation he must pour out in love, but amends it for Zen to say "pour out in work," for work is, he says, "the active and concrete realization of love." This is the responsibility which every man has toward himself and others. As long as you are eating our rice, take the broom and sweep out the courtyard.

Is Zen anti-scientific?

I THINK THE FAIREST ANSWER to this question is this: In principle, Zen is by no means hostile to science; in fact, there *is* a certain hostility, and how deep you judge it to be depends, I suppose, on your general sympathies with regard to both Zen and science! In principle there is no opposition, because what Zen is insisting on in this connection is no more than what we find in our own scientific philosophies, like pragmatism and logical positivism. It is not the inadequacy of the scientific mentality for dealing with genuine problems, but rather the pointlessness of directing that mentality toward religious and metaphysical questions. The existence of God, the freedom of the will, the immortality of the soul—all the substance of theology and theological metaphysics—these questions have been ruled out of court by most of the major Western philosophies since Kant. Unlike Kant, however, Zen is not limiting reason to make room for faith; it just wants nothing to do with the whole mess. Zen does not arrive at its position on any theoretical basis—neither a Kantian transcendental logic nor a positivistic or pragmatic semantics. It sets itself only to undercut the motivation for entering upon such speculations. It does not undertake to prove that the task is an impossible one or even ill-defined, but only to confer the realization that there is just no point in entering upon it.

So much for the principle. But the fact is that any position which persistently attacks in one area any reliance on the abstract intellect is likely to be carried by the vigor of its own attack into other areas, and evoke at least a profound distrust of the uses of reason. (So it is that most positivists espouse an emotivism with regard to questions of value.) Even in the most sophisticated exponents of Zen one can find, as in Suzuki, many strictures against modern science. Science is blamed for the predicament in which we find ourselves today and for the spiritual emptiness of our way of life. This is loose talk, and I think dangerous, for of course it is the use we make of science, the ends we have it serve, that is subject to criticism, and not the scientific temper itself. In my experience there is quite a good deal of confusion on this score in Zen. But it is by no means limited to Zen, and in all fairness I must add that it does not belong there.

In what way does Zen affect Japanese life?

HISTORICALLY SPEAKING, the influence of Zen on Japanese culture has been enormous. As I mentioned at the very beginning, most of the characteristic elements of that culture developed under the more or less direct influence of Zen. What we most easily identify as Japanese architecture, for instance, derives from that of the typical Zen monastery and contrasts sharply with the ornateness traceable to Chinese sources. But I take it that what is relevant here is not the matter of historical origins but the question of Zen style. How does the Zen point of view express itself in the patterns of a culture?

Obviously Zen makes for simplicity, directness, intensity; it is more concerned with what is left unsaid than with explicit statement; it values singleness of purpose, and concentration of effort. Japanese speak of the quality of *wabi* which may be found in a work of art, an action, or in nature itself. It is a composite of profundity of expression, naturalness of form, and economy of means—the kind of poverty that is spiritually rich in its harmony with itself and with all that is. And this is pure Zen. It is easy to recognize a Zen painting: just a line or two, a bare hint, almost an unfinished sketch, and yet all the more compelling and vivid, conveying the whole essence of whatever has been painted. A shivering bird in the dead of winter on the branch of a tree—one line for the branch, another for a leaf, a few feathers, and the unpainted whiteness of the scroll for the snow, and that's it—the painter has caught it all. The haikku has this same quality—seventeen syllables with which to take hold of the whole life of man. "They were silent all three: the host, the guest —and the white chrysanthemum." With such a miracle before them, how could they speak; and as for the poet, what more is there for him to say?

Zen is a style of life, not just of art, and indeed can find expression in art only because of its roots in life. Painting and poetry, architecture and ceramics only render in their materials what Zen aims at with the material of action. The tea ceremony, for instance, is, from one point of view, the most stylized art form imaginable. Every gesture, literally every motion, appears to be rigidly controlled and calculated. Yet the whole ceremony was summed up by one of its greatest exponents—a man who, not incidentally, was also a Master of Zen— as consisting only of this: you boil water, make tea, and drink it. The tea ceremony, like all else in Zen, is, if you will, only a matter of form; but form must be understood in the sense in which we speak of it in sports—a player has good form when he does whatever the game calls for with perfect ease and naturalness. And this, as every duffer knows so well, is the hardest thing in the world to achieve: to master Zen is just to live life like a pro.

Living by Zen is thus a tissue of paradox: restrained intensity, formalized naturalness, sensitivity without sentimentality, concentration but not intellection. Yet when we are confronted with it, there is no mistaking it. There is a striking instance in a recent Japanese film, *The Magnificent Seven* (also exhibited under the title *The Seven Samurai*). One of the seven is a master of swordsmanship, and quite obviously of Zen as well. Challenged by a boor to demonstrate his mastery, and with naked blades, he at first refuses, since the outcome of the fight is a foregone conclusion; but when he is given no alternative—not as a matter of personal pride but of loyalty to his professional standing—he kills his opponent with one blow, so swift and sure that the onlookers are scarcely aware that it has been given; and he turns to walk away even before the man has fallen. In a heavy rain, he leaves his shelter in order to take advantage of the opportunity to practice his swordsmanship in the mud. When the need arises to secure a gun from the band of brigands with whom he and his fellow samurai are fighting, while ways and means are being discussed, he says simply, "I'll go," and is already well on his way almost before the words are out; returning from this dangerous mission after some hours, he presents two guns and makes his report, "Got two," and then promptly settles himself to sleep. This is not unlike the behavior of the strong, silent hero of our Western epics (the film has, in fact, been translated effectively into a Hollywood Western). What he exhibits is the Zen tactic of "living as though dead"—if we can really feel that there is nothing more to be lost, we can put our whole being at stake, and with that we win; or if we lose, nothing has been lost after all, unless we have been deceiving ourselves from the very beginning. In the West we are told that the great thing is to live as though today is our last day on earth, and this has much to recommend it; Zen suggests instead that it was yesterday.

What is the basis of the great current interest in Zen?

FIRST I MUST MAKE A DISCLAIMER, for this is plainly not a philosophical question but a sociological one; but I will venture to offer my opinion for what it is worth.

I think there are two major reasons for the present popularity of Zen. One is that in the past decade or so—especially, of course, since the end of World War II—a great many Americans have become acquainted with the Japanese culture, many of them through direct personal experience. Now for some time our own society has been undergoing rapid and, in some respects, radical transformations; I need not elaborate on the disorientation to which this process has given rise. New cultural materials, whatever their content, hold out a promise of providing new meanings to replace those whose loss we feel so keenly. Something of this kind seems to have played a part in the spread throughout the declining Roman Empire of the new religion from Palestine. I think it extremely likely, however, that in these terms the impact of Zen on the West has been, and will remain, negligible.

But from another standpoint, Zen has had a widespread though superficial impact. And this, I think, is due largely to a serious misunderstanding of its teaching. It is interpreted as a justification for the dissolution of all restraints on conduct, and on this basis presents great attractions to the rebellious adolescents of all ages. For indeed, one might suppose that what Zen is urging is, in psychoanalytic terms, a repudiation of the ego functions of the self and a regression to the condition in which the personality has not differentiated itself from an external reality. Satori is identified with what Freud called the "oceanic sense," and the way of Zen is thought to be nothing other than the unthinking release of impulses which a moment's reflection would understandably inhibit.

I hope I have said enough to make it clear that nothing could be further from Zen. If anything, just the contrary holds true of it: the concentrated directness of experience at which Zen aims is just what emerges only from the utmost discipline of all our faculties. Its goal is not a life dominated solely by the pleasure principle, but a submission to the reality principle so complete, that nothing of subjectivity remains to be set in opposition to an objective reality. Sheer irrationality and nonconformity have no more Zen in them than their opposites, for they are also contrivances, also guesses at the riddle. The beatnik is not interested in acquiring good form but contents himself with a scornful "Who wants to play *that* silly game?" So he plays another, just as badly, and is endlessly engaged in assuring himself that such bad play is exactly what the game of life calls for.

I don't believe it.

I cannot conclude without a few words to correct any false impression I may have left that I have been trying to convey a Message to you. There is no point in my trying to deny a certain sympathy for Zen, but I must warn you that it is for Zen as I see it, and what I see has undoubtedly in turn been shaped by my sympathies. I have no doubt whatever that other writers could—and *have*—given accounts of Zen more accurate than mine and revealing it to be much less attractive than I may have made it seem. But in any case, my purpose in this lecture, as in the others, is only to offer you food for thought and not to interfere with either your taste or your digestion. All the philosophies which I put before you—with the sole exception of communism—agree in repudiating such interference; and this repudiation is especially appropriate to Zen. I know of no better way to convey this to you than with one last Zen story.

A blind man spent the evening at the home of a friend, and as he was about to leave, the friend offered him a lantern to take along. "It is not for you," he explained, "but so that others may see you coming." The blind man took it and went his way; he had not gone far when someone bumped into him. "Couldn't you see my lantern?" he exclaimed. "My friend," was the reply, "your candle has gone out.". . . I have no way to relight it; we must each of us find his way as best he can.

INDEX

Index

INDEX

Abraham Kaplan, who describes himself as "a positivist by training, a pragmatist by inclination," was born in Russia and came to the United States as a child. He was educated at the College of St. Thomas in Minnesota, the University of Chicago, and the University of California at Los Angeles. He has taught at various times at N.Y.U., the University of Michigan, Harvard and Columbia, and is currently a Professor of Philosophy at U.C.L.A. where in 1960 he served as a Fellow at the Center for Advanced Study in the Behavioral Sciences. A recipient of both Guggenheim and Rockefeller fellowships, Mr. Kaplan has published papers in numerous philosophical journals, and is co-author of the book, *Power and Society.*